T0384072

Project: Communication

All teamwork is grounded in effective communication. *Project: Communication* enables project managers, leaders of project teams, and team members to get their ideas heard, facilitate effective teamwork, and create a culture of openness and creative thinking—in short, a culture of effective communication within their team.

The book opens with an orientation on what group dynamics and interpersonal communication entail, particularly in terms of management teams. It then guides the reader on a personal journey whereby different theories and concepts in group dynamics, communication, and project team management are gradually introduced. Readers are encouraged to use the book to explore and improve their personal communication style, with the aim of sustaining growth and development within project teams and their respective organisations.

Project: Communication is an ideal companion for professionals, specialists, and project managers who are leading or working in teams within all types of organisations, businesses, NGOs, and governmental and transnational institutions. The book should be of interest to all those who want to use psychological knowledge to improve their teams. It is also a practical guide that can be used as a training course in interpersonal communication in general, with a special focus on project teams.

Haukur Ingi Jonasson is a professor at Reykjavik University, a consultant, and Certified Stanford Project Manager. His background is in theology, philosophy, and psychology, which he applies to engineering and management. He is the author of several books on leadership and management.

Helgi Thor Ingason is a professor at Reykjavik University, a consultant, and Certified Senior Project Manager. He is the author of several books on management and his work has been published in the *Project Management Journal*, *International Journal of Project Management*, and *Journal of Metals*.

Project: Communication

Haukur Ingi Jonasson and
Helgi Thor Ingason

LONDON AND NEW YORK

First published 2019
by Routledge
2 Park Square, Milton Park, Abingdon, Oxon OX14 4RN

and by Routledge
52 Vanderbilt Avenue, New York, NY 10017

Routledge is an imprint of the Taylor & Francis Group, an informa business

British Library Cataloguing-in-Publication Data
A catalogue record for this book is available from the British Library

Library of Congress Cataloging-in-Publication Data
Names: Haukur Ingi Jonasson, author. | Ingason, Helgi Thor, 1965- author.
Title: Project communication / Haukur Ingi Jonasson and
Helgi Thor Ingason.
Description: 1 Edition. | New York: Routledge, 2019. |
Includes bibliographical references and index. |
Identifiers: LCCN 2018058245 (print) | LCCN 2018058834 (ebook) |
ISBN 9780429441554 (eBook) | ISBN 9781138338654 (hardback: alk.
paper) | ISBN 9780429441554 (ebk)
Subjects: LCSH: Project management. | Teams in the workplace–
Management. | Communication in management.
Classification: LCC HD69.P75 (ebook) | LCC HD69.P75 H3783 2019
(print) | DDC 658.4/022–dc23
LC record available at https://lccn.loc.gov/2018058245

ISBN: 978-1-138-33865-4 (hbk)
ISBN: 978-0-429-44155-4 (ebk)

Typeset in Goudy
by Deanta Global Publishing Services, Chennai, India

This book is dedicated to our families

Contents

· ·

Figures

· ·

Tables

Acknowledgements

· ·

Special thanks to our beloved families for their encouragement, patience, and their contributions. Very special thanks to Jonathan Norman at the Major Projects Association Knowledge Hub for his unceasing support, guidance, dedication, and friendship. Thanks to Tim Morissey who read through the text and gave us some great suggestions for the content. Our thanks also go to Lara Jonasdottir, Jon Asgeir Sigurvinsson, and Jane Appleton for their help with translations and to Olof Embla Eyjolfsdottir for her help in initiating the project with Routledge.

We also want to thank some of our friends and colleagues within the project management community for the many inspiring discussions: Bob Dignen, Beverly Pasian, Darren Dalcher, Mark Morgan, Miles Shepard, Rodney Turner, Steven Eppinger, Sharon De Mascia, Tom Taylor, and Yvonne Schoper. Also, we extend our thanks to our co-workers in the Master of Project Programme (MPM) at Reykjavik University: Asbjorg Kristinsdottir, Benedikt Arnason, Agnes Holm Gunnarsdottir, Gudfinna Bjarnadottir, Ellen Gunnarsdottir, Florence Kennedy, Greta Maria Gretarsdottir, Hannes Petursson, Yr Gunnarsdottir, Pall Kr Palsson, Pall Jensson, Pauline Muchina, Marta Kristin Larusdottir, Morten Fangel, Markus A Zoller, Thordis Wathne, Throstur Gudmundsson, and Thordur Vikingur Friðgeirsson. We want to thank the University of Reykjavik and all our co-workers there and our students for an ongoing invaluable input, support, and encouragements. Special thanks to Aslaug Armannsdottir MPM and Iris Hrund Thorarinsdottir MPM and our co-workers on the Project Leadership and Project Management programme at the University of Iceland, Kristin Jonsdottir Njardvik, Kristin Birna Jonsdottir, Elin Julia Sveinsdottir, and at University of Akureyri, Elin Hallgrimsdottir.

We thank also Gudrun Hognadottir, Gunnar Stefansson, Kristjan Kristjansson, Kristinn Orn Vidarsson, Ingolfur A. Johanneson, Margret Bjornsdottir, Petur Maack, Runolfur Smari Steinthorsson, Kristinn Orn Vidarson, and Tryggvi Sigurbjarnarson for their support.

Special thanks to CCP Games in Reykjavik, its CEO, Hilmar Veigar Petursson, and its SVP of Human Resources, Sophie Froment, for their help in funding the translations. We want to thank JPV Publishing in Iceland, particularly our editor Oddny S. Jonsdottir and CEO Egill Orn Jonatansson, for their encouragement and co-operation.

Last but not least we want to thank Halldor Baldursson for his wonderful illustrations and friendship and Amy Laurens and Alexandra Atkinson at Routledge for their patience, suggestions, and support.

Haukur and Helgi

Preface to the series

....

Transparent leadership and sustainable project management

This book is a part of a series of four that are written for anyone who needs to be able to lead and participate in different kinds of projects and the human, technical, and communication aspects of projects, programmes, and portfolios, using a style and techniques adapted to the context and the environment of each one.

The series is tailored to help you strengthen four key proficiencies in a very creative way; strategy, leadership, implementation, and communication. Use the advice they contain to develop your personal leadership and managerial style and your ability to take ideas and advance them through planning and execution—with the transparency and accountability that successful project management today demands. We put equal emphasis on the technical and human elements of effective management. Success will require you aligning the objectives of the project leader, team, and organisation within the project's social and environmental context.

We've written this series primarily for the next generation of project, programme, and portfolio managers. The models, techniques, and advice within the books have been taught for many years in the most popular and successful management education and training program in Iceland. They reflect the integrated nature of this successful program, which is designed with the needs of those who want to lead well in both their professional and private lives in mind. To do that you will bring a degree of self-awareness and self-realisation to the leadership of businesses, public bodies, NGOs, and society in general.

We have aligned the books to the most recent version of IPMA Competence Baseline ICB4. The idea is to provide something that is practical as handbooks and as supporting documentation for anyone aiming to become certified ICB 4.0.

We wanted to make sure the series will be of interest to an international readership since projects today are typically planned and operated across international boundaries and involve teams from different disciplines and cultures.

Our aim is to transform you into an international and transparent leader. Someone who is intellectually and emotionally ready to manage others in a spirit of self-reflection; has the values and ethics to guide them in often complex and difficult environments; and has the flexibility and confidence to listen to and make use of criticism and communication, in all its forms. Transparency implies leading in a way that shows constant, considered awareness of the project's content, context, and consequences for you, your team, your organisation, as well as the society and environment within which you live and work. The series is based on this vision.

Foreword

···

Project: Communication forms part of a series of four books that each individually focus on one of the following broad topics: "*Leadership*", "*Strategy*", "*Communication/Teamwork*", and "*Organisation/Planning*". Although the overall approach taken in this series is strongly influenced by the authors' involvement in the field of project management, we believe that the material presented has wide appeal and is relevant to a broad constituency of readers who wish to become better leaders, managers, planners, and strategists. Our combined background and experience lends itself to a novel cross-disciplinary approach and there is a strong focus on the human element in management and leadership in general. As such, these books are intended to complement the large body of general management and project management literature available that is more technical in nature. With this perspective, our aim is to provide more depth to these topics by: (a) discussing them within a very broad context; (b) referencing a diverse array of academic sources; (c) including frequent examples to support the various points made; and (d) describing practical tools for real-life applications. The material is written with both the student and experienced practitioner in mind and each book can be read as a whole or used as a handy reference guide to be dipped in and out of as the occasion demands.

In this book, we focus on *Communication* and *Teamwork*—essential elements in how teams carry out their activities and achieve their goals. As soon as there is more than one person involved in an activity, then communication comes into play as information is necessarily exchanged through whatever medium is most effective; e.g. through the spoken word, written word, visual signals, or various other forms of nonverbal communication. While this is largely a conscious process, there can often be a significant unconscious element to it, and it may be difficult to hide our true feelings as our body language and speech patterns may communicate messages that are at odds with the strict meanings of the words we are using. Many of the topics that we discuss in the book *Project: Leadership*, relating to our conscious and unconscious selves, are relevant here.

The ability to communicate well is something that we develop over many years, beginning in earliest childhood, and is something that benefits greatly from real-life experience. There are many different types of situations, each of which calls for different forms of communication. For example, different types of people may: (a) excel at one-on-one communications where sensitive issues are being discussed in depth; (b) excel in round-table discussions involving small teams of informed individuals; and (c) excel in communications with larger audiences. Anyone managing a project team will benefit from mastering a broad range of communication skills that they can adapt to the particular situation in which they find themselves while performing a certain task. There are many ways in which you can develop your communication skills and we have provided frequent practical exercises throughout this book for personal development and team training. We encourage you to apply yourself fully to these exercises and to explore how to master the communication skills of both yourself and of your team.

Success in teamwork is based on many factors. In this book a range of perspectives are introduced and you can also follow up on the original references to explore any aspects of the subject further. You'll find theory and practice on everything from team formation to role assignment, team cohesion and motivation factors here, and we have emphasised the importance of effective two-way communications between all relevant parties with a variety of different examples.

As is the case for all of the other books in this series, the aim is to provide a comprehensive view of the subject matter and to open your mind to a broad range of considerations, some of which may be entirely unfamiliar and even unexpected. As well as the practical exercises running through the text, we offer some reflective exercises at the end of each sub-section to stimulate your critical thinking and encourage you to question the approach to teamwork, co-working, and communication that you currently use. We hope that you will enjoy reading the book and that it will provide you with new insights and further your skills as a current or future manager and team member. Happy reading.

Haukur Ingi Jonasson
Helgi Thor Ingason

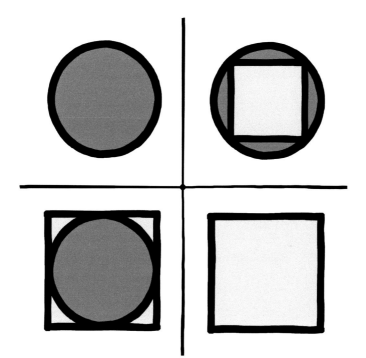

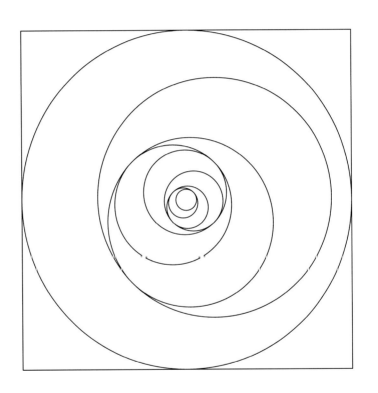

1 Teams and their dynamics

● ●

In the following chapters we will systemically discuss many different aspects relating to the interpersonal dimension at the heart of teams and organisations. We will explore how insights from *social psychology* and the discipline of *group dynamics* can be used to improve team performance. The gathering together of highly talented individuals to undertake a project and achieve goals may not always suffice as a recipe for success. Pertinent issues include: How does the team encourage individuals within it? How do individuals perform within the team? What keeps the team together? What is the effect of one individual on another within the team? From where does the team derive its sense of power? How can communication within the team best be facilitated? It is our aim in this book to describe and discuss these challenges.

In this first chapter, we look at teams' social entities and seek to deepen your understanding of what constitutes a team and what characterises them. We will then embark on a journey that will show how to strengthen your communication skills in order to excel at personal communication with your co-workers and turn your team into a communication training lab alongside getting things done.

Teams and team dynamics

While the contents of this book may relate to all kinds of human activities, the main focus here is on those factors that impact upon the productivity and contentment of *teams* and their members. Thus, we need to have an understanding of what a team is and also what it is not. We consider a *team* to be a collection of people who have placed themselves in certain *special relationships* with each other in order to closely co-operate and achieve set goals. This collaborative structure may be ongoing, with no set time limit attached to it, and part of the everyday operations of an organisation. Alternatively, it may be associated with particular *projects* that are defined by having a set of specific goals outside of routine operations and a defined lifespan. Simply having three individuals together in a work environment does not mean that they have formed a team. These three people may not know each other and may work separately in their rooms on unrelated projects. An arrangement of individuals working in the same area, but there is no relationship between any of them and they do not see themselves collectively as a unit, is not a team. These three people would form a "team" only if the situation changed so that, for instance, everyone began to work on the same project, recognised a common goal, and were in close communication on a regular basis.

Organisations and teams are categories of groups where there is a greater degree of structure and co-ordination in relationships and interactions. With sporting reference, for example, a *group of supporters* may provide much-needed encouragement for a player to perform to the best of their abilities, but a *medical team* will be needed in order to put them right for their next match if they get injured. A team is here defined as a group of people with different skills and different tasks that work together on a common endeavour, and who mutually interact and support each other. An *organisation* is a more permanent entity where a number of individuals co-operate to achieve ongoing success, such as in business, and whose lifespan is greater than that associated with individual projects.

To sum it up, a team is therefore a group that works consciously and purposefully together towards meeting common goals and objectives. Project teams work on a certain task or tasks within a defined structure that includes variables such as cost, time, and any other special attributes unique to that project. The word "task" is used here in relation to projects in the sense of being "*a unique series of interconnected components that have one goal and one purpose. A task needs to be completed within a certain time, according to budget and in accordance with the specified description of the project*" (Wysocki et al., 2000).

Classical studies of social psychology, which we reference heavily here, have a direct bearing for understanding team *dynamics* and their performance. In physics, the word dynamics refers to the movement of objects due to the forces that act upon them. While interactions between inanimate moving objects have clear physical laws that can be used to determine outcomes, there is less certainty in the case of interpersonal interactions although management experience in this area has shown a number of clear trends that have predictive value. Team dynamics, therefore, relates to the interactions between individuals and the associated events that follow. We will use the term *team dynamics* to mean the behavioural relationships between members of a group that are assigned connected tasks. This will mean both the behaviour of individual team members when they are influenced by the team and the collective behaviour of a team within its environment. In this book, we discuss *team dynamics* and *team communication* in order to heighten general awareness of these terms and their implications and to show the impact that positive interpersonal relations and communication can have.

The quality of the interpersonal relations between team members working together towards a common goal greatly affects team performance. Managers, leaders, and team members will, therefore, benefit from having a sound knowledge of interpersonal team dynamics and also be able to harness the communication skills of both individual team members and the team as a whole.

Types of groups and teams

Modern life requires that we spend a large part of our time interacting with other people within groups, teams, and organisations. There are differences in the level and nature of these interactions depending on how we define our relationships. A *group* is a collection of people who are aware they belong together in some form and have social ties (Figure 1.1). Most people probably belong to more groups than they realise at first glance. These groups can range from families to group associations on the Internet, political parties, associations, sports clubs, professional groups, working groups, or large collective groups defined by ethnicity, or opinions, as in the case of protesters.

Groups have been classified, more formally, in various ways (Forsyth, 2019: pp. 5–7). Usually, the function of a group, or specific common features that are intrinsic in groups, is to unite individuals together. At the end of the 19th century, the sociologist Charles Horton Cooley separated groups into two main types: primary groups and secondary groups (Cooley, 1909). By Cooley's definition, family, friends, close associates, and even work teams that work intimately together can be classified as primary groups. They are usually small

Figure 1.1

Group is a collection of people with social ties.

with direct person-to-person communication and interaction, their life cycle is long, and there is a strong cohesion between individuals belonging to the group. Sometimes people become members of a group without having decided to do so. Individuals do not choose their families, for example, but are rather born or adopted into them. Primary groups often protect individual group members, taking care of the sick and sheltering them. Based on his observations, Cooley concluded that the main significance and purpose of primary groups was to bridge the gap between individuals and society.

Secondary groups, by contrast, are usually larger and more formal than primary groups; interaction is less intimate and more focused on goals and objectives. They are usually formed to perform functions and personnel would usually be interchangeable. Members can share interests or activities and work carried out will typically be associated with monetary reward, although volunteering is also common. This description covers, for instance, typical for-profit business with its owners and employees being rewarded for their contributions, as well as unpaid members of a volunteer organisation. Operational or project teams are, in most cases, more secondary in nature than primary. It can be useful for managers to understand the different kinds of belonging that people seek out by joining groups. Linking oneself to the collective life and attempting to gain social status can be an important factor relating to your motivation and sense of self.

Teams can also be understood according to how they are formed (based on Cartwright & Zander, 1960). *Organised teams* would then be created with a specific purpose in mind. They can be formed internally or externally and include project teams, sports teams, committees, councils, study groups, support groups, and commercial organisations. Organised groups are usually well defined and formalised, and their work has clearly-set goals.

Circumstantial groups (or *ad hoc groups*) are formed when people come together and relationships emerge on this basis. The group is formed without an "express resolve" among members to form a group. Examples of such groups are those formed for informal audience events, or people who find themselves stuck at an airport together, due to a delay. While these groups are not systematically assembled, they often form unwritten rules of interaction between the individuals within them.

Informal groups commonly crop up within organisations and they may have particular interests or beliefs that may differ from those leading an organisation. For example, they can be concerned about the direction in which an organisation is being steered and seek to gain gradual influence. These groups can have blurred outer boundaries, making it hard to discern who belongs to the group and who lies outside of it.

Teams can also be classified as mixed teams, created teams, situational teams, and self-generated teams (based on Arrow *et al.*, 2000) and their classification based on their size, duration, permeability, interaction, and importance; team classification can also be based on the intuitive understanding of how people perceive their participation (Lickel *et al.*, 2000). The following list of types of groups illustrates this, and is here modified as to apply to teams (based on Forsyth, 2019):

- *Concocted teams* are planned by someone outside the team.
- *Founded teams* are planned by someone within the team.
- *Emergent teams* get created when people come together repeatedly and relations form and they unconsciously begin to organise themselves.
- *Circumstantial teams* get created when external circumstances provoke interaction and mutual action.
- *Self-organising teams* get formed when people come together and willingly organise themselves.
- *Intimate teams* are small teams where there are strong relationships between individuals.
- *Task teams* are teams with strong emphasis on well-defined mutual goals.
- *Weak associations* are a collection of individuals who informally form, for a short time, a team randomly.
- *Social categories* are collections of individuals that share common features.

Reflection points

- What characterises the teams that you belong to?
- Try to find examples of teams to which you have belonged under each of the categories provided in the list above.

The size of a team can range from two people to a very large number of people but, in most cases, teams are relatively small (see Figure 1.2). Team size is important for many reasons and its size can have different effects on performance. In smaller teams, all the members can easily interact with one another but, as the team grows in size, it may become more difficult for each individual to interact with other team members. Thus, the complexity of the team's structure increases as it gets bigger, and the same is true of the interpersonal and managerial challenges the team faces. It is not only size that makes a team more complex; the nature of interpersonal relationships can also have a significant impact.

Relations in teams can be based on weak or strong emotional ties that can both increase and undermine success. If there are no feelings at all, people get bored quickly and feel work to be dry and dull. On the other hand, the team can also be successful precisely because of the weak emotional ties between team members. This is more likely to be the case when you are looking at the purely technical aspect of projects where objectivity and objective forthrightness in views expressed among team members are particularly necessary. The technical design of a pharmaceutical drug trial is an example, but even here, politics and emotions may influence the team

Figure 1.2

Teams come in many sizes.

and its members. On the whole, fewer or a lack of emotional connections between team members can lead to weaker connections and a decrease in enthusiasm and incentivised co-operation. If there is no desire, there is no fun, and a lack of engagement and strong emotional ties can create a sense of bonding and belonging.

The connections between individuals within a team can be either direct or indirect. A direct connection means that individuals have close interpersonal interaction, whereas an indirect connection means that individuals are aware of each other but do not have close interpersonal interaction with each other. Indirect relationships are more common in larger teams, partly because the number of connections needed to link all members to each other grows very rapidly as the team expands in size. For example, six connections would be needed to connect everyone together in a four-person group (a with b, a with c, a with d, b with c, b with d, c with d) and 66 connections would be required for a group of 12 people.

Reflection points

- Give examples of direct and indirect relationships within a team to which you belong.
- Think of a team that you have recently worked as part of. What was the common purpose of the team members? What were the team's main objectives?

Team attributes

All teams have some common characteristics but to identify them we need to look beyond the sole characteristics of individual teams and examine team commonalities. Teams are systems that create, develop, and maintain interpersonal communication between individuals. These communications can be of various kinds: members engaging in conversations, providing information, answering questions, arguing and fighting, working together, making decisions and learning from each other. These interactions can be task-oriented, on the one hand, where the emphasis is on teamwork and getting things done, and relation-oriented, on the other hand, where the aim is to achieve a better relationship or contact with other individuals within the team (Bales, 1950).

In all teams, members are inter-dependent, which means that a team can only be sustained if individuals within it are active. Teamwork necessarily depends on team members' contributions; actions, thoughts, feelings, and experiences of each member are partially dependent on other members, both individually and collectively. Thus, members are inevitably affected by each other and, invariably, they influence each other. The effect can be mutual or one-way and, in some cases, the influence shifts between individuals, one after another, as in a chain reaction.

Teams have a structure and how this structure develops is not purely random. In most teams, the structure is clearly defined and determines who talks to whom, who takes on which role, what is allowed, and what is seen as normal. The development of the team's internal structure and relationship dynamics also reflect the norms, roles, and relationships that shape the activities of the individuals within the team.

The emergence and existence of teams are usually dependent on the goals and objectives that shape the team and its work. Thus, for example, a particular project team can aim for creativity, problem solving, social support, or resilience.

Teams are not just a collection of individuals but groups of independent social agents that stick together. The "force" that keeps the team together can be called team cohesion. This cohesion is a feature that requires cultivation and can diminish if problems remain unaddressed and members drift apart or fall out with each other. Cohesion welds the team together and the level of cohesion in a team determines how strong the "glue" is that keeps the team together and its strength depends on each individual's relationships with other team members, and with the team as a whole. Managers need to be aware of this force and be able to use it to the advantage of the team and its work.

Reflection points

- What are the characteristics of the team/teams to which you belong?
- How has the structure of a team which you belong been developed?

Teams and social psychology

The study of team dynamics is inevitably part of social psychology. Research methods from many other fields, such as political sciences, economics, anthropology, education, management, and organisation behavioural studies can also be of relevance. Researchers have investigated, for instance, team selection, team development, team leadership, team cohesion, team conflicts, and team success. Understanding team dynamics is of crucial importance for understanding individuals as well as managerial and social realities. It can be argued that individuals define themselves by the teams they belong to, and teams in return offer individuals a confirmation of identity.

Even though research may approach teams differently, they are all based on the basic premise that teams play a fundamental role. Teams are essential to getting things done and this justifies the importance of investigating their nature, impact, and function. Research on team dynamics can look at small task teams, larger project and programme teams, relations between teams, and how teams may play a role in international relations and influence international politics.

Teams can be studied from a social perspective and a narrower view on individual psychologies. When researchers began to study groups in the early 20th century, they adopted different approaches. Sociologists tried to explain how groups functioned as the political, economic, religious, and educational foundations of society, and how they maintained their status in doing so. Psychologists wondered what the impact of groups on individuals might be and vice versa. Both attempted to answer questions regarding functions and meaning of groups and they often reached very different conclusions. Initial research on the nature of groups contributed to the idea that in order to understand society and individuals within it, researchers would have to understand groups. This initial study also laid the foundations for the methodologies that are applied today in research on groups (Forsyth, 2019).

The sociologist Émile Durkheim theorised of a collective group mind (Durkheim, 1897) and argued that the power of this collective "mind" was sometimes so strong that it could overcome the willpower of the individual. On the other hand, social psychologist Floyd H. Allport believed that there were no scientific reasons for studying groups separately (Allport, 1924). Applied to teams, he believed that the teams' contribution was equal to the sum of the contribution of the individuals and that the behaviour of the individuals within the team would be best understood by studying the psychology of the individual members. However, this idea prompted researchers to argue that groups have an independent life of their own and should be dealt with in their own rights as independent psycho-social realities; and that they constitute something more than just the sum of the individual elements within them.

Reflection points

- How is the desire for attention and love met within a team of which you are part?
- What are the team dynamics within a team of which you are part?
- How does the group mind (conscious and unconscious) manifest itself in a team of which you are part?

Norms in teams

Collective norms in teams are the informal understandings that govern the behaviour of team members. They are not only based on the combined individual opinions of members, but on a mixture of conscious and subconscious consensus that seem to overrule extreme views, even when they happen to be the rights ones (Sherif, 1936). In a famous experiment, by the Austrian psychologist Muzafer Sherif, individuals in a group were asked to assess the distance that a light dot in a dark room appeared to move. In fact, what made the light "move" was a psychomotor function called the "autokinetic effect", so that although a light dot in total darkness is still, it still seems to move. The experiment illustrated that people gradually accepted the viewpoint of the group instead of trusting their own individual assessment. It was also revealed that even when individuals were later given the opportunity to assess the distance privately, each person still accepted the opinion of the group. The experiment also showed how once group norms have formed, members of that group can be changed without this having an impact on the norms within the group. This process prevailed even when all of the original members were gone. This experiment demonstrated that the group is, in fact, an independent phenomenon because, if the norms remained after the individuals who comprised the group in the first place were no longer members of it, then the norms must belong to the group and not to the individuals within the group (Sherif, 1936; Forsyth, 2019).

The German-American psychologist Kurt Lewin presented the equation $B = f(P, E)$ where the behaviour of individuals in a team (B) can be understood as a function (f) of the interaction of personality (P) and environmental factors (E). In other words, individual behaviour is a function of personality and environment (Lewin, 1948). Other studies have confirmed Lewin's theory, including studies of cohesion. The cohesion of a team may be stronger than that which individuals experience on their own and, for instance, the power of a team can be more than the combined power of individuals within the group (Hogg, 1992). Thus, a team may in fact achieve a lot more than the sum of individual effort of the individuals in that team. Moreover, teams can make bad and even appalling decisions that individuals on their own would never make due to strong cohesion and groupthink (Janis, 1972, 983; Hackman, 1987; Forsyth, 2019). Based on these findings, the basic understanding is that teams have, to some extent, lives of their own and that team dynamics are forces that have a very real impact.

Reflection points

- How might the opinion of a team of which you have been part differ from the combined individual views of all of those within it?
- How would you summarise the theory of Kurt Lewin?
- What impact can one person in a team have on the whole?
- What experimental research would you be interested in conducting on teams?
- What experimental research would you be interested in conducting on groups?
- How would you perform these studies?

Team evolution

Teams are not mechanical structures but organic communication systems that continually change and exert outside influences of all kinds. They are dynamic because they involve human attitudes and are dependent upon their environment. Teams evolve over time and are influenced by internal activities as well as external influences and other factors. An example of such an influence is described in the writing of the American psychologist Bruce Tuckman on group development (Tuckman, 1965). He outlined the team life cycle as divided into five stages—the forming, storming, norming, performing, and adjourning stages. During the forming stage, team members get to know each other and initially begin to learn about each other in the new context of the team. At the storming stage, disputes can arise within the team when members aim to prove themselves, define their roles within the group, and set objectives. As the team progresses, shapes up, and reaches a plateau, fewer disputes arise and the team begins to focus more on their work. This is the norming stage. If disputes are more or less happily resolved, this also moves the team to the performing stage. The team works together at the performing stage until it comes to separation, which defines the adjourning stage. Further detail on these stages in team situations is provided in Chapter 4.

Along with Tuckman's view, this process is necessary and inevitable as the team grows, deals with challenges, resolves problems, finds solutions, organises itself, and finally yields the results that are achieved. While the Tuckman theory is interesting, there is also a strong case to be made for the development of a team that does not always follow a straight line. Some teams repeatedly go through the same stages in a search for a balance somewhere between, for instance, task-targeted action and relation-related behaviour. In those projects that have a strong political aspect, for example, the path to achieving an acceptable outcome invariably involves compromises from different team members involved. This can require extensive back and forth discussions that need to avoid damaging sensibilities and can be difficult to execute as a result. Another observation is that in order for a project to be successfully completed, it needs to be driven by those people who benefit from the completion of the adjourning stage. These people can be users, business owners, contractors waiting to get paid, or a range of other stakeholders.

Reflection points

- What happens to individuals who know they are about to start working in a new team?
- How have you experienced the five stages described by Tuckman, each in turn, in a team (or teams) that you have been part of?

Impact of teams

Teams not only help organisations to define and execute their strategies and reinvent themselves through innovation. Teams can create in individuals a sense of belonging to something that is special and this can greatly inspire and motivate and bring out the best in people (Figure 1.3). Such drive is usually what gets start-up enterprises off the ground. Ideas are born and owners and early employees alike are willing to make things happen and even make

Figure 1.3

Teams can create a sense of belonging.

sacrifices when navigating through turbulent times. This can mean employees are willing to accept late wage payments or to work frequent unpaid extra hours. In research projects, many of those carrying out the work as part of research teams have a strong sense of commitment and are willing to work extremely long hours for little or no monetary reward as a result. Of course, in these examples there can be an expectation of greater rewards in the future, but this may not be the main driving source as people have a genuine desire to belong, challenge themselves, and contribute to the greater good.

They can also have a very strong impact on the organisational culture and individual team members and even shape their behaviour, thoughts, and feelings. Most people who study teams would now accept the viewpoint that in order to understand the individual needs of people in a team, they need to be seen in the context of the team they are working within and vice versa. "No man is an island"—according to poet John Donne—and the behaviour of individuals is often shaped significantly by others. It is difficult to take the two out of context.

Reflection points

- How have teams you have belonged to benefitted society?
- What led you to participate in these teams?
- What impact did your team have on you?
- What effects did teamwork have on you?
- What kind of team (or teams) would you put together in order to make a positive impact on society?

Communication is key

Good interpersonal relations are essential in effective teamwork. This means that you need to have the personal competences to self-observe, self-reflect, and learn and the social competence to initiate, sustain, and enjoy the interaction with others. Social competence is the ability to establish and maintain healthy, constructive, and fruitful relationships with other people. Deeper understanding of how teams function and thrive is also helpful. We'll in later chapters discuss a whole range of approaches and methods to help your team members to master their personal and social competences.

When working in teams you, and all other team members, send out messages (e.g. talking and writing) and receive messages (e.g. listening and observing) and this two-way nature of effective communication will be emphasised throughout the book. It is invariably the case that "actions speak louder than words" and leaders, in particular, need to be cognisant of this. For instance, what message does it send out if a lively enthusiastic lessons-learned exercise that generates suggestions for improvement by team members is followed by a complete failure to implement any of the feedback in the systems or processes associated with your projects?

As technology develops and enterprises change their operations, the ways in which people interact with each other will also change and it is worthwhile for organisations and individuals alike to reflect periodically on how they conduct their daily business. Having a low-cost customer service call centre at the far side of the world may please those who are focused on keeping business overheads down but can lead to widespread misunderstanding, frustration, and customer leakage at the same time, if not properly managed. Both enterprises and individuals need also to understand that unguarded or unwarranted comments or actions can end up becoming widely distributed in the digital age and damage reputations. Although many aspects of good communication and teamwork would be considered timeless and independent of technology and innovation, there are nonetheless important classical considerations to be aware of that relate to the modern world and we will refer to these where appropriate.

Communication as team competence

Communication is the key competence that enables us to work with others in a team. Understanding the nature of teams and human interactions within them does not necessarily come naturally, nor can it be learnt by just reading books on the subject. Interpersonal skills building can only be gained through actively working and communicating with others. A good way for you—and your team—to acquire these skills is to participate in specially designed training exercises where a focus is put on mastering communication skills. There are certain essential things that must be considered initially when it comes to fostering communication competence amongst participants in a team. In our discussion on interpersonal skills in project teams we are in particular indebted to the American professor Gerard Egan's and the insights he provided in his book Interpersonal Living (Egan, 1976).

Firstly, you need the willingness and commitment among team members to develop their communication skills. That means willingness to learn about communication, discover new things about themselves and others, understand better their role within the team, and gain deeper insights into the interpersonal aspects of the team's work. This requires trust, openness, confidentiality, and the commitment to develop. One way to start is to encourage this sense of trust and openness by inviting each member to practise self-expression by talking to the team as a whole. The team could then give a feedback to the person who expressed him or herself, describing what they experienced and how they understood what was expressed. The team can also work on an exercise involving each person speaking directly with another person, one at a time, while everyone else in the team observes the exchange and then gives constructive feedback. This can sharpen the communication skills among the team members. The aim of both exercises is to make team participants more competent in interpersonal interaction.

Secondly, an important aspect of good communication within teams is the ability of team members to be present and able to tune in to what

Figure 1.4

Tuning in to what is happening "here and now" is crucial.

is happening "here and now" (see Figure 1.4). This means that members express their opinions, experiences, and feelings about what is happening at any given moment in a constructive way and avoid losing themselves in the detail of events in the past or future, or in what is happening outside the team. If you are deliberately aiming at developing the communication skills within a team, it is best to keep the team unchanged over the course of the training. Consistency enables the team members to create a sense of closeness that will subsequently grow stronger. It also builds a sense of trust within the team and allows people to become increasingly open to one another. A team that is dedicated to focusing on the interpersonal aspects of teamwork gives its participants the opportunity to try things that might ordinarily not be so easily tested and this will challenge and develop the communication culture.

Thirdly, the communication of opinions within the team should be honest and purposeful. If people are not accustomed to this, it can be useful and may even be necessary to have an experienced facilitator to manage the training. He or she observes, listens to the conversation, sets boundaries and even takes part. It is common for people to feel anxious at the beginning of such training, but that is very natural and must be acknowledged. The benefits of communication training will be even greater if the participants practise what they have learned both within their team on a day-to-day basis and in their interactions with people outside the team.

The special emphasis on communication training within your team is to enable participants to act constructively in their interactions and this takes practice. The training provides an opportunity for participants to get to know themselves better and to evaluate and master their communication skills and needs. It also helps participants to respond constructively to comments, feedback, and criticism and it also provides them with valuable feedback on various aspects of their personality.

Reflection points

- What do you need to consider in a team that focuses on developing the communication competences of its members?
- Describe a situation when you participated in a team in a way that enabled you to develop your communication skills.
- How can communication skills be developed within a team?
- What can you expect to learn in a workshop on communication?

Values and self-actualisation

Personal values are reflected in interaction, behaviour, and conduct. When considering values associated with communication, it is useful to distinguish between actual values and desired values. Actual values are those that are already implemented and lived by. Desired values are ideals that we might not live up to now, but that we want to live up to in the future. For example, a person may pay lip service to the value of helping others, but when asked for help, he or she might not respond because he or she is afraid of standing out from others. In this example, helpfulness is not an actual value, but a desired one. One way to ascertain the actual values of an individual is to look at their behaviour rather than asking them to describe their values. One study on values concluded that behaviour reflects the real values of an individual if the individual is consistent in these values; their behaviour does genuinely reflect these personal values and priorities; and these values are apparent in the person's communication style and will actually affect how the person treats others (Raths *et al.*, 1966).

As part of their skills development, participants may pledge to work in constructive ways in order to learn from each other. The group gives participants the opportunity to view their actual values and to compare them with their desired values. Tensions can arise from different values, both within the individual and as conflict and disputes between individuals within the group. Competing values within an individual can pull them in different directions.

When values compete, both positive and negative consequences can ensue. In the context of management, it is the task of the manager to analyse what is happening and deal with the problem in time. Disputes can be constructive and need not necessarily become destructive unless they are poorly managed. It is important to know that conflict is a normal part of human interaction and can lead to personal and team development. As someone grows up, they unconsciously imitate their caregivers and pick up on their behaviour. When it comes to higher consciousness in adulthood, we can begin to recognise the extent of these early influences in our attitudes, values, and behaviour. We can then examine what we have acquired, either accept or reject it, and take more responsibility for our actions.

Under normal circumstances, we should gradually realise that we are, first and foremost, responsible for our own behaviour and have the ability to shape our future. We do not control the behaviour of others but we can potentially change and affect our own. In some cases, this happens relatively effortlessly but, in other cases, we need to deal with the painful process of reforming the emotional programmes that previous experiences have established in our minds. Participating in a team that has dedicated itself to the development of communication skills can help us to explore the values, attitudes, behaviour, emotions, and other factors that determine how we behave in our interactions with others.

Understanding ourselves and our feelings affects the way we communicate with others. The team can help us to look inward and understand how we feel. Responses and feedback from others provide participants with a mirror-view of their identity and gives them the opportunity to appreciate factors they were not conscious of. Participants can look inwards and appreciate their social strengths and weaknesses and will have opportunities for further development and training. Good self-esteem leads to a healthier self and the ability to develop relationships with others based on strong self-confidence, and vice versa. The Canadian psychologist, Nathaniel Branden, amongst others, has argued that it is particularly the self-confidence of a person that defines their behaviour (Branden, 1971). The humanistic psychologist, Abraham Maslow, believed that in order to develop, the individual needs to satisfy different levels of needs that range from biological primary needs, through relational and social needs, to self-actualisation needs that enable the development of personality (Maslow, 1968). Maslow's hierarchy of needs presents these levels based on necessity and importance (Figure 1.5).

Figure 1.5

Maslow's pyramid of needs.

At the bottom of the pyramid, you'll find the basic needs such as the biological necessity for food and shelter. This is followed by safety needs, social needs, and finally self-actualisation needs. Included within self-actualisation is the need to educate yourself and to be inspired creatively. Maslow believed that if the lower needs are not met, the individual in question will have little interest in, or capacity for, fulfilling needs higher up in the pyramid. He also theorised that if the basic needs of an individual were not being met in their upbringing, then the individual would have to try to meet their needs themselves first, before being in a position to aim for satisfying higher needs.

Interpersonal communication in teams

The ability to communicate well allows individuals to co-operate more effectively with others, cultivate interpersonal relationships, and meet their social needs. The ability to express views, respond to the demands of others, make demands on others, and allow others to influence them underlies this endeavour. This self-awareness also helps individuals to respect the legitimate claims of others and to prevent and solve disputes. In short, the ability to communicate well fosters our emotional and social intelligence.

People who have participated in our communication training teams are well aware of the intensity that can characterise the experience of working with others. Many participants experience anxiety at the beginning, but moderate anxiety is a normal part of the process. Communication training is naturally, at first, felt as a journey into the unknown. If members know each other, this might lead to additional anxiety as one might fear the others' reactions based on previous experience.

The contribution of team members during communication training may also vary greatly but, if a participant is overly withdrawn, then the team may wish to focus their attention on them. Participants may question why the person in question is not fully participating; whether this is because they are shy, find the conversation inappropriate, or are thinking of other matters. It may also be possible that something else is dominating their thoughts. When people are encouraged to become more involved, however, they normally become more active and will benefit more from the team. If a deeper issue is bothering them, then they may also give an indication of this, which will help the rest of the group to show understanding.

At the outset, conversation can be slow and it is common to see the team drift somewhat and focus instead on the project on which they may be working. The attempt to process the team experience and relationships within the group may feel uncertain and difficult and this sense may be sustained over the course of the project life cycle. To solve this issue, the teams could design formal limits on what is to be discussed or define rules of communication, e.g. that individual contributions take the form of one speaking after another in a circle. Both approaches can yield success but a greater flow between participants is generated in groups that are not overly concerned with such formalities.

The managing of interpersonal explorations within your teams requires flexibility and the understanding that different teams have different needs. While in some teams members will experience a lack of ability to talk and will remain quiet, in other teams they may experience strong and rewarding interpersonal interactions. Some teams may need the support of supervisors regularly whilst others will not welcome such intervention.

Participants that take on the challenge of processing interpersonal experiences within their team will learn how individuals can differ greatly in how they experience and interpret the same incident. Communication training can also teach many valuable lessons about prejudice. It can happen that team members will have formed strong opinions about each other that are unjustified and understanding this can change the experience of interconnectedness of the team as it evolves.

Participants in teams where there is a focus on developing interpersonal skills can experience various emotions and feelings as part of this process, while learning to be in the "here and now". It often takes teams some time to reach this stage and it can also be difficult to stay there. Participants come to realise that the more individuals submit to the team, and the more constructive interpersonal risks they take, the more the team will gain as a whole. Do remember, however, that some people may be wary of participating, for example, if they feel that their input may not be rewarded or appreciated. Countering such fears is an important aspect of team management.

Finally, experience has shown that participants find it challenging to express themselves face-to-face in the first person. People tend to engage in small talk and discussions of less relevant opinions or general theories of communication with the group as a whole, rather than discussing what is really happening "here and now" within the team. This may be driven by forceful personalities who spend a disproportionate amount of time airing their opinions, while others, who may even be more knowledgeable, remain quiet. People can also find it hard to continue expressing themselves via the "I think" and "I feel" modes, which entails maintaining both the voltage and connection in the conversation. Overall, teams are an interesting laboratory both in interpersonal communication and in group dynamics and the next chapter focuses on research methods that can be used to understand teams better.

Reflection points

- What suggestions do you have for developing your people skills?
- If you had to develop a workshop in communication skills, how would you do so?

References

Allport, F. H. (1924). *Social psychology*. Boston, MA: Houghton Mifflin.

Arrow, H., McGrath, J. E., & Berdahl, J. L. (2000). *Small groups as complex systems: Formation, coordination, development, and adaptation*. Thousand Oaks, CA: Sage.

Bales, R. F. (1950). *Interaction process analysis: A method for the study of small groups*. Reading, MA: Addison-Wesley.

Branden, N. (1971). *The disowned self*. New York: Bantam Books.

Cartwright, D. & Zander, A. (1960). *Group dynamics: Research and theory* (2nd ed.) New York: Harper & Row.

Cooley, C. H. (1909). *Social organization*. New York: Scribner.

Durkheim, É. (1897/1966). *Suicide*. New York: Academic Press.

Egan, G. (1976). *Interpersonal living*. Belmont, CA: Wadsworth Publishing Company.

Forsyth, D. R. (2019). *Group dynamics* (6th ed.) Boston: Cengage.

Hackman, J. R. (1987). "The design of work teams" in J. W. Lorsch (Ed.), *Handbook of organizational behaviour* (pp. 315–342). Upper Saddle River, NJ: Prentice Hall.

Hogg, M. A. (1992). *The social psychology of group cohesiveness: From attraction to social identity*. New York: New York University Press.

Janis, I. L. (1972). *Victims of groupthink*. Boston: Houghton Mifflin.

Janis, I. L. (1983). "Groupthink" in H. H. Blumberg, A. P. Hare, V. Kent, & M. F. Davis (Eds.), *Small groups and social interaction* (Vol. 2, pp. 39–46). New York: Wiley.

Lewin, K. (1948). *Resolving social conflicts: Selected papers on group dynamics*. New York: Harper.

Lickel, B., Hamilton, D. L., Wieczorkowska, G., Lewis, A., Sherman, S. J., & Uhles, A. N. (2000). "Varieties of groups and the perception of group entitativity" in *Journal of Personality and Social Psychology*, 78, 223–246.

Maslow, A. H. (1968). *Toward a psychology of being*. New York: Van Nostrand Reinhold.

Sherif, M. (1936). *The psychology of social norms*. New York: Harper & Row.

Tuckman, B. W. (1965). "Developmental sequences in small groups" in *Psychological Bulletin*, 63, 384–399.

Wysocki, R. K., Beck, R., & Crane, D. (2000). *Effective project management*. New York: John Wiley & Sons Ltd.

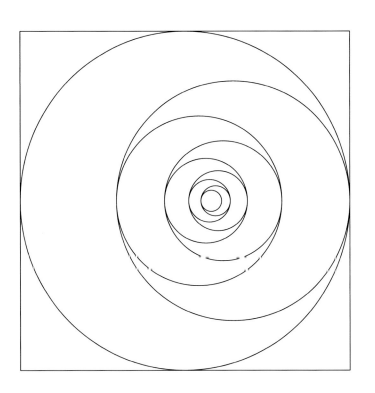

2 Understanding teams and interpersonal communication

· ·

Team dynamics refer to everything that happens when people come together in teams. Since the early 20th century there has been considerable research to understand what happens when individuals collectively come together. In this chapter we will discuss some of the methods that can be used to gain a better insight into teams. Various forms of research into social psychology and group dynamics has led to a wide variety of theories that provide us with an understanding of teams and offer practical perspectives to enhance their performance. Team research requires curiosity and a detailed attention or "tuning in" to the reality that is being scrutinised. Such "tuning in" links in well with the communication skill of active listening that we discuss at the end of the chapter.

Understanding teams

Team leaders should be interested in understanding their teams. Usually, this knowledge is gained informally through participation, co-working, and observation. Any formal research of teams, however, demands reliable and accurate methods. Metrics and methods of data collection must give consistent data under repeated measurements and in terms of what they are intended to measure. In *quantitative research*, data is collected in numerical form and this kind of research can have various statistical features. In *qualitative research*, data is collected by inspection, interviews, and other methods, which aim to capture the subjective experiences of people. Examples are *structured observational measures* and *self-reporting measures*, where people give feedback on their personal experiences (Forsyth, 2019) (Figure 2.1).

Systematic research of teams involves monitoring them in an organised and precise manner. It can entail recording both behaviour and interactions within it. It can look at verbal expression and written statements of team members, and non-verbal expression, such as physical and facial expressions. The researcher can either be outside the team, or part of it. If the team is aware that it is the object of study, this is called *overt observation*; if the team

Figure 2.1

There are many ways to study teams.

is not aware of the research, it is *covert observation* (Forsyth, 2019). Any systematic study of teams will need to consider the *Hawthorne Effect*, which refers to some seminal research that took place in Chicago in the early part of the 19th century and concerned the tendency of people to change their behaviour when they are being closely monitored, which means that the behaviour the researcher witnesses may not necessarily reflect typical behaviour. Thus, for example, if a team's performance is being measured, the team's awareness of the attention of the researcher might raise ambitions within the team. In real-life research in commercial retailing, for example, many managers like to employ "mystery shoppers" to help secure objective results.

When using systematic observation in qualitative research, the data comprises the observations of the researcher as they monitor the team, and their descriptions of interacting with the team. Data can also be collected through interviews with members of the team who answer questions that are often open-ended (i.e. those that do not allow for a simple yes or no answer). In such questioning, the researcher should try to stay as objective as possible so as to avoid bias. In the systematic use of quantitative research, however, researchers use instruments that enable them to classify, for instance, behaviour as coded into predefined categories. This results in information being translated into numerical form. Two well-known methods that can be used to measure team dynamics are the *Interaction Process Analysis (IPA)* and the *Systematic Multiple Level Observation of Groups (SYMLOG)*.

The American social psychologist, Robert Freed Bales, introduced the IPA method first in 1950, and this was followed by an improved version in 1970.

In it, people's interpersonal behaviour within a group was observed, classified, and scaled based on the following categories (Bales, 1970):

1 Seems friendly.
2 Dramatises.
3 Agrees.
4 Gives suggestion.
5 Gives opinion.
6 Gives information.
7 Asks for information.
8 Asks for opinion.
9 Asks for suggestion.
10 Disagrees.
11 Shows tension.
12 Seems unfriendly.

Bales continued to develop the IPA method with the SYMLOG model representing an evolved version of the original (Bales & Cohen, 1979; Forsyth 2019). Applied to teams, the method classifies people on the basis of the behaviour that they tend to show within team activities. The model assumes that the interactions of people can be mapped in three dimensions. The three principal positive axes relate to degrees of *friendliness*, *expressiveness*, and *dominance*, while the negative axes relate to the respective opposites. Overall, a variety of different personality types are outlined and within these are numerous descriptive terms including: extrovert; task-leader; assertive; authoritarian; domineering; egocentric; provocative; dramatic; entertaining; egalitarian; co-operative; analytical; legalistic; cynical; emotional, affectionate; appreciative; gentle; obedient; self-punishing; resentful; self-doubting; depressed; contented; passive; etc. The possible combinations that come from mapping behaviour in three dimensions define behavioural tendencies within the team and repeated measurements can illustrate changes in team behaviour.

Self-reporting can be a valuable means of collecting first-hand data about how team members feel, and to get a sense of the attitudes, beliefs, or reasons behind their behaviour. Participants are approached directly and asked to record their answers in a systematic way. The questions put to participants can take various forms, but the approaches most commonly employed are personality tests, questionnaires, surveys, and interviews. One example of a measure that requires people to be interviewed is the so-called "sociometry" method that can be used to gather information about the relationships between individuals within a team (Moreno, 1934; Forsyth, 2019). By making team members answer questions about their relationships with others in the team, the connections between members of a team can be mapped out, as well as the status and role of each member. An example of a question might be: To whom do you go for advice in solving problems? The results can then be presented graphically as a connected network, as is seen in Figure 2.2, where

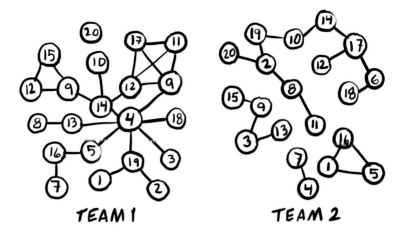

Figure 2.2

Circle represents individuals and lines indicate their relations.

each circle represents an individual within the team and the lines show the principal connections.

These approaches and their graphic representations can help to reveal what is going on within a team and how people position themselves within it. They can show, for instance, popular participants (*populars*), unpopular participants (*unpopulars*), participants who are isolated (*isolates*), positive participants (*positives*), negative participants (*negatives*), pairings participants (*pairs*), groups of participants (*clusters*), as well as others. The frequency of certain factors can then be calculated, such as how often one person is selected by other team members, and other factors that show their status within the group. The reliability of the method is based on asking the right questions and on the group members' consistency in their answers.

Reflection points

- List as many methods as you can that can be used to obtain information about teams.
- What questions could be submitted to members of a team in order to better understand the team?
- Draw a diagram of a team that you belong to and put yourself in the place of all others in the group. Try to work out how interpersonal relations between members could be presented visually in your diagram.

Assumptions about teams

We all make assumptions about our teams and, if based on purposeful curiosity, such assumptions can be turned into hypotheses and be tested. The first stage in this process is to define the research question to be answered and a research methodology that describes the strategy to be used in testing the hypothesis. Remember the GIGO (garbage in, garbage out) principle and make sure that the information recorded is both representative and useful. Good measuring is not enough to ensure good research as in-depth articulation is just as important. For instance, a researcher who is observing a team might interview its members and be able to give a detailed description of the team, but in order to explain the team behaviour, he or she may have to delve deeper. Once data has been collected in an objective manner, it can be used to build a theory.

A variety of methods can be used to produce research on a team. According to the American social and personality psychologist Donald R. Forsyth, the most common are probably *case studies*, *experiments*, and *comparative studies* (also known as correlation studies) (Forsyth, 2019).

In a *case study*, the behaviour of an individual team and individuals within it are studied in as much detail as possible. Case studies are well suited to researching project teams and have led to major discoveries on the nature of groups. One classical case study, conducted by Irving Janis, enabled the researcher to come up with the concept of "Groupthink", the social dynamic within groups that can lead individuals and the group as a whole to put the cohesion of the group above the quality of their decision-making; eschewing debate and avoiding criticism of ideas that don't fit with what the group wants to do (Janis, 1972). Case studies of teams are usually conducted on real teams that have already formed and are viewed in their typical environment. Such teams could be named "real teams" (or *bona fide* teams) to distinguish them from teams that are formed specifically for research purposes and then dissolved after the study's completion. Project teams are good examples of *real teams* and can be fertile ground for studying, for instance, how decisions are made, how interactions change over the course of a project life cycle, and how the power structure within the team is implemented and maintained. When using case studies to learn something valuable about a team, it should be kept in mind that the team under observation may be somehow special, so the findings might not be directly applicable to other teams. Consequently, case studies may therefore provide only limited information on the general behaviour of teams and may not be ideal to demonstrate causal links between variables, for example.

An *experiment* is a research method where there is at least one variable—the primary variable—whose impact on another predefined variable—the secondary variable—is explored. Experiments involving teams might require that the team is specially assembled, or its circumstances are specifically tailored for the study. In order to state the effect of one variable on other variables it is important that all conditions are stable and that nothing is changed apart from the primary variable. Experiments can indicate total causality in situations that are staged but might not be able to predict with absolute certainty team behaviour under non-tailored circumstances. A classic example of an experiment on team behaviour is the study by the social psychologists Kurt Lewin, Ron Lippitt, and Robert White that showed how different leadership styles can influence the behaviour of a team (Lewin *et al.*, 1939; Forsyth, 2019). The authors put together three groups of 10 and 11-year-old boys who were each assigned arts and crafts projects. Three boys were asked to lead the groups, each with their own leadership style. One boy managed his team with an autocratic leadership style, another by using a democratic approach, and the third employed a laissez-faire management style. The leadership style of the leader was the primary variable in the study but the aim was to examine the effects of leadership style on work and aggressiveness, which were secondary variables. The experiment showed that if the leadership was autocratic, the team would spend 74% of their time working. If the leadership was democratic, the group worked actively 50% of the time, while the corresponding result for a laissez-faire leadership style was only 33% (Forsyth, 2019). Based on this, one could conclude that the autocratic leadership style was most effective but, although this style was the best in terms of work time, other factors were also revealed. For instance, it was found that contributions from team members in the democratic approach were of the highest quality. One could also examine other variables such as the composition of a team using this approach. Such a study could be used to examine responses to different management styles within project teams.

In a *comparative* or *correlative study*, at least two variables are measured and the relationship between them is examined by using statistical methods. The so-called "correlation coefficient" assesses the strength of the relationship and whether the correlation is positive or negative.

All of the above methods have their advantages and disadvantages. The results of a case study are rarely typical for most teams. They can be subjective but they can nonetheless stimulate interesting theories. It is important to bear in mind the ways that a researcher can affect the behaviour of individuals in a team if the trial is conducted openly, with the knowledge of the team. Experiments are staged and therefore the team is "not real" and might not be in its typical environment. Experiments investigate specific causal connections in teams. Correlation studies look at real teams and offer up fewer ethical problems. They provide limited information about causal relations though they are well suited to analysing the relationship between two variables (Forsyth, 2019).

Reflection points

- Come up with a hypothesis about team dynamics.
- What is a case study?
- What is an experiment?
- What is correlation research?
- What methods might you use to explore your hypothesis?
- What are the pros and cons of each method?

General theories applicable to teams

Not only do prominent researchers create and use authentic methods to try out their hypotheses; they also construct theories based on their findings, and a theory that organises knowledge in some way often warrants further research. What follows is an overview of some of the key theories of social psychology that are of relevance to how teams perform (based on Forsyth, 2019).

Biological theories focus on the individual as an organism that responds to its surroundings on the basis of their biological, biochemical, and genetic nature. The heart beats faster when disputes arise, stress causes physical symptoms, and various other biological factors can influence how people interact and communicate in teams. Evolutionary psychology is a subgroup of biological theories. Here, it is claimed that team behaviour is determined by genetics and that the development of mankind is based on the fact that good social skills help individuals to survive. This has caused us to respond to a variety of situations with learned social behaviour. In developmental psychology, explanations behind various processes that occur in teams, i.e. bonding, conflict, and aggressive tendencies, can be found.

Psychoanalytical theories. In 1921, Sigmund Freud published a paper entitled *Group Psychology and the Analysis of the Ego* in which he compared the psychology of the individual and the group. Aside from monetary considerations, Freud believed that what primarily keeps people together in groups is a longing for the attention and love (or indeed respect) of the groups' leaders. To illustrate this idea, he used the example of a military leader who has authority, gives his soldiers love to encourage them, and punishes them by withdrawing his love. When the soldier does his duty, he receives the love of the leader—or even the love of the national leader. When the soldier fails to perform his duty, then he is deprived of such love. Thinking about teams in the business context, we could say that one of the things that motivate team members is the desire to make their leader proud of the team and to receive their attention and love (or respect).

The field of psychoanalysis and its practitioners have much to offer that is applicable to the study of team dynamics. The psychoanalyst Wilfred Bion, who discussed the conscious and unconscious life of teams, noted, amongst other things, that while a team can plan consciously through defining conscious objectives and aiming for results, there can be various unconscious motives at play too, beneath the surface. Bion believed that teams worked on two levels: firstly, on a *conscious level* where the emphasis is on completing tasks, and secondly, on a *subconscious level* where members behave as though they have objectives that might be very different from their conscious goals (Figure 2.3). He describes both areas as interdependent. In his view, unconscious fears create the desire among members to escape each other, fight among themselves, pair up, and so on. This can cause groups to avoid doing the tasks that are at hand and these emotions can also hinder teamwork (Bion, 1961).

Figure 2.3

Teams work on two planes: the conscious and the subconscious.

Bion contributed much to the scientific study of the behaviour of groups. He used the concept of group dynamics to describe the forces that are unleashed when individuals come together in a group. Cartwright and Zander (1968) defined *group dynamics* as the increase in knowledge of the nature of groups, and the laws governing their development and internal communication—both among individuals within a group and between groups.

Behavioural theories derive from pioneer work carried out by B. F. Skinner (1953) and other advocates of behaviourism. Skinner believed that psychological factors such as instinctual drive might condition the reactions of people within teams. He noted, however, that such factors could be difficult to identify accurately and, therefore, he recommended that in order to understand human endeavours, one should only observe people's manifested behaviour, rather than try to investigate underlying psychological factors. Skinner's research showed that behaviour followed by positive rewards would foster recurrent behaviour, such as people's willingness to contribute; negative feedback, however, discouraged people from participating. One theory developed by the social psychologists John Thibaut and Harold Kelly (1959), known as "social exchange theory", is based on Skinner's contribution and assumes that, as people are pleasure-seeking, they will strive to maximise their own rewards while minimising their efforts. When people work in teams, the results will be a compromise.

Motivational theories seek to explain what motivates people when working in teams. Why do some strive for leadership roles in teams whereas others are content to follow? Why are some teams more creative than others? Motivation has to do with human desires and needs, as well as many other psychological factors that combine to determine why people will react in one way rather than another. The "level of aspiration" theory put forward by Kurt Lewin (1939) is an example of a motivational theory. According to this theory, people work in accordance with what they think will make them meet their objectives best. Studies show that goal setting is encouraging for teams and that it motivates teams to achieve their objectives. On the basis of their experience, teams that reach their goals tend to set yet higher goals where team members contribute more. Teams that do not achieve their goals, however, gradually decrease their level of aspiration, team spirit worsens, and members leave the team more frequently.

Cognitive theories are based on the idea that team dynamics can be explained in terms of the cognitive processes that occur within individuals in teams. Cognitive processes are concerned with how people receive information, organise it, and integrate it. People are constantly processing information, placing it in the context of past experiences, and memorising it. Individuals in teams are constantly "reading" each other's behaviour, making judgements and assumptions that affect the way they perceive other members, the team, and themselves. An example of one cognitive theory is the "expectation-states theory" of Joseph Berger and his team (1992). This theory is meant to explain how individuals come to be defined in different positions or take on different roles within groups. According to this theory, there are mainly two determining factors: (1) the quality of the individual and their ability to perform a task that awaits the attention of the team, and (2) the personality traits of an individual that seem likely to contribute to success in general. Individuals who are thought to have the most qualities will achieve a higher position than others within the team.

Systems theories try to explain the team as an integrated system. Researchers in various fields such as engineering, biology, and medicine have found out that better performance is often achieved when a system is established in such a way that it sets up relationships between factors that were previously independent. A systems theory of teams would imply that teams are systems in which individualised elements together form a complex whole. Teams are, hence, active systems that, for instance, collect data, process this data, and come to a conclusion. Systems theories propose models to understand many aspects of team activities, including team development, team functions, and internal disputes.

All of the above theories have their advantages and disadvantages (Figure 2.4) (Forsyth, 2019). In the context of managing teams, *psychoanalytical theories* are rather speculative, theoretical, and inspiring. *Motivational theories* demonstrate the importance of encouraging team members and relate to setting challenging but realistic goals for success. Goal setting can be ambiguous, as objectives have to be both challenging and also felt to be obtainable by the team members. *Behavioural theories* show that it is not guaranteed that the team will bring out the best in an individual if they cannot see the personal benefits of participating. *Systems theories* view teams as systems where different tasks are ideally assigned in such a way that the system as a whole functions at its best. Team members can compensate for each other when working together, and the team as a whole is more capable than individuals on their own. Within the team, there is extensive knowledge that can only be activated for the common good when contributions are made towards mutual

Figure 2.4

All team theories have their advantages and disadvantages.

benefits. *Cognitive theories* shed light on the designation of roles that team members inevitably undertake when working in teams. The manager needs to pay attention to this and to manage the process in such a way that it benefits the team and their work. *Biological theories* show that project team members are driven, amongst other things, by an inherent need to protect themselves against others. The consequence of this is the tendency of many teams to focus their efforts primarily on maintaining the power the team might have acquired. For real teams, some difficult factors to determine theoretically, but which can nonetheless be very influential, are the preceding history of a group and the established culture, as well as the nature of external circumstances the group as a whole is exposed to.

Reflection points

- What theories do you know about teams?
- What theories do you have about groups?
- What kind of theories are your theories?
- What are the pros and cons of each of these theories?

Importance of project teams

Project teams are in the unique position of being created to solve defined problems. If they are professional teams, they define tasks and have well-defined objectives in terms of time, cost, and quality. When project teams fail, the main reasons will be that the project was not adequately defined from the beginning, that the team was not given full authority to do what it needed to, that risk assessments were not completed or undertaken at all, or that insufficient attention was given to the project stakeholders. On top of this, it is necessary to examine team dynamics and define how this might affect a project and its outcomes. Project management is a fertile ground for anyone who wants to gain a better knowledge of team dynamics. A variety of psychological, social, and biological factors can affect projects and it is beneficial to make use of scientific research on the subject. All professional project managers should have a basic understanding of team dynamics and make use of them in management (Figure 2.5).

We have seen that many methods can be employed for the study of teams. No single method stands solely out as the best and arguing that one method is more scientific than another is not overly useful. Ideally, the subject of the research should define the research method and the variables should define what needs measuring and how. The multifarious aspects of team dynamics are reflected in the many theories about group dynamics. Different theories seek explanations for different aspects, they do not necessarily contradict each other. These different theories should be seen as complementary in advancing our understanding of teams.

There is no doubt that research on team dynamics can be both multi-faceted and complex. Team research can, for instance, be more complicated statistically and logistically than research where one individual is being

Figure 2.5

Project managers need to understand team dynamics.

investigated. The dynamics within teams can change rapidly and these changes can be both substantial and unpredictable. Relationships between members can be so complex that it becomes difficult to grasp their scope. These problems are not insurmountable, however, and, in order to understand teams, it is essential to be familiar with fundamental research methods, and to be able to assess their appropriateness. It is important throughout to bear in mind what the most important issues are that team research is meant to aid. For example, an HR department may recognise that employee turnover in a particular division of a company is unusually high and seek to understand what the main causal factors are in order to prevent this in the future. If the resulting work is not thorough and does not ask probing questions, then the real reasons for this may not be uncovered and the problem may become chronic.

Reflection points

- What matters most in the study of teams?
- What is the practical value of scientific research into teams?
- How might a project manager conduct research into the performance of their project team?
- On what, if any, research have you based team management that you have undertaken?

Teams as platforms for communication enhancement

Teams and teamwork are based on effective communication. They are also a fertile ground for learning about, and developing, interpersonal communication skills such as the ability to appropriately self-disclose, respond well towards others, and have the confidence for active engagement. Good communication skills begin with your *self-presentation* (Egan, 1976). One of the main objectives of communication is to establish and build relationships with others through, for instance: Spending time with your team doing things such as talking, sharing experiences, or discussing situations at ease; fostering respect for team members and showing that you like them and care for them; strengthening a sense of mutuality within the team through mutual give-and-take exchange and acceptance; discussing your challenges with team members and showing them that you are ready to help; and taking on activities together outside of formal employment.

Everyday relationships are certainly something that "happen" but are not necessarily something that we work systematically on building up. Professional relationships, however, with colleagues, customers, or clients can easily become emotionally charged and hence the need to manage interpersonal communications in professional settings. In managerial teams, a variety of interpersonal relations build up and the interactions associated with these can have a purposeful meaning if well managed. They are also a great opportunity to improve communication competences within the team.

One of the key skills of good communication is the ability to listen attentively to others, in other words being an active listener when others talk. This also includes the ability to respond with integrity to others when they have expressed their opinions, experiences, and feelings. Active listening creates trust and will gradually enable others to invite you into their personal space of personal meanings, experience, and insight. Active listening also *earns you a hearing* so that you will be better heard when it comes to telling others what you think or how you feel. Good listening is also a great sign of appreciation.

A dedicated team in which team members work mutually on improving their communication is a platform for human expression and performance. Open communication enables members to share with others, get feedback, and to find out what might be improved in the team communication. Once you've established trust, you can easily let your team know what you like and what you would like to see changed. In that kind of team atmosphere, team members can help each other by providing feedback on how they see the quality of communication and interaction with each other. This can also help process feelings and emotions that manifest themselves within the team and might, if not dealt with, affect the team's performance.

Your aim is to create a great culture of communication within the team. In order, however, to turn them into a platform for communication competence-training, all team members need to understand what that implies and be happy to each commit to the initiative to make it happen. For some this will be intuitive but others might be uncertain and sceptical. We will discuss this challenge in further detail later in the book.

Reflection points

- How would you describe your communication style in the working environment?
- What do you get out of your interpersonal interaction with others?
- How do you disclose information about yourself to others?

Five levels of communication skills

We suggest that, based on insights from American communication expert Gerard Egan, that when it comes to using your teams as platforms for communication skills training, there are essentially five levels to which you can aspire (Egan, 1976). At the *first level*, all team members will need to commit to the learning process by discussing and defining the mutual agreement that will be the foundation for the training. Here, the main aim is to build trust and mutual understanding based on the curiosity to learn.

The *second level* involves interpersonal interaction where participants are encouraged to express themselves clearly in front of others, and to demonstrate their ability to listen actively. Here, participants gradually learn how to deal with trust and risk in interpersonal communication. Try the following exercise to get you started: Form teams of threes, sitting down facing each other or standing and facing each other. While one participant talks (self-expression), another listens, and the third observes what takes place between the two, and is ready to give feedback on what was done well and what could be improved. What you are practising here is competence in self-expression and listening to others with understanding and respect. This requires the person speaking to use their intuition to express themselves appropriately and in accordance with the circumstances. Self-expression includes expressing appropriate feelings alongside opinions, facts, judgement, etc. The listener should try to respond with *empathy* and sincerity (Figure 2.6). Empathy is probably the most important communication quality that any of us possesses and we'll come back to it in more detail in later chapters.

The *third of the five levels* involves developing competence in providing constructive feedback and confronting others. In other words, it is an exercise in taking the necessary risks that, if done right, will enable your fellow team members to understand themselves better. It can help participants greatly in developing communication skills if they observe each other and are able to provide constructive feedback to one another. Try inviting participants to help each other to identify strengths, weaknesses, and inconsistencies as part of a feedback session on a given piece of work.

Figure 2.6

The listener should try to respond with empathy and sincerity.

It is important that the person providing feedback starts by focusing on the strengths before moving onto any weaknesses; a weakness is often an exaggerated strength or an under-developed strength. For example, the ability to organise and plan consistently is definitely an attribute for project managers. If you can't organise or plan, then you are going to struggle managing a project (an undeveloped strength). On the other hand, over-organisation can lead you to spend far too much time and effort on planning or even to plans that are over-detailed, difficult to implement, and totally inflexible (an exaggerated strength).

When using this model to explore a perceived weakness, take time to unpack the strength before you tackle the weakness. Thus, in our example about planning and organisation, you might say:

> You are a master planner. No one produces the quality or detail of plans as well as you do, however, on some occasions [cite an example], when you take your planning a little too far, I see people turning off, ignoring the plan as impractical or showing frustrating because they want to move forward. Is that something you recognise and how can we help you make sure your plans are excellent without being over-developed?

At this stage, you can use the opportunity to practise the ability to show empathy with care and compassion and, by doing that, help participants to gain deeper self-understanding. If done well, this also enables participants to criticise and suggest that colleagues view their behaviour in more detail. The final goal of this stage is that participants acquire the skills necessary in building and maintaining *open and direct communication*.

At the *fourth level*, the team should focus on using specific communication competences for improving their teamwork; learning how to establish and maintain relationships, encourage each other, and confront one another when needed. This is something that takes considerable practice and is best carried out with the team as a whole rather than person-to-person exercises. Competence in this level of communication requires two key skills. The first is the ability to *participate actively within the team*. Instead of being a passive spectator, each team member needs, beyond the responsibility for themselves, to be responsible for the functioning of the team as a whole. Regardless of who starts a conversation or what happens within the team, each member must participate and respond effectively to one another. The second skill is to learn *how to take the initiative actively* within the team. This can be done by showing interest and empathy, acting in an appropriate manner, and by engaging in communication with others in a constructive and supportive manner. Furthermore, you must be willing to be challenged and to be called for an opinion. Taking the initiative means not only waiting for comments from others but also actively asking them to participate and advise each other how to strengthen relationships and co-operation between individuals.

The *fifth level* involves *working in earnest* on the basis of the team's mutual communication training contract. The nature of this agreement is discussed in more detail in the next section. At this fifth level, the communication experimentation can be less structured, as all team members intuitively try out all the new skills that they have acquired. Emphasis should be placed on creativity and on the more direct use of all the communication competences (of all the five above stages) that are introduced in this book. All team members should continually evaluate their personal communication approach, give and receive feedback, and work to establish and develop interpersonal interaction with others in the team.

Reflection points

- What personal communication competences do you think you could develop using the five-level approach?
- If you were leading this training exercise, what approaches would you take to encourage greater interaction among participants and build trust?

Communication contract

It takes a lot of discipline to work with a team to foster communication competences and it takes courage as well. To train in this way, the team needs to establish a mutual commitment. This is best achieved by having the team itself, as a whole, creating either a formal or an informal contract that expresses this commitment (Figure 2.7). The aim is to build a place of safety and trust in which participants can explore and learn, as well as establish a shared understanding of their expectations for all. If the programme is unclear, misunderstanding may arise and the chances of success will decrease.

The agreement should require all team members to promote the communication skills of the participants and the team collectively. It should emphasise a commitment to *self-reflect* in such a way that everyone can examine themselves and share with one another how each of them interacts

Figure 2.7

Formal or informal agreement should express team commitment.

and works with the others. This means that members may need to change their personal style as they become aware of weaknesses and build on their strengths. The agreement should both define the learning communication objectives of the team and the methods that might help each member to achieve these objectives. To sum up, the agreement should involve that all team members commit to: Build and maintain their relationships with one another and all team members; participate actively in the process of creating a strong communication culture; establish and develop their relationships with all other team members; pay special attention to their own communication style and change it if needed; give each other constructive feedback and a chance to experiment with new behaviours; and support each other in changing communication behaviours to enable more effective communication (based on Egan, 1976).

In projects where the stakes are high, it can be useful to put the protocols and rules of conduct that the team has jointly decided to follow down on paper. Such an agreement could also define the values to be upheld and ways of dealing with conflicts and crises. A written agreement will have greater awareness amongst the group and more chance of being respected. In agreeing to it, participants will know what is expected as desirable behaviour and what boundaries should be respected.

Team success is based on a mutual commitment and efficient communication. Communication competence can, however, only be gained through introspection, self-reflection, and interaction with others. It requires you to take the initiative and have the courage and sensitivity to engage with others through empathetic communication. It also involves a considerable interest in others, and a willingness to understand them and respond to them in a professional and yet sympathetic manner.

Reflection points

- Discuss your co-operation in terms of how you communicate within your team.
- Draft a communication agreement for your team.
- What are trust and confidentiality?
- How far does your freedom extend within the team?

Communication journal

Anyone involved in a team that has committed itself to developing the communication skills of its members is, in fact, undertaking research on themselves with the help of others. It is, therefore, useful to write down all your findings in a communication diary where you can document events, thoughts, feelings, experiences, behaviour, and what stands out in meetings. The aim is to scrutinise your own behaviour and that of others, and to reflect on it

Figure 2.8

Record your experiences of communication or lack thereof in your journal.

following any meetings so that each subsequent meeting is more rewarding and successful.

You'll find it useful to record the experiences of communication or lack thereof in your communication journal, for example: "Carl ignored me throughout the meeting and it hurts. I will check what's going on at the next meeting". You can also record observed behaviour, for example: "I asked Susan a lot of questions at the meeting but did not understand her answers without asking her to clarify. I noticed that I do this quite often". Or you can write down your feelings, for example:

> I've let myself down yesterday and few people in the team have since contacted me and no one made me feel bad even though I lost my temper. I haven't accounted for my inappropriate behaviour and need to apologise to them. (Figure 2.8).

The communication journal also helps to keep track of all the factors relevant to your objective of building communication competence. These then need to be expressed in a constructive manner to the team during the next meeting. When you contribute to the team, endeavour to be both clear and thorough. It is quite common for participants to write good notes but then ignore them in subsequent meetings. If this happens, you may wish to discuss this and encourage the participant to state their concerns. Some journals have a special communications page for each participant in the team, which allows you to monitor each individual's communication style with a special focus on their relationship with each of the other team members. This is an effective means of giving feedback to team members. It is also good to create a task list to record planned improvement, based on the notes taken. Good notes increase the probability of success and will help to make the training more effective.

Reflection points

- In your communication journal, describe your observations on communication skills within your team.

- In your communication journal, describe what you notice regarding your own interaction with other members.
- Describe both your experience and your critical view of these experiences. Keep your attention focused on your own behaviour rather than the behaviour of others. Compare and discuss your experiences with others by listening to and sharing them within the team.

Active listening

Active listening is a core communication competence that involves focusing your attention on the person speaking in such a way that they are aware that you are doing your best to understand them. Active listening both encourages others to reciprocate and listen to you and to express themselves. When you listen actively, you should be able to summarise what has been said and, by doing this, check your understanding of what they mean and make them feel that you are sincerely trying to see their point of view.

By listening actively, you increase the likelihood that those you are talking to will reciprocate and listen when it is your turn to put forward views (Figure 2.9). If your two (or more) viewpoints are opposing, it is best to keep the interaction short and to state your views as objectively as possible. Try to identify common ground and demonstrate your willingness to look for possible solutions together. When another team member has presented ideas for a solution, you should try to build on them, refer back to their points, and then put forward your own ideas in the context of what he or she has proposed.

It is useful to practise the basics of active listening in a four-step exercise. Step One: listen to another participant without showing any reaction or interest, sitting completely passively. This enables the person speaking to

Figure 2.9

Active listening will enable you to earn a hearing from others.

practise self-expression without being supported by the listener. They may find this uncomfortable as the exercise reveals how unnatural it is to not react to or support another person when they try to express themselves. The speaker will also experience how difficult it is to talk if the listener does not respond or show any interest. Step Two: repeat the conversation but this time support the speaker by simple gestures and minimal responses such as "yes", "interesting", and "aha". You'll understand how much easier it is to listen and to express yourself when at least a minimum amount of support is allowed for. Step Three: helps the speaker to express him- or herself with short, open ended questions (questions that do not allow yes-or-no answers, such as those beginning with "how …", "when …", "what …" and so on.). At this stage, try to refrain from using "why …" questions, as they might be interpreted as being critical, or require reasoning, and this might not always be appropriate or timely. Step Four: summarise what the speaker has said using, as much as possible, their own words. It is important to understand that *active listening* and *empathy* are closely related, both stemming from respect for others and their views. We'll return to this connection in later chapters.

Reflection points

- Have one person speak and another listen without giving any feedback or support and discuss the impact on both.
- Have one person speak and another support them by gestures and minimal support and discuss the impact on both.
- Have one person speak while the other encourages them to express themselves by asking open questions and discuss the impact on both.
- Have one person speak while the other listens and then, when the speaker has finished, the listener recounts what was said, discuss the accuracy of the recount.

References

Bales, R. F. (1970). *Personality and interpersonal behavior*. New York: Rinehart and Winston.
Bales, R. F. & Cohen, S. (1979). *SYMLOG: A system for the multiple level observation of groups*. New York: The Free Press.
Berger, J., Wagner, D. G., & Zelditch, M., Jr. (1992). "A working strategy for constructing theories: State organizing processes" in G. Ritzer (Ed.), *Studies in metatheorizing in sociology* (pp. 107–123). Thousand Oaks, CA: Sage.
Bion, W. R. (1961). *Experiences in groups*. London: Tavistock.
Cartwright, D. & Zander, A. (1968). *Group dynamics: Research and theory* (3rd ed.). New York: Harper & Row.
Egan, G. (1976). *Interpersonal living*. Belmont, CA: Wadsworth Publishing Company.
Forsyth, D. R. (2019). *Group dynamics* (7th ed.). Boston, MA: Cengage Learning.
Freud, S. (1921). *Massenpsychologie und Ich-analyse*, Leipzig, Vienna and Zurich: Internationaler Psychoanalytischer Verlag. *Group psychology and the analysis of the ego* 1922. London and Vienna: International Psycho-Analytical Press.

Lewin K., (1939). "Field theory and experiment in social psychology" in *American Journal of Sociology*, 44, 868–897.

Lewin, K., Lippitt, R., & White, R. (1939). "Patterns of aggressive behaviour in experimentally created 'social climates'" in *Journal of Social Psychology*, 10, 271–299.

Moreno, J. L. (1934). *Who shall survive? A new approach to the problem of human interrelations.* Washington, DC: Nervous and Mental Disease Publishing Co.

Skinner, B. F. (1953). *Science and human behaviour.* New York: Macmillan.

Thibaut, J. W. & Kelley, H. H. (1959). *The social psychology of groups.* New York: Wiley.

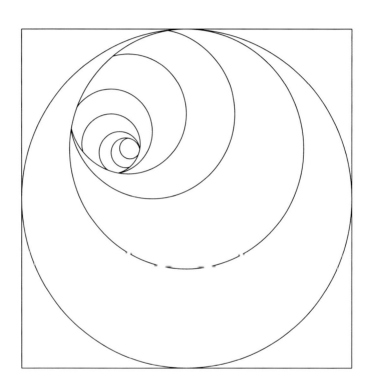

3 Team selection and team communication

······································

Teams are formed for many different reasons and to serve many different purposes. They can involve people with a wide range of expertise performing very different roles, or people with limited expertise and performing a broadly similar role. Project teams are formed to manage often complex undertakings and are created around specific projects with a beginning and end date and with a purpose to achieve certain results. House-building projects, for instance, require a range of contributors—e.g. architects, foremen, block-layers, labourers, carpenters, roofers, plasterers, electricians, plumbers, painters, and so on—as it is in most working environments. An individual's involvement in a particular team may be up to their personal desire or necessity, or due to orders from superiors. Teams can be formed for socially beneficial purposes, such as is the case with rescue teams or teams that want to promote political change. Teams are also formed as a response to circumstances, such as a crisis situation or to transform the fortunes of a company. In all of these cases, if you know what makes a person want to participate in the group you'll have a better understanding of what motivates them and what the team must provide to keep that person committed.

Personalities and team participation

Teams are formed to accomplish things, and with this comes a gradual sense of belonging. Our motive for participating in teams can be founded on a common purpose, personal aspiration, a desire to identify with the team and its mission, interest in the network or experiences that the team might provide. The psychologist Richard R. Moreland, in his theory on group formation, stated that groups form gradually when people realise that they are repeatedly meeting the same individuals (Arkin & Burger, 1980; Moreland, 1987; Forsyth, 2019). Repeated interactions promote a sense of unity, cause participants to see themselves as a team, and cause others in the area to begin to treat them as a team. Not everyone will be as keen on team participation and personality may play a role, if for example, there are introverted or extroverted people.

Individuals have many reasons for wanting to join teams. These include working style, previous experience, and personality, but circumstances also play their part. In terms of basic personality traits, some people are naturally *extroverted*, and seek empowerment from others to maintain their sense of self. Others are *introverted* and prefer to be alone to maintain their sense of self. The Swiss psychologist Carl G. Jung (1924) developed the basic concept of introverted and extroverted personality types. He argued that a tendency to engage with, or move away from, others was a basic element of human personality. Introverted individuals may avoid teamwork, are less inclined to workplace chat, and sometimes find it hard to express themselves to others, preferring to be alone. Extroverted people are attracted to other people, are good at self-expression, and are more likely to enjoy working in teams. Culture influences whether introverted or extroverted personalities are preferred in a determined social setting. Extroverted people, for example, are often favoured in the U.S., while introverted characteristics are considered a virtue in some Asian communities.

Extroverts are predisposed to work in teams because relationships with others encourage them to express themselves and engage others. Extroverts are usually positive in temperament as well as being more quarrelsome, energetic, and happier than introverts (Forsyth, 2019). When teams are selected, extroverts are often chosen because they seem more willing to participate, take action, get straight to work, and are easier to motivate than introverted individuals. However, when choosing extroverted individuals for a team you might not necessarily be conscious of their underlying skills. It is hard to judge competency and being extrovert, alone, does not necessarily mean that an individual will make useful contributions to a team. Whilst there are various traits associated with introverts and extroverts, remember these are often archetypes and you should be careful to avoid stereotyping people on this basis. There are lots of different kinds of people who are extroverts and the same is true of introverts. Depending on the circumstances, there can be a very broad range of personality traits that are desirable for filling team roles. Teams benefit from having members with a complementary mix of personality traits. For example, a festival management team will need outgoing and connected people to attract sponsorship and encourage participation by communities, while it might also benefit from having others who operate quietly in the background ensuring effective planning and logistics.

The crucial factor in selecting an individual to join a team is the extent to which that person will contribute value to the team. It is up to the team leader to provide clear goals and instruction at the beginning of a project, and then to ensure that individuals in the team stay on track and can see how their individual contribution will benefit the overall intended outcome. Understanding what individuals seek from the team and appreciating their personality and communication style enable you to be a better team leader for each and every member in the team.

Reflection points

- Would you describe yourself as an introverted or extroverted person? Can you be both?
- What kind of personality do you have?
- What motivates you to participate in teams?
- What personal needs would you like to be met in a team?

Social needs and teams

The theory of social motivation can help us to understand that it is primarily social need—the need for relations, intimacy, and power—that define people's personal willingness to join teams. People with *higher social needs* and a *stronger need for intimacy* will (generally) be more willing to join teams. They are also more likely to express concern for others, look for friendship, team spirit, and want to be helpful. Likewise, those who have a strong need for power may also seek to join teams because they see them as a locus to influence others (Figure 3.1) (Green, 1995; Murray, 1938; Winter, 1973; Forsyth, 2019).

Figure 3.1

People with a strong need for power may also seek to join teams.

The American psychologist/philosopher William C. Schutz (1925–2002) measured the integration of the need for different levels of inclusion, power, and affection with his *Fundamental Interpersonal Relations Orientation* (FIRO) scale (1958, 1992). His research indicated that group participation is based on at least three basic needs, which works well when applied to teams:

- *Need for inclusion* indicates a desire to feel a part of the team, to be approved within a team and be able to interact with other members. This need can motivate a person to work with others and enjoy teamwork.
- *Need to control* indicates a desire to take initiative and show determination and can be fulfilled by any actions that involve leading the team, for example, by organising it and maintaining its processes. This need can be expressed both as an interest in controlling, and being controlled, by others.
- *Need for affection* indicates a desire to open up and show and receive kindness, i.e. the need for warm and positive relationships with others. *Kindness* involves friendliness, generosity, and consideration, and may be driven by a number of factors such as altruism, the desire to get along with others, or to be recognised as likeable.

The needs of team members will affect the behaviour of the team and have a decisive influence on how people treat others and how they want to be treated themselves. Understanding how teams can give people an opportunity to meet some of their basic needs is useful when it comes to managing them. Individuals who have a strong need to belong will want to get things done with others rather than on their own. If they have a need to control, they will look for teams that they can control. If they have a need to be controlled they will prefer to work in a team with a strong leader and clear direction. If they are looking for affection, then they will want to work with individuals who are warm and friendly. The stronger these needs are, the more likely these needs will make a person want to join a team. It's worth paying some attention to these needs, for instance, by allowing your team members to take on different roles and by ensuring that the team culture meets the social needs of participants, where this is possible. Success is more likely if these needs are recognised and roles assigned accordingly. Changing roles or expanding roles in some way on a regular basis enables team members to feel that they are not stuck in a rut and helps them embrace the challenges that the team faces. A sense of being trapped in unchallenging circumstances can be especially demoralising for creative and driven people and managing such people can be both a challenge and great fun.

Reflection points

- What social needs do you have?
- What needs do people try to meet by participating in teams?
- How do you try to meet the social needs of others in your team?

Willingness to participate in teams

Aside from obligation, financial, and other inducements, various other theories can be used to understand what makes people want to work with others in teams. The Self-Evaluation Maintenance (SEM) theory developed by American social psychologist Abraham Tesser (1941–) suggests that two people in a relationship each aim to keep themselves feeling psychologically healthy through an ongoing comparison with the other (Tesser, 1988). The theory explains how outstanding performance in others can affect our own behaviour via this process of comparison and self-reflection (Figure 3.2). This is a complex area and the comparison process can impact our sense of self-esteem in many ways and often unconsciously. You may, for instance, be delighted if a sibling scores a goal for a team because of your sense of close association. Someone else experiencing the same circumstances may be despondent because they feel that their sibling's success highlights their own failure. The high performance of someone close to you, in a relevant area, can invite comparisons with your own achievements and this can be why individuals will often choose not to interact with people who are better than themselves in areas that are important to their sense of self-worth.

Closeness and *relevance* are key concepts in the SEM theory. Studies indicate that we are less willing to help people who are close to us in areas that have a high relevance for our own self-evaluation. Instead, we may be more

Figure 3.2

Performance of others can affect our own behaviour.

willing to assist strangers. If the activity is of low relevance, the opposite tends to be the case and we like to be associated with the success of others close to us. In this way, a pit crew member working for a Formula One team is more likely to be jubilant at a team race victory than the other driver on the team who did not win. This raises an interesting question: How is the performance of individuals within a team affected if they have to work with someone who strongly affects their self-confidence? The short answer is that this can lead to a reduction in self-esteem, and individuals can find themselves excluded within teams, which can have a negative impact on their performance. This may be unavoidable to a certain extent but the negative effects can be mitigated with a mature understanding of the potential impact.

Individuals who resemble each other in some way, or have similar interests, seem to be attracted to one another and this promotes bonding between them. American social psychologist Leon Festinger (1919–1989) argued that individuals often turn to others for information about themselves and their environment (1950, 1954). Although it is sometimes enough to be convinced on our own, we tend to look to others to verify our convictions. We thus take part in social comparison to determine whether our opinions, beliefs, or attitudes are consistent with those of others.

Social comparison can work in a very peculiar way when people are in danger or become desperate. When someone encounters dangerous or difficult situations, they tend to seek strength in the company of others. Discomfort will make people seek out the company of those who are faced with similar problems. Difficulties, danger, and threats often encourage individuals to seek the support of others facing similar situations, and bond with them. When faced with threatening situations, you will naturally begin to form relationships with others to gather information, compare what they know, and to try to determine whether your understanding is correct, valid, or justified (Goethals & Darley, 1987). The American psychologist Stanley Schachter (1959) illustrated that the majority of individuals want to wait with others when facing an emergent threat (63%). Schachter claimed that this proved that anxiety awakened a need for companionship. Schachter also found out that 60% of individuals wished to wait with people who were about to undergo the same ordeal rather than with people who were not. This suggests that the need for further information and consultation was a critical factor. There are many real-life examples of people who desperately look out for people in a similar situation for information and support. Other studies showed that when individuals find themselves in awkward situations and are not surrounded by others in similarly awkward situations, they socially withdraw, are less willing to interact with others, and prefer not to discuss these situations with others.

An individual who is faced with uncertainty will seek out a likely outcome by means of social comparison. In one study, participants in groups of four to six people were asked to take part in an experiment in a situation that provoked uncertainty and shame (Morris et al., 1976). The groups were observed without their knowledge and details such as members' *interactions*, *actions*, *withdrawals*, and *controlled non-reactions* were recorded. Participants tended to talk about something other than what feelings or thoughts the objects in front of them provoked and sought to *escape* from the situation. If the results of this experiment are applied to teams in general, then we may say that people tend to make social comparisons when anxious. When teams work under circumstances where team members expect they might feel ashamed, they refrain from connecting with other members of the team. If, however, the need to obtain information outweighs the fear of embarrassment, they will try to obtain the information that they need (Buunk & Hoorens, 1992; Davison *et al.*, 2000).

An individual with little experience in teams will try to imitate what others do. In very competent teams a part of the socialisation of a new member will involve them observing and learning from the others. This can either motivate or intimidate the new member, who might even change their style, such as clothing and demeanour, to fit in better. *Downward social comparison* is when we compare ourselves to others who are less capable or worse off than we are in an area that is fundamental to our self-esteem. In a positive sense, this can increase an awareness of your own merits and abilities and can foster a positive sense of self. On the flip side, it leads to arrogance. *Upward social comparison* happens when we compare ourselves with others who we see as better, more able, or more respected than ourselves. In a negative sense, such a comparison can make us feel incapable and discouraged. In a positive sense, it can reset expectations of your abilities, motivate and encourage you to improve.

Reflection points

- What attracts people to teams?
- What effects does anxiety have on teams?
- How has downward social comparison affected a team of which you have experience?
- How has upward social comparison affected a team of which you have experience?

Resistance in teams

Resistance to participate in teamwork can have different causes and manifest in many ways. Some find working with others to be difficult, beyond their abilities, or simply of little or no interest. Others may just not see the benefits to themselves of team participation and may want to ensure their needs will be met in advance by negotiating their terms of engagement. Others may have had negative experiences of teamwork and participate only hesitantly.

Shyness is an innate personality trait that can lower interest and participation in team activities. Shyness manifests itself in individuals from very early on in life. Children demonstrate fear or shyness when they meet someone they do not know. Some constantly seek to interact with others, while others are reserved and shy when amongst people they don't know. Shyness can be very unpleasant and if you suffer from it, you may find it nerve-racking to communicate with others. Most people largely overcome shyness when they grow older but, for some, it can evolve into a social phobia, a condition that is characterised by persistent anxiety when interacting with others. The underlying cause is often the desire in the person in question to make a good impression, associated with a concern that their efforts will fail and others may dislike them. These negative expectations increase the unpleasant emotion with escalating psychological consequences that manifest in anxiety-related behaviour; individuals may become excited, feel strange, awkward, or unwanted by others. Physical symptoms can include a raised pulse, blushing, sweating, as well as the dreaded blank state of mind and the loss of our train of thought.

Shy individuals are more unlikely to want to join teams and once they do, often remain on the periphery of any social activity. They can be silent, look downward when speaking, talk with a quiet voice, and are more likely to function effectively within teams that do not challenge them. Such a person's interest in team activities is limited, they may agree with the views of the whole, make little of their own participation in the team communication, and often need help of others to get their views across. Such non-engagement can naturally have an impact on team performance but when managing shy people, you should be considerate and show care. It is good to know that most people who are shy and anxious are able, and willing, to reduce these impacts. You should support shy individuals with appropriate assistance if it is possible.

Resistance to working with others can also be influenced by previous experiences and choices (Figure 3.3). Negative experiences in working with others may discourage team participation. A talented individual, for example, may have contributed greatly to a previous team but been overlooked when the time came for rewards and promotions. Feeling of resentment over this may even overshadow their response when their abilities *are* recognised and acknowledged in a new environment.

Insights into what impact previous experience of interpersonal encounters can have on team members can help you to give those with bad experiences the chance to have a better one through positive orientation and socialising. Organise your team activities in such a way that you avoid the recurrence of negative experiences and foster more positive attitudes. Part of your responsibility is to ensure that team members stay active and committed at the necessary, desirable, and appropriate levels. By creating a positive atmosphere and engendering a sense of excitement towards finishing each phase of work, you should help encourage a positive attitude from team members.

Resistance to participation may also come from external forces and this can stem from societal attitudes around who should do what. Gender, religion, status,

Figure 3.3

Resistance can be influenced by previous experiences and choices.

stereotyping, and cultural background of those who participate can play a role and even overshadow any criteria based on merit. In terms of gender, research shows that there are certain gender differences when it comes to willingness to participate in teams but these differences are more tendencies rather than being absolute. There are indications that women tend to be more willing to participate, especially in areas where personal warmth and team building occur. Most researchers agree that women recall more specific aspects of their relations with others and remember more details about their social life. However, even though women, in general, do seem to put more emphasis on interpersonal relations, it does not necessarily follow that they have stronger social needs than men. In terms of leadership roles, statistics from different countries and different sectors indicate a significantly higher percentage of men are leading teams. These may be, for example, professional teams, organisations, political parties, and military units. This is commonly linked to the "glass ceiling effect" (related to gender) and Cotter *et al.* (2001) provide a useful description of this phenomenon. Stereotypical attitudes and conventions may result in capable women not getting the chance to participate in managerial challenges to the extent that they would like to, when they might, in fact, do things better than others. Cultural norms are often deeply rooted, such as the idea that women should stay at home after they become mothers or, in more extreme forms, where women are seen as having no rights at all. Professional managers, whether male or female, are often at the coalface with regard to human rights, and their attitudes, stances, and actions with regard to gender equality should reflect modern times where meritocratic criteria predominate.

Reflection points

- What is shyness?
- What makes you shy?
- How has shyness manifested itself in teams you have participated in?
- Why might some people not want to participate in project teams?

The supportive team

There are a number of other factors—psychological or social—that have an impact on whether individuals will be interested in working in teams and how they then work within the team. When people worry that they might be held responsible for bad decisions or poor outcomes, they will often come up with a team decision-making process in order to evade personal responsibility and "hide" within the group, particularly when they feel disempowered. They may also refer to team dissatisfaction with the lack of action and believe that change will only be achieved by mobilising a joint force. Such things lean toward the negative implications of team participation. On the more positive side, teams can also be fertile ground for social support and consolidation. Teams can, in general, provide their members with at least five types of support:

- *Recognition support* in when the team as a whole approves a member and clearly affirms that they are part of the team.
- *Informative support* is when team members provide each other with information and advice, guide each other on specific issues, and propose solutions for each other's problems. Support is given by providing information about the problems to be dealt with, and advice on methods or ways of managing certain tasks or project phases is provided.
- *Problem-solving support* is when team members help each other to solve problems by doing each other favours or giving each other tools to solve an issue.
- *Emotional* and *spiritual support* is where the expression of feelings and emotion is used as a means of social support, appraisal, and encouragement. Emotional support means active listening to each other, showing each other understanding and empathy, allowing members to state their concerns and discuss their problems, share their feelings and even, if appropriate, express affection by nodding, touching, or hugging. The related spiritual support is when the team provides existential or ideological direction in order to help them gain a sense of importance, meaning, and purpose.

Some teams have to deal with crises, disasters, or other major challenges. Such situations can generate sympathy and the formation of deeper bonds amongst the team's members as they try to console each other and this social support is important. Man is a social creature so it is not surprising that this quality appears when people feel overly challenged or under pressure.

Teams react to challenges in two basic ways. Firstly, when faced with an immediate threat they may either "fight" or "flee" the situation. A sudden challenge may unite the team and encourage the team members to work together to overcome the challenge or to escape it collectively. In such a situation, the team needs to decide what course of action to take and, in order to give themselves the best chance of success, team members will have to agree on how to react. When consensus is reached, ties are strengthened and this enables the team to achieve things that were unthinkable without co-ordinated teamwork. Secondly, if challenged over a longer period, the members of a team are more likely to begin to "tend" and "befriend" each other. This tendency is more likely if the threat is long-term and long-lasting effects occur. Team members seek to strengthen their ties and will support each other to deal with the challenge (Figure 3.4).

Project teams can "fight" or "flee" at different stages in a project life cycle. When the workload increases, they may "attack" the tasks at hand in a unifying effort or become withdrawn. Success or failure to perform in such a situation depends on the quality of the interpersonal relationships formed and the team's loyalty towards the project. If the strain is prolonged, the team might start to show "tend to" and "befriend" reactions where members rely more on spiritual and emotional support from each other.

Figure 3.4

Team members can support each other to deal with challenges.

Reflection points

- How might social support manifest itself in teams?
- Describe a situation where a team reacts with a "fight" response when challenged.
- Describe a situation where a team responds with a "flee" response when challenged.
- Describe a situation where team members "tend to" each other when challenged over a longer time period.
- Describe an incident where team members have "befriended" each other when facing challenges over a longer time period.

Collaboration in teams

Teams are created in order to achieve goals that individuals cannot achieve on their own. Some tasks are too difficult or time-consuming for one person to accomplish and most projects are simply too complex for one person to be in possession of all the knowledge needed to solve the problems. *Self-generated project teams* are those created by one or more members who remain part of the team until the project is finished. *Organised project teams* are those formed by someone other than the members of the team. Within organisations, there will be both self-generated and organised teams.

Teams are more likely to succeed if their members put their energies together instead of each working independently on their own. In general, as tasks become more complex, it is more likely that a team will need to solve them by a concerted effort rather than by personal initiative (Karau & Williams, 1993; Zander, 1985). For example, certain projects can be very broad in scope and can require considerable manpower and time. As a project can take months, years, or even decades, it is wise to design the project team in such a way that work will continue even though individual members leave or are otherwise unavailable. A key question for all projects is: How complex is the project? One person cannot perform a symphony or play a football match. Individuals can solve certain tasks but complex projects require a number of work phases that must be organised in a co-ordinated way.

The work undertaken must be sufficiently challenging to keep the team engaged. Assignments that do not stimulate team members can de-motivate them. If the tasks are overly easy, a manager may try to create excitement or even competition within the team to reach the end-point quickly. A manager also needs to make sure that communication within the team is sufficiently open, ensuring that members express their real opinions instead of having the team uncritically accepting whatever a member suggests. It is important for teams to use constructive dialogue to discuss, explain, and understand all views expressed, bearing in mind the progress of their work.

Reflection points

- What makes people want to withdraw from a team?
- What might be accomplished better by working as a team? What might not?

Attraction in teams

The American psychologist Theodore Newcomb (1903–1984) was interested in examining how affection and hostility influenced people. One experiment he conducted involved putting several strangers in a group and monitoring their interactions and bonding as they stayed together over a long period. The aim was to see how spontaneously groups were formed, who each individual was attracted to, and how. Newcomb then observed how the participants—who were allocated rooms randomly—interacted, formed relationships, became friends, and formed groups. The result was that most developed close ties with their roommates and liked them the best. Newcomb also noticed that the group divided into subgroups (Newcomb, 1960; Forsyth, 2019). The experiment showed that groups are often based on mutual attraction between their members. Newcomb's research also showed that individuals are more likely to like those who are closer to them, express similar attitudes to theirs, and provide them with positive feedback (Figure 3.5). This attraction leads to group formation and continuity. Three fundamental principles recognised by Newcomb are outlined below.

Figure 3.5

We are more likely to like those who provide us with positive feedback.

The *proximity principle* is related to physical closeness as people tend simply to be more attracted to those who are next to them. Individuals who regularly meet gradually takes shape of a group, the reason being that as interactions increase, people get to know each other, and begin to like one another. Based on this, we can speculate whether team members are more likely to prefer their fellow team members over people in other teams.

The *elaboration principle* proposed by Newcomb, when applied to teams, sees them as self-organised dynamic systems and could be used to understand how they might grow. A team that is composed of only two members at the beginning could grow over time as the individuals within it connect to more and more individuals outside the team. Over time, as the individuals within the team relate to more individuals outside the team, the group affiliated with the team grows and becomes more complex. Interaction will also develop when individuals who have not connected to each other directly are attracted to one person who then becomes the heart that nourishes the relationships of others (Redl, 1942; Forsyth, 2019).

The *similarity principle* states that the interests, beliefs, and values of members who join a particular group are similar. In one team, the members who are engineers or who all came from the same geographic area might bond as they share a similar understanding of how to work and have similar values. Such bonding might evolve around education, background, political and religious views, and so on. Newcomb found strong evidence that people will seek out others who are similar to themselves, and have similar values, appearance, sense of humour, or interests.

Reflection points

- How might the proximity principle play out in your teams?
- How might the elaboration principle play out in your teams?
- How might the similarity principle play out in your teams?

Likes and dislikes in teams

In some teams, people work in the same location. In other teams, people are spread around geographically, sometimes across the globe. It is useful to bear in mind that proximity to other people can function as a kind of a social magnet that pulls people together. As previously indicated, we tend to interact more with those who are nearby. More engagement makes them more interested in the relations and fosters a sense of belonging. If a team that has become uniform needs to be reduced in size, the first member to leave is often the one who is most different from other members. Thus, relationships in teams are stronger amongst people who resemble each other and are quicker to dissolve between people who are different from each other.

The *conformity principle* states that we tend to like people who are similar to ourselves and this leads to uniformity (Forsyth, 2019). Various psychological and social factors seem to promote uniformity and strengthen relationships between people who possess similar characteristics (McPherson *et al.*, 2001). When others adopt similar beliefs and values to our own, we experience this as confirmation that our beliefs and values are justified, and thus interaction with those people is felt as rewarding (Byrne, 1971). Interactions with similar people are more likely to lead to co-operation and are less likely to turn into conflict (Insko & Schopler, 1972). Team members who have a lot in common might also experience a greater connection amongst themselves (Arkin & Burger, 1980). Disliking someone who is similar to one's self is confusing and can cause inner turmoil. It is also a common assumption that if someone is like us, they must be likeable so uniformity breeds more uniformity (Festinger, 1957; Heider, 1958). Since location, education, and workplace bring people together who are similar in one way or another, people often choose to connect with others who already have similar opinions to their own (McPherson *et al.*, 2001).

The *complementary principle* indicates that people may prefer to associate with others who are different from them. For example, it is not likely that someone who has a strong need to control others will be drawn to people who also want control. According to this principle, we are drawn to individuals who complement qualities that we lack (Kerckhoff & Davis, 1962; Levinger *et al.*, 1970; Meyer & Pepper, 1977).

When combined, the conformity principle and the complementary principle would indicate that we are more likely to respond positively both to those who we think like us and to those who seem to compliment us for what we lack. Being attracted to people who have qualities that we lack enables us to feel that we are similar to these individuals and we can be attracted to people who are like us in some ways but unlike us in other ways (Dryer & Horowitz, 1997). Studies show that individuals prefer to interact with those who show a similar level of friendship, warmth, and positivity as they do. People also seem to tend to respond to dominance with compliance, and compliance is usually met with authority. This might explain how leaders find followers and followers find leaders, as the conformist complies to people with authority and vice versa (Tracey *et al.*, 2001; Forsyth, 2019).

The American psychologist mentioned before, William Schutz (1958), made a distinction between *interchange compatibility* and *originator compatibility*. Interchange compatibility would exist in a team where team members have similar expectations of intimacy, control, and approval. There is *strong interchange compatibility* when all members assume that the team is formally managed and intimacy is kept to a minimum. There is *weak interchange compatibility* if someone wants to share their immediate feelings while others do not want such interaction. *Originator compatibility* would exist in a project team when members have dissimilar, but complementary, needs with regard to expressing and receiving control, intimacy, and approval. Thus, originator compatibility takes place when a person with a strong need for control joins a team of people who are looking for a strong leader. Schutz tested these theories by putting together groups with different compatibility attributes. He created the conditions for originator compatibility by inserting one person in each group with a strong need for control, and another person with a high need for approval, along with three individuals who had less need to control or seek approval. Schutz created conditions for interchange compatibility by putting together a group of individuals with similar needs for intimacy. All groups in the study reflected strong compatibility and, though a great intimacy developed in half of the groups, it did not develop in the other half. Schutz also put together a group of individuals who did not have anything in common, including individuals with varying degrees of the need for intimacy, from strong to very little. As predicted, Schutz discovered that *cohesion* is higher in teams with strong compatibility than in the others, and compatible teams are more productive when it comes to teamwork.

The *reciprocity principle* states that when we feel liked by another person, we are more likely to like them. When we discover that people like us—for instance by giving us friendly advice, praise, or telling us how much they like working with us—then we usually react by also liking that person (Jones, 1973; Shrauger, 1975; Forsyth, 2019). Negative reciprocity also takes place in project teams—we do not like those who seem to dislike or reject us. In one study, students were asked to discuss controversial issues in groups. Two to three participants in each group belonged to the research team and were either for or against the topic and objected strongly to the opinions of others. In the breaks between the discussions, participants shared their experiences and how they had experienced the others. Those who belonged to the research team deliberately blocked the others out, talked only among themselves, and looked only from time to time, and with disapproval, towards the others. Rejected members were attracted to each other. The rejection also had the effect of decreasing the self-esteem of those individuals who were rejected (Pepitone & Wilpinski, 1960).

The *min-max principle* asserts that people will participate in teams that provide them with the greatest rewards for the least cost (Figure 3.6)

Figure 3.6

People may participate based on the greatest rewards for the least cost.

(Thibaut & Kelley, 1959, 1978; Forsyth, 2019). Rewards can be of many kinds, for example, the appreciation of others, new friends, achieving personal goals, social support, participation in exciting discussions, and the opportunity to work with people who are interesting. It also involves an opportunity cost to join teams, i.e. time, energy, and money that could have been used for something else. The potential *opportunity cost* of participating could mean sacrifice of time and money, having to deal with social pressure or possible trauma, illness, or facing unrealistic demands from the team. Overall, however, people tend to see more benefits, through participation, than sacrifices (Brinthaupt *et al.*, 1991; Moreland *et al.*, 1993; Forsyth, 2019). Team members are also an important source of reward and opportunity cost. People are attracted to teams in which members possess qualities that are highly valued and, concurrently, they avoid teams that reflect negative social values. We are usually more willing to associate with people who are generous, motivated, reliable, useful, credible, and wise (Bonney, 1947). We have a tendency, however, to dislike people and to refuse to associate with them if they possess negative social qualities such as vulgarity, complacency, or boredom (Gilchrist, 1952; Iverson, 1964; Kowalski, 1996). Nor will people be interested in working with those who lead discussions beyond the topics at hand, show little interest, or are too serious or too preoccupied with themselves (Leary *et al.*, 1986).

All this plays out in what can be called the *economics of membership*, which is based on the idea that members participate in teams to maximise the utility of joining. Members will participate if they can get more out of being on the team than it costs them to join, and they will leave if the cost or effort outweighs the reward. Based on this, the willingness to participate in a team is based on two things: on comparable level (what are the alternative options that I have?) and the comparable level of alternatives (how much do I like the alternative options?). If able to choose, the team with the greatest benefits and lowest cost is the one that the individual will join as long as it is comparable to other options. The results from comparing such options will determine the willingness to join or leave a team. Their satisfaction of belonging to the team depends mainly on whether participation meets the expected comparisons.

The American management experts Bill Fischer and Andy Boynton described what they called "Virtuoso teams" (Fischer & Boynton, 2005) as teams that are built up from the very best experts and thinkers in their fields, and who stand out starkly in terms of their ambitions and successes, compared with traditional teams. These teams show far-sightedness and deep consideration of all aspects of a project while traditional teams place more emphasis on execution rather than thinking. They argued that thinking is the most important factor in promoting stellar results. However, the prerequisite for such results is that team members must be chosen for their talent and their desire to deal with challenging tasks at hand. More discussion on how to facilitate creative, ethical, and critical thinking can be found in our book *Project: Leadership* in the same series.

Team leaders need to understand why people may want to participate in a team and why they may not. Team members often have other responsibilities, commitments to other managers, little time, or even limited interest in participation. Hence, it is useful to know what stimulates their performance and motivates them. This knowledge can have significant impact. If you know who they want or need to have in your team, then you can change or influence conditions and thus increase the potential team member's interest in engagement. For example, challenging tasks, learning opportunities, the promise of promotion, the possibility of visiting an attractive place, or a visit from a notable leader could all affect an individual's interest in team participation. Several factors define when people deem the benefits of teamwork to be positive and compelling enough for them to join. You should try to optimise the satisfaction of your team so that you can motivate the individuals you want to be part of the team to join it and work together with the rest of the team.

Reflection points

- Discuss these ideas with your team and come up with examples to illustrate each idea.
- How can these ideas be used when it comes to managing your team?

Attachment in teams

Developmental psychologists have found that babies and young children respond differently to their parents. Some children are secure in who they are, feel comfortable communicating with their parents and trying out new, unknown situations as long as they have their parents in sight. Other children seem to rely less on the support of their parents, and still others seem to be more able to take care of things themselves. These observations form the basis for *attachment theory*, which describes how individuals relate to others. According to this theory, attachment has its roots in infant-parent relationships that play out in different attachment styles in adulthood, and this defines how we respond intellectually and emotionally to other people. According to the theory, there are at least four types of attachment styles in adults: security-driven, avoidance-driven, and anxiety-driven (Forsyth, 2019).

- *Security-driven personalities* enjoy being in close contact with others. They do not worry about being abandoned and are confident in intimate relations. Their relationship style is characterised by security and comfort. They find it easy to become emotionally close to others, are comfortable in depending on others and having others depend on them. They do not worry about being alone or others not accepting them.
- *Dismissive-avoidance personalities* avoid close contact with others and feel uncomfortable having to rely on other people. They feel that close

relationships require deeper and a greater level of intimacy than they can provide. They are comfortable without close emotional relationships, want to feel independent and self-sufficient, and prefer not to depend on others or have others depend on them.

- *Anxiety-preoccupied personalities* crave intimacy with others but worry that their loved ones will abandon them. They rarely establish intimacy; instead feeling bad speculating whether their emotions will last or will be repaid/rewarded. They are uncomfortable when not in close relationships, but they might also worry that others don't value them as much as they value others.
- *Fearful-avoidant personalities* are uncomfortable in getting close to others. They want emotionally close relationships, but have difficulty trusting or depending on others.

These four types of relationships and their variants are based on two underlying factors: (1) anxiety about intimate relationships and (2) a phobia of intimacy and dependency on others (Brennan *et al.*, 1998). An individual's attachment style naturally affects their love and family life, but also the teams to which they belong and in which they work. One way of measuring people's attachment style is to use the *Group Attachment Scale* (Smith *et al.*, 1999). If this is applied to a team, it could ask, for instance, whether team members find it difficult to trust the team; whether they fear being hurt; and whether they feel they are closer to the team than they feel comfortable with.

Individuals who are anxiety-driven are prone to doubt that the team approves of them as members and feel that they do not deserve to be admitted to the team. These individuals spend less time in the team, participate in fewer events, and are less satisfied with the support the team can provide them with. Individuals with a *social phobia* are less connected and thus more likely to state that they want to leave the team (Smith *et al.*, 1999). Individuals with a more secure relationship style, however, will contribute more to teamwork and general interaction within the team than people with a less secure relationship style. Individuals with an anxious relationship style will contribute less work within the team, and individuals with an avoidant style will both contribute less to teamwork and be less likely to form relationships within the team. Try to be aware of the relationship styles of each member of your team and bear this in mind both with regard to work tasks and other kinds of interaction within the team.

Whether voluntarily or involuntarily, we continually signal our feelings. Feelings manifest themselves in our behaviour, attitudes, and expression. Even when not necessarily stated in words, feelings about situations and events, whether relating to one's self or to others, will leak out, even when you think you can hide them.

How and why do feelings and emotions matter in teams? How can feelings be expressed? How should they be expressed appropriately? We will discuss all this in greater detail in the subsequent chapters when we will explain how important it is to be able to express feelings and emotions in a clear and constructive manner when working with others in teams. We will provide tips for those who want to foster their skills. This is particularly important as the performance of the team is largely determined by how well team members communicate, how they avoid the obstacles inherent in vague and forced communication, and can, consequently, reach the core of the matter quickly.

Reflection points

- What kind of a personality are you in terms of attachment theory?
- Make a list of feelings.
- Make a list of emotions.
- Identify personal emotions and feelings and tell others in your team what they are.
- What are the shortcomings of not being able to identify and express emotions and feelings?
- What are the benefits of being able to identify and express emotions and feelings?

References

Arkin, R. M., & Burger, J. M. (1980). "Effects of unit relation tendencies on interpersonal attraction" in *Social Psychology Quarterly*, 43, 380–391.

Bonney, M. E. (1947). "Popular and unpopular children: A sociometric study" in *Sociometric Monographs*, No. 99, A80.

Brennan, K. A., Clark, C. L., & Shaver, P. R. (1998). "Self report measurement of adult attachment: An integrative overview" in J. A. Simpson & W. S. Rholes (Eds.), *Attachment theory and close relationships* (pp. 46–76). New York: Guilford Press.

Brinthaupt, T. M., Moreland, R. L., & Levine, J. M. (1991). "Sources of optimism among prospective group members" in *Personality and Social Psychology Bulletin*, 17, 3643.

Buunk, B. P. & Hoorens, V. (1992). "Social support and stress: The role of social comparison and social exchange process" in *British Journal of Clinical Psychology*, 31, 445–457.

Byrne, D. (1971). *The attraction paradigm*. New York: Academic Press.

Cotter, D. A., Hermsen, J. N., Ovadia, S., & Vanneman, R. (2001). "The glass ceiling effect" in *Social Forces*, 80:2, 656–681.

Davison, K. P., Pennebaker, J. W., & Dickenson, S. S. (2000). "Who talks? The social psychology of illness support groups" in *American Psychologist*, 55, 205–217.

Dyer, D. C. & Horowitz, L. M. (1997) "When do opposites attract? Interpersonal complementarity versus similarity" in *Journal of Personality and Social Psychology*, 72, 592–603.

Festinger, L. (1950). "Informal social communication" in *Psychological Review*, 57, 271–282.

Festinger, L. (1954). "A theory of social comparison processes" in *Human Relations*, 7, 117–140.

Festinger, L. (1957). *A theory of cognitive dissonance*. Stanford, CA: Stanford University Press.

Fischer, B. & Boynton, A. (2005). "Virtuoso teams" in *Harvard Business Review*, 83(7), 116–123.

Forsyth, D. R. (2019). *Group dynamics* (7th ed.). Boston: Cengage.

Gilchrist, J. C. (1952). "The formation of social groups under conditions of success and failure" in *Journal of Abnormal and Social Psychology*, 47, 174–187.

Goethals, G. R. & Darley, J. M. (1987). "Social comparison theory: Self-evaluation and group life" in B. Mullen & G. R. Goethals (Eds.), *Theories of group behaviour* (pp. 21–47). New York: Springer Verlag.

Green, R. G. (1995). *Human motivation: A social psychological approach.* Pacific Grove, CA: Brooks/Cole.

Heider, F. (1958). *The psychology of interpersonal relations.* New York: Wiley.

Insko, C. A. & Schopler, J. (1972). *Experimental social psychology.* New York: Academic Press.

Iverson, M. A. (1964). "Personality impressions of punitive stimulus persons of differential status" in *Journal of Abnormal and Social Psychology*, 68, 617–626.

Jones, S. C. (1973). "Self- and interpersonal evaluations: Esteem theories versus consistency theories" in *Psychological Bulletin*, 79, 185–199.

Jung, C. G. (1924). *Psychological types.* (transl H. G. Baynes). New York: Harcourt, Brace & World.

Karau, S. J. & Williams, K. D. (1993). "Social loafing: A meta-analytic review and theoretical integration" in *Journal of Personality and Social Psychology*, 65, 681–706.

Kelley, H. H. & Thibaut, J. W. (1978). *Interpersonal relations: A theory of interdependence.* New York: Wiley.

Kerckhoff, A. C. & Davis, K. E. (1962). "Value consensus and need complementarity in mate selection" in *American Sociological Review*, 27, 295–303.

Kowalski, R. M. (1996). "Complaints and complaining: Functions, antecedents, and consequences" in *Psychological Bulletin*, 119, 179–196.

Leary, M. R., Rogers, P. A., Canfield, R. W., & Coe, C. (1986). "Boredom in interpersonal encounters: Antecedents and social implications" in *Journal of Personality and Social Psychology*, 51, 968–975.

Levinger, G., Senn, D. J., & Jorgensen, B. W. (1970). "Progress toward permanence in courtship: A test of the Kerckhoff-Davis hypothesis" in *Sociometry*, 33, 427–433.

McPherson, M., Smith-Lovin, L., & Cook, J. M. (2001). "Birds of a feather: Homophily in social networks" in *Annual Review of Sociology*, 27, 415–444.

Meyer, J. P. & Pepper, S. (1977). "Need compatibility and marital adjustment in young married couples" in *Journal of Personality and Social Psychology*, 35, 331–342.

Moreland, R. L. (1987). "The formation of small groups" in *Review of Personality and Social Psychology*, 8, 80–110.

Moreland, R. L., Levine, J. M., & Cini, M. A. (1993). "Group socialization: The role of commitment" in M. Hogg & D. Abrams (Eds.), *Group motivation: Social psychological perspectives* (pp. 105–129). London: Harvester Wheatsheaf.

Morris, W. N., Worchel, S., Bois, J. L., Pearson, J. A., Rountree, C. A., Samaha, G. M., Wachtler, J., & Wright, S. L. (1976). "Collective coping with stress: Group reactions to fear, anxiety, and ambiguity" in *Journal of Personality and Social Psychology*, 33, 674–679.

Murray, H. A. (1938). *Explorations in personality.* New York: Oxford University Press.

Newcomb, T. M. (1960). "Varieties of interpersonal attraction" in D. Cartwright & A. Zander (Eds.), *Group dynamics: Research and theory* (2nd ed.) (pp. 104–119). Evanston, IL: Row: Peterson.

Pepitone, A. & Wilpinski, C. (1960). "Some consequences of experimental rejection" in *Journal of Abnormal and Social Psychology*, 60, 359–364.

Redl, F. (1942). "Group emotion and leaders" in *Psychiatry*, 5, 573–596.

Schachter, S. (1959). *The psychology of affiliation*. Stanford, CA: Stanford University Press.

Schutz, W. C. (1958). *FIRO: A three-dimensional theory of interpersonal behaviour*. New York: Rinehart.

Schutz, W. C. (1992). "Beyond FIRO-B. Three new theory-driven measures—Element B: behavior, Element F: feelings, Element S: self" in *Psychological Reports*, 70, 915–937.

Shrauger, J. S. (1975). "Responses to evaluation as a function of initial self-perceptions" in *Psychological Bulletin*, 82, 581–596.

Smith, E. R., Murphy, J., & Coats, S. (1999). Attachment to groups: Theory and management. *Journal of Personality and Social Psychology*, 77, 94–110.

Tesser, A. (1988). "Towards a self-evaluation maintenance model of social behaviour" in *Advances in Experimental Social Psychology*, 21, 181–227.

Thibaut, J. W. & Kelley, H. H. (1959). *The social psychology of groups*. New York: Wiley.

Tracey, T. J., Ryan, J. M., & Jaschik-Herman, B. (2001). "Complementarity of interpersonal circumplex traits" in *Personality and Social Psychology Bulletin*, 27, 786–797.

Winter, D. G. (1973). *The power motive*. New York: Free Press.

Zander, A. (1985). *The purposes of groups and organizations*. San Francisco: Jossey-Bass.

4 Team cohesion and expressions of emotions

••

Now you have a better understanding of what makes people want to participate in teams, you might ask: What keeps a team together? We could start by saying it is the goal of getting things done, but there are other things at play too. Goals are, of course, an important part of motivation but it is clear that there is something else that will keep the team together and this "something" is the team's cohesion. Cohesion is not easy to explain and no single definition can cover everything the idea entails; we are not going to attempt to define it too rigorously nor limit the definition. Instead, we will take a look at teams and their development, go a little deeper into outlining the differences between groups and teams, and discuss the functions of teams in organisations. Towards the end of the chapter, we will explore the basis for the appropriate expression of emotion within a team setting; something that takes into account different character types.

Team cohesion

What holds together a project team working on constructing a bridge is unlikely to be the same as what holds together the team in a theatre or a mountain rescue team. This suggests that team cohesion is not necessarily a universal concept and that an archetype of a cohesive team may not exist. As we explained in the previous chapter, some teams cling together because of the attraction that exists between members; when friendships build up and connect the members of a team together. Other teams might stick together because their members feel it is important to belong to that team, their attitudes are similar, and their spirit, commitment, and sense of "we-ness" is high. Yet other teams stick together because their members like to compete and believe that a united force is stronger than a single effort. In the latter of these kinds of teams, teamwork may create cohesion in the absence or instead of social ties with other team members. Even though attraction, a united purpose, and teamwork are common characteristics of cohesion, not all teams possess these characteristics but they manage to stay together anyway. Financial considerations as well as work obligations can be factors that influence people to remain in teams even when they see the work as not particularly relevant or personally worthwhile. In professional teams, if members feel they are not being rewarded fairly for their work, then this can become a reason to leave.

It is not easy to measure team cohesion. Researchers have used different methods to assess cohesion in groups, either by monitoring them or by asking their members to self-evaluate the level of cohesion (Forsyth, 2019). The different methods can yield different results and often conflicting conclusions. One option is to employ an approach developed by Kurt Lewin and Leon Festinger in the early 1940s. They defined *group cohesion* as: "the total field of forces which act on members to stay within the group" (Festinger *et al.*, 1950). For them, attraction is a special force, and they completed numerous studies that showed that cohesion was proportional to the number of positive connections made between team members. Applied to teams, team cohesion would hence be contingent on the nature and strength of the positive emotions between the individuals within the team. Attraction can arise and have an impact in two ways. Positive feelings may arise between individuals within a team or these feelings may arise out of positive attitudes towards the team itself. It is often difficult to distinguish between these two types of attraction, and they undoubtedly affect each other. Friendship between individuals in a team will result in the individuals' feelings sharpening and sparking feelings towards the group itself and this in turn prevents members from leaving the team. However, where team members feel loyalty towards other team members, rather than towards the team, this can be problematic if those individuals leave the team.

Reflection points

- What attracts you to belonging to a group or team?
- What attracts people to join teams?
- What drives people to participate in work teams?
- How does participation in professional and voluntary teams differ?

Team co-operation

In a team that sticks together, cohesion prevails and individuals will be committed to maintaining the team's unity and to supporting each other. Teams of this type are more likely to defend their interests to prevent individuals or groups from outside the team from threatening their unity. They are also more likely to refer to themselves collectively saying "we" rather than "I". Members of such teams will have a stronger sense of belonging to the team and are more committed to the team and its activities.

Team cohesion is more likely to occur in teams that have worked together successfully on other projects or over a long period of time. A leader may also have strengthened the cohesion by focusing on the positive aspects of the teamwork and on the things that unite the team members. You can also do this by encouraging a team culture of honest communication and by solving disputes as soon as they come up. Thus, the team's efforts are not wasted in destructive conflict. The team's cohesion will also be strengthened if all members feel appreciated and the questions they ask within the team are answered, or if they spend time in activities that may seem unrelated to their work but are nevertheless important for cohesion (Scholtes *et al.*, 2003).

By way of example, when it comes to accomplishing goals, sportspeople and rescue team members often refer to the quality of the team's co-operation as the defining factor. It could then be argued that team cohesion that enables effective work is based not so much on attraction but rather the *will of team members to work together* to achieve the team's goals. Hence, it will be the quality or strength of a team's co-operation that underpins the cohesion of the team. Such teams are also characterised by a strong collective efficiency based on the team members' positive expectations that the team has the competence to accomplish the mission on which it is working. Here, cohesion is linked to what has been called *esprit de corps*, team spirit or team morale. Thus, it is not enough that the team has confidence and believes that members can handle the task in question but they must also be willing to say "yes we can!" and to be ready to fight for the team and the task if necessary. This "spark" is hard to define in any detail but it can be the defining factor for whether or not a team will succeed. Take, for example, those companies, often in the construction and manufacturing sectors, that place special emphasis on the importance of health and safety and build up a strong safety culture. A common approach is to highlight the number of hours worked without a serious incident occurring. This helps focus the minds of all the individual teams, involved in different aspects of the overall work, on maintaining consistently high standards of performance. Alternatively, a sports team that has not splashed out money on bringing in expensive players, but rather has focused on building up a strong capable squad of local talent, will find the team members are willing to go that extra yard for each other and are mentally strong in the face of adversity, driven collectively by their shared sense of team membership.

Reflection points

- What is team unity?
- What creates unity in a team?
- How might you develop unity in a team?
- What are the advantages of unity in teams?
- What could the disadvantages be of unity in teams?

Tuckman's five stages

Different theories can be applied to understand the development of teams and their life cycle. These theories indicate the importance of the team leader in appropriately addressing the different expectations and needs of the team throughout its life cycle. Most of these theories suggest that teams go through certain developmental stages. One of the most cited, mentioned in Chapter 1, is the theory of Bruce W. Tuckman (1938–2016; Forsyth, 2019), which describes five stages in the life of groups: forming, storming, norming, performing, and adjourning (Figure 4.1). Tuckman's research on the behaviour of small groups in different environments showed that they go through several distinct developmental stages before collaboration between members begins to yield results (Tuckman, 1965). Let's discuss what this looks like when applied to teams.

Forming

The *forming stage* occurs as the team is assembled and members of the new team begin to interact with each other. There are often feelings of tension, communication is tentative, and members may be on their guard towards each other. Many of these feelings will not be outwardly expressed but are part of the team's life nonetheless. Members are naturally cautious while they assess the pecking order within the team and determine which protocols are to be respected. At this point, members may stop looking at themselves solely as individuals and start to identify as part of the team. Clearly, this stage tests the skill and capacity of the team leader to manage group expectations and activities. Members can experience various emotions within themselves, towards the team and other members. These may include pride at having been chosen, or anticipation, optimism, hesitation, as well as doubts, fears,

Figure 4.1

Tuckman's stages of team development.

and anxieties, all of which you may need to acknowledge. During this stage, the team is also trying to define their goals and the means to achieve them. Members will actively seek out what information is needed and will begin to conform to team behaviour. Procedures will be established that determine how disputes should be resolved.

In *The Team Handbook* by Peter R. Scholtes, Brian L. Joiner, and Barbara J. Streibel, the authors discuss how to manage teams successfully through the formative stage. They encourage leaders to build trust and a sense of safety by helping team members to get to know each other, stating objectives and the team's mission clearly to the team, and by giving members the opportunity to participate in designing work plans themselves. They suggest that leaders should clearly explain the role of each member, encourage the member's co-operation, provide the information and working framework needed for the team to start working, and help members to answer the following questions: (1) What is expected of me?; (2) Do I belong to the team?; (3) Do I want to belong to the team?; (4) What will I get from joining this team?; and (5) What is the purpose of the team's activities?

As members begin to express themselves to each other as individuals and as a team, the collective understanding of the purpose of the team builds. The team leader gradually gains more recognition if they are deemed by the team to be a worthy candidate for the role. The forming stage ends when interactions within the team are characterised by trust and the team members have begun to relax with each other.

In terms of communication, the focus can initially be very wide and include dialogues about events and issues that may be unrelated to, yet confusingly identified with the work. Other topics can include difficulties in surmounting implementation obstacles and criticism of the organisation overall. Since the formative stage might not seem to be part of the overall work, you may be tempted to ignore the importance of managing this stage or feel impatient with this part of the process. It can be tempting to roll up your sleeves and start working on the project but you may regret something in the team dynamic or organisation that you overlook now if you don't allow enough time to explore all appropriate eventualities. If the team does not successfully navigate and complete this stage, it may be much harder to succeed and finish your work in a satisfactory manner (Scholtes *et al.*, 2003).

In some teams—although this is unusual in project teams—participants are made to pass tests or some kind of social initiation (which members may find painful) to be accepted into the group. The American social psychologist Leon Festinger (1919–1989) studied such initiations. He discovered that the suffering imposed on the participants is designed to force prospective members to commit to the team. One of the groups that Festinger investigated were the followers of the religious leader Marian Keech, who proclaimed the end of the world and imposed rituals for preparation. Each ritual pulled the participants closer to each other (Festinger, 1957). In ancient cultures, induction into the group can involve arduous initiation rituals to enable a new member to establish respect within an established social order that values toughness and loyalty above all else. This can be seen in the various warrior initiation ceremonies among indigenous African tribes and is widely observed in gang culture, for instance. By passing such tests, individuals become accepted team members. The tests themselves may not involve a defined form or structure but instead are experienced in the form of particularly trying circumstances that are, in turn, experienced by established team members in their own group initiation. In the case of a rescue team, for example, new team members may be required to participate in a particularly harrowing rescue, which is entirely separate from any prior training stages. In the context of a project team, proving your ability to handle a particularly demanding deadline, make a difficult or painful decision, or establish rapport with a notoriously critical stakeholder may all serve a similar purpose.

Storming

The *storming stage* comes next in the team's development. The mild uncertainty and insecurity towards your fellow team members that characterised the forming stage has eased, and the focus has now shifted towards work objectives. During the stage, individuals seek to establish their personal role and responsibility for the work of the team. Personal conflict may arise between members with disputes regarding work challenges and disagreement around the strategies and solutions for tackling them to. Competition for power, roles, and status can arise. This may interfere with team cohesion and performance. Alliances will also begin to form. Participants need to decide if they should resist or conform to the team. This process continues until stability is achieved in the distribution of power, attraction, and relationships. It is important to realise that some *conflicts* may in fact be necessary at this stage because they will, if constructive, promote team cohesion and prove to the team that it has workable methods to process and solve disputes. Disputes that escalate out of control and that the team cannot manage may degenerate into open warfare which will damage trust in the team and compromise their ability to co-operate. Niggling conflict may diminish interest among team members to engage in teamwork (Figure 4.2).

As you lead the team through the *storming stage*, focus on the twin issues of power and responsibility. This includes preventing individuals within the team from dominating at the expense of others. Encourage the team to develop a consensus over how they make decisions. Your leadership role is also evolving at this stage. Endeavour to develop the role in a way that enhances the independence of the team and encourages members to take on responsibility. You'll need to establish procedures and processes that ensure opportunities for everyone to participate and help team members to answer the following questions: Who is in charge? Can I have an impact? How do I go about communicating my opinions and getting results? (Scholtes *et al.*, 2003).

Figure 4.2

Conflict may diminish interest to engage in teamwork.

Norming

The *norming stage* begins once you have achieved greater stability within the group and teamwork becomes more coherent and better organised. Support and mutuality begin to characterise the interaction of team members. As the team prepares to solve their challenges they now find common ground. The team has also defined its norms, standards, rules, and the procedures that should support teamwork. Roles, goals, and the distribution of power have also been more or less defined by this stage. In terms of leadership, encourage co-operation between members, encourage everyone to participate, and help facilitate the team so that members can make use of their talents, experience, and knowledge to the fullest extent. This is the time to encourage members actively to begin to work together in a consolidated fashion. As a leader, you are responsible for ensuring the team establish their procedures and for helping them answer these questions: How should we deal with conflicts? How should we support each other? (Scholtes *et al.*, 2003).

Performing

The *performing stage* is established once the team has developed yet further, is genuinely co-operative and increasingly efficient. At this stage, the team is ready to take on the work at hand with full force. It is not self-evident that all teams reach this stage. If they do, their members now spend less time on exploring the work environment. They focus instead on their project work. At this stage, as a leader, you should aim to foster and maintain a positive attitude, work on updating the methods and procedures to support the team's co-operation, and deal with necessary changes. You should monitor their progress and encourage them to celebrate when milestones are reached. Letting the team know how close to goals they are, or when they have achieved them, can provide a psychological boost to all, particularly where the overall work is highly compartmentalised and it is hard for individuals to see the bigger picture.

Adjourning

The final stage, according to Tuckman, is the *adjourning* stage, where the team has accomplished their objectives (or their work has been cancelled) and is subsequently dissolved (Figure 4.3). This stage can be characterised by the emergence of separation anxiety on the part of the team members, nostalgia, and even grief, when members look back on the challenges, co-operation, and successes. The end of the project and the end of teamwork is often pre-determined but it can also occur at short notice. Members can even dissolve the team and commit to other teams prematurely or choose not to work with other teams if they believe this might benefit them. Regardless of how this occurs and what happens, separation from the team can cause both stress and relief on the individuals and this should be acknowledged. Your role as a leader during this stage is to be aware of the impact that dissolving the team can have on people, and to facilitate an appropriate ending and "goodbye" with, for instance, the appropriate thanks, exchange of contact information, and future blessings.

The Tuckman model is very helpful in understanding the nature of team development and teamwork. While primarily relevant to projects, it is also a practical management tool that can be used to lead teams and groups in all organisational settings regardless of their objectives. On the other hand, it has its limitations and the notion that teams develop in such a linear fashion has been challenged. We could also argue for the addition of at least two more stages in project team development. The first might be called a *preparation*

Figure 4.3

Adjourning is when the team life comes to an end.

stage—a stage that exists before the team meets and that is characterised by the *expectations* of the team members prior to meeting the team. Inevitably, these expectations can have an impact on the team and, therefore, they should be acknowledged as representing a specific stage in team development.

The second is a *grieving stage* that occurs after a team has been dissolved, as is typically the case for isolated projects. Here, team members grieve the loss of their relationships with other members of the team and of the association and sense of belonging that the team provided them with. This can, for instance, have an impact on how members act and behave within their department, or in the next team to which they are assigned. Knowing this stage will occur can also affect team dynamics with the team trying to avoid the inevitable loss. At this stage, you also often see attempts to recreate the team in another context, such as by members organising activities themselves or holding reunions. Sometimes, such attempts are successful but equally, they can feel awkward as the team is not the same in this new context. The *grieving stage* is not uncommon among people who have taken part in exciting, productive, and meaningful projects involving many people. The teamwork was very meaningful at the time and what prevails afterwards is a sense of loss and emptiness. The role of the project leader may be limited at this stage though you can help ease the transformation for team members by leading them towards something new.

As a final word on the different stages in team development, we advocate an *informing stage* that occurs on those occasions when a team struggles to get information, to define itself in terms of its environment, and finds it difficult to understand the context in which the team members find themselves. This might be part of the forming stage or it could be a continuous situation.

Reflection points

- Go through the Tuckman stages and discuss how they have manifested themselves in your experience of team environments.
- Discuss how a team leader should operate in each of the stages.
- What other stages could there be in a project team life cycle?

Team development in context

The original Tuckman model assumed that teams go through the team developmental stages outlined above in a linear fashion, progressing forward from one level to the next. However, not all teams go through the process stage-by-stage. Teams can easily skip certain stages and the distinction between stages may not always be so clear. It can be argued that teams go through the stages in a circular manner, especially teams that have a long life cycle. In this case, the team progresses, turns back to an earlier stage, regresses, or even jumps over some of the stages. Teams that develop in a circular fashion tend not to evolve significantly over time, but hopefully reach a satisfactory equilibrium. A spiral trajectory on the other hand can be looked at in two ways. If the starting point is at some distance from the centre, then the resultant inward spiral development represents the evolution of a team into a tighter knit group with the distances between members shrinking over time. Alternatively, team development may be viewed beginning in the centre of a spiral where various others gradually join a small core team, and so the increasing distance of a point along the spiral from the centre reflects the increased complexity of a developing team, increasing in an outer spiral until circumstances are met that impact upon this growth. Mathematically, this evolution can be studied in phase space diagrams and these are widely employed in biological systems studies and population studies.

Robert Freed Bales created the *equilibrium model of group development* in which group members try to maintain a balance between the aims of the group on the one hand and improve their relationships with other group members on the other (Bales, 1970; Forsyth, 2019). According to this model, a team constantly moves between the Tuckman stages of *norming* and *performing*. The dynamics within a team that struggles to find a balance between work objectives and the interpersonal needs of its participants can change quickly. This struggle can have a major impact on the group, relationships, co-operation, and team cohesion. Such a situation is often characterised by what is called *punctuated equilibrium*.

In most cases, positive experiences of teams—such as increased enjoyment, lower member turnover, and less stress—are associated with team cohesion. Cohesion may, however, lead to increased tension in team development. If the team clings together, its members will inevitably be under more pressure from one another. They rely on each other, expect action and responses, and will be more affected by each other. Under certain circumstances, teams with strong cohesion evolve in a negative way. One example is the *old sergeant syndrome* where members find it difficult or are unwilling to accept new members to replace those who have left. Such teams can also show negative behaviour such as seeking "scapegoats" and hostility towards individual team members. So, while teams may evolve and become more competent and cohesive, team development in the longer term is inevitably a dynamic process and there needs to be mechanisms in place to allow newer members to be given the opportunity to perform and gain acceptance by their peers. For example, almost invariably, where a country, region, or specific team is known for producing a conveyor belt of talented sportspeople, you will find a strong system in place where juniors are nurtured and given the proper opportunities at the right times to break into the senior arena. A caveat here, of course, is that we are only referring to those situations where performance-enhancing drugs or any other unethical practice do not lie behind individual and team success. To bring this idea into the context of general management, it can mean involving junior members in a stepwise process of increased responsibility, allowing them to make decisions on goals, activities, and direction in the process. They should be given the space to make acceptable mistakes and to learn from them in the process.

Loyalty can be a difficult notion to define and can mean different things in different contexts, e.g. customer loyalty versus military loyalty or community loyalty. Essentially, it refers to the strong support and dedication to a particular cause that people adopt, sometimes to the extent that they may even be willing to sacrifice their life for it. Consequently, it can be a very powerful force and can be an essential component of team cohesion in fraught situations. Having a strong sense of team loyalty means that many potential sources of conflict are bypassed and team members are willing to put themselves out for their team mates and these combined factors can make the overall process of achieving goals far easier. Loyalty can originate for many different reasons and can involve a mix of feelings and emotions including a sense of connection, belonging, trust, and obligation. If you have colleagues who are there when you need them, give you the help and support that you need, particularly in difficult situations, you are likely to become loyal to them. Alternatively, consumers with a strong feeling of national pride may well choose to buy products manufactured or sourced from their home nation even if there is a price penalty for doing so.

Unsurprisingly, there is a strong correlation between team cohesion and performance, as solidity can advance the successful team and united teams usually perform better than disparate ones. The norms and rules of a team also have a significant impact on their performance. As their leader you'll need to work out how to guide your team step by step through its development— whatever the precise progression is. Look for opportunities to promote team unity and make team members feel proud of belonging. Team performance needs to be defined by the *requirements* of their work, the *resources* that your team possesses, and the *processes* and the *norms* that are cultivated within it. There are times when the demands of work will stretch and test your team's interpersonal relationships. You'll sometimes need to make tough decisions, but these can be widely accepted if done in a fair and appropriate manner. Therefore, in order to achieve a balance between the needs of the project and the needs of the team, learn how to detect the variety of emotions and feelings that arise as a team evolves and how the individual personalities and the dynamic of the team respond to different managerial approaches. By keeping a certain distance from team members, you'll provide yourself with the latitude to respond in different ways to different circumstances. Getting too close to team members or behaving in an irresponsible fashion can leave you exposed at times when their integrity and standing may be challenged.

Reflection points

- Discuss what characterises a team development that is circular or spiral.
- Discuss how these theories might be improved.
- Come up with examples of the old sergeant syndrome in teams.

Diversity in teams

We have seen that the agenda of a leader needs to evolve along with the team's development. In the *forming stage*, your task as leader is to build trust and confidence among team members by helping them to get acquainted with each other, explaining the purpose of the work and providing good information. In the *storming stage*, you are aiming to make the team self-reliant in their work by explaining the role, mandate, and status of each member, and processing this information within the team. In the *norming stage*, you become a facilitator who seeks to promote mutual respect between members. The aim here is to plug fully into the skills, knowledge, and experience of the team. During the *performing stage*, look out for necessary changes and improvements in the norms and procedures of the team to facilitate still better co-operation. Finally, in the *adjourning stage*, your role is to maintain focus all the way to the end of the work, tie together all loose ends, thank the team, acknowledge the feelings that might be at play, allow the team members to say goodbye to each other, and send them off to new challenges. In the context of project management, this stage can include the formal process of handing over to the owner, as well as project evaluation and production of a final report. Throughout this stage, allow time to consider and address all the interpersonal aspects of your shortly departing team.

Modern teams can be very diverse, multi-disciplinary, and multi-cultural, with members from different backgrounds, with varying education and diverse experience (Figure 4.4). Members may be different ages, sexual orientation, ethnicities, and nationalities. Respect these differences and take them into account in your approach to managing the team. It is both the ethical thing to do as a project professional and you'll find that it will also pay dividends in terms of the performance of individuals and the team collectively.

The composition and organisation of teams is a significant factor in everything from their creativity, their performance, and their resilience under pressure. Diversity of thought and background is an important part of this and you'll need to work actively to develop a culture that values diversity during the forming stage. You're looking to challenge ignorance, lack of understanding, or insensitivity in how individuals and the team respond to differences in others. Social events, discussion, and sharing cultural heritage (pictures, languages, dance, symbols, movies) are all great ways to foster respect for diversity within the team. It will take time for your team to reach peak work performance. Allow for incremental learning and development in the team to make sure you are creating the right conditions to encourage members to share their experience and expertise (see Figure 4.4).

Within the International Red Cross and Red Crescent organisations, there are many project teams that consist of experts in emergency prevention. They all have different areas of expertise and they come from all around the world. One such team is the Disaster Management Working Group (DMWG) founded in 2002 (Lynch *et al.*, 2006). Its purpose is to develop and implement best practices in the emergency situations within which the

Figure 4.4

Modern teams can be very diverse, multi-disciplinary, and multi-cultural.

organisation works. The team meets every year in order to introduce and discuss new approaches based on their research, share experiences, create a plan, and organise their work. Members work together on projects between meetings and they are open to new members who volunteer on the basis of their expertise. The International Red Cross and Red Crescent formally approve the team. Things were all straightforward until the team started experiencing accelerating interest in participation from large numbers of people from different parts of the world.

At a recent meeting of the team, members were concerned about co-operation, admission requirements, and team efficiency in light of the increased interest of people in joining. It was very natural for this team to celebrate increased diversity, wider perspectives, and resources. At the same time, the team needed to maintain its core identity. Greater diversity could have been managed through formal procedures, but this was a team culture that had been characterised by informal procedures, personal interest in the topics at hand, and pleasure in having one's say. After discussion, the team appointed three members to survey what team members thought about a project charter and entry criteria for new members, and to define a future vision for the team. These three then came up with a description of admission requirements and objectives that they saw as requisite for the further development of the group (Lynch *et al.*, 2006). The survey results were presented and the project charter was redefined, expanded, and improved on the basis of this research.

This is a good example of *punctuated equilibrium* and the *old sergeant syndrome* that was provoked by cultural differences and the strong desire of people outside the team to participate. This unexpected change in the team's situation meant that the team had to adjust its development. In fact, the team was forced to take a step backwards in its development and move from the performing stage back into the storming stage, before being able, once again, to mature through the norming stage and return a second time—in a slightly different form—to the performing stage. Once the team had stabilised, the project leader restated the project mission and they were able to move forward.

Reflection points

- How would you work with diversity within a team?
- What should be kept in mind when people from different backgrounds come together in a team?
- What could the consequences be if diversity within a team is not acknowledged, recognised, and respected?

Team functions and organisation

Recent developments in management theory have been reflected in the concept of *human capital*, which indicates that team members—their welfare, knowledge, expertise, interpersonal skills, emotions, and feelings—are to be highly valued. Organisations increasingly rely on teams to get things done via projects. At the beginning of the book, we defined groups as entities consisting of two or more people who have social interaction. Teams, on the other hand, were defined as organised groups that focus on specific goals and objectives. Many modern business organisations can better be understood as a network of interconnected teams rather than as hierarchical systems built up of individuals.

Not all teams are project teams and, within organisations, there can be different kinds of teams. But what are teams particularly good for within organisations? What do teams do? How can you bring out the best in them within an organisational context? Management teams include examples that manage daily operations, analyse problems, make decisions, and form policy. Teams can also be groups of consultants, quality groups, steering groups, audit committees and working teams, production teams, and customer care teams. Finally, there can be expert teams and specialised groups such as rescue groups, surgical teams, and bands who work together with great co-ordination and co-operation (see Figure 4.5).

Teams that have now become the norm in project management are often cross-functional, bringing together the many competences needed for a project. Their role may vary; project teams can be formed to construct a building, bridge, or a space shuttle, to identify new approaches to business, find solutions

Figure 4.5

Expert teams work together with great co-ordination and co-operation.

to problems or challenges, to develop new products or services, policy making, and so on. Project teams are, therefore, types of groups with specific, albeit varied, characteristics. They can operate at all levels within an organisation and their activities often have a profound impact.

Team members possess a variety of competences, skills, and abilities that they bring to their teamwork. The success of a team depends on how well its leaders can make use of, and co-ordinate, the contributions of everyone within the team; the clarity and feasibility of goals. They require the appropriate organisation, team identity, and unity. But it is not enough to have competent individuals; the team needs to be orchestrated so all its members can perform together. The success of the team is further determined by how well the team is able to co-ordinate its efforts. To progress fast and efficiently requires team members to interact and communicate in a clear, frank, and constructive manner. This allows individuals to perceive and understand each other, and to appreciate the particular strengths of each of their co-workers and peers. You can also help your team thrive by fostering a learning culture or environment. Encourage and enable your team members to try new things and to experiment; to ask questions, challenge traditions, and make recommendations for changes, without the fear of ridicule or censure. A relaxed atmosphere where people are allowed to "think aloud" helps the team share the knowledge and experience of the individuals within it. This accelerates both the learning and the performance of the team. In organising project teamwork, you'll find the following factors helpful:

1   Within the constraints that exist, take time to identify and select the right people for the team.

2   *Set clear team goals* so that team members understand the purpose of the team and what is expected of them. Effective teams know their targets and know what needs to be done to achieve them; preferably through objectives that are clear and measurable.

3   *Select the appropriate organisation.* As there is no such thing as "a" typical team, and all teams are different. Each team requires a tailored plan that is based both on the team competence and the project at hand. Several criteria are important when organising any team, not least, the proposed lifetime of a project and the available resources. You'll need to establish the appropriate number of participants, as well as agree on how members should relate, what their mandate, authority, and division of labour should be.

4   *Be sure that the team gets what it needs in terms of training and the opportunity to practise their competences.* This applies to technical and managerial skills but also to interpersonal communication skills. All these things are needed to ensure good performance and to reduce anxiety and stress. Members who do not have the skills at the outset need to have the opportunity to learn them. Given the importance of communication within project teams, people should also be guided and given the opportunity to practise a range of these skills too; competences. These including the ability to adjust, accommodate, align, support, delegate; express themselves and listen actively to others, show assertiveness and responsibility; deal with change, conflicts, and crises; and give and receive feedback and express gratitude. The most effective communication training is social learning; team members working together to make it happen. In this way, over time, they will learn to build on the strengths of others.

5   *Work out how you can create cohesion and unity within the team to ensure effectiveness.* The team needs to stick together and it also needs to have an atmosphere and conditions that encourage mutual trust and rapport. The promotion of unity, team spirit, and positive attitudes, as well as respecting the confidentiality of participants on sensitive issues, are important responsibilities for the team leader.

Reflection points

- What are human resources in the context of an organisation?
- What is human capital?
- What kinds of teams have you worked within?
- What are the similarities and differences between a group and a team?
- How would you organise a team in order to make it succeed?
- What else could help a team to succeed?

Emotions and feelings

Clear and positive expression of emotions and feelings towards each other—whether positive or negative—have a big impact on any team. Are there times when giving free rein to negative emotions can hinder or delay team success? There is certainly little doubt that strong feelings play a big role in the cohesion and development of teams, which makes it useful for both you and your team members to realise and acknowledge the environment within which you work and reflect on how you all might unite and contribute to the development of the team. At the beginning of a project, for example, if the team members have not worked together before, introduce them to each other, invite them to describe their background, and outline the contribution you hope each of them can make. But should you encourage them to express their emotions and feelings towards each other?

This might not depend so much on whether emotions and feelings are expressed—they are likely to come out in one way or another—but rather on *how* they are expressed. Here's a list of some common feelings and emotions (see Table 4.1). You might share this with the team and ask them to pick a few examples and tell stories of their experience of feeling or observing these emotions at work.

Table 4.1 Emotions that are common to most workplaces and teams

Common feelings and emotions

Tenderness	Receptive	Exhausted	Bored	Shamed
Helpless	Suspicious	Bitter	Safe	Aggravated
Defeated	Inferior	Relaxed	Fearful	Infatuated
Rageful	Hateful	Interested	Depressed	Shocked
Cheerful	Excited	Depressed	Preoccupied	Embarrassed
Sympathy	Interested	Insecure	Happy	Restless
Powerless	Cautious	Insulted	Anxious	Concern
Bored	Confused	Relieved	Hopeless	Panicked
Outraged	Scornful	Intrigued	Angry	Humiliated
Content	Amused	Hopeless	Love	Grumpy
Adoration	Delighted	Disgusted	Worried	Trust
Dreading	Disturbed	Indifferent	Sorrow	Afraid
Rejected	Grief-stricken	Hopeful	Jealous	Disgraced
Hostile	Spiteful	Absorbed	Lust	Awkward
Proud	Elated	Sad	Scared	Liking
Fondness	Shocked	Pity	Uncertain	Nervous
Distrusting	Overwhelmed	Pleased	Envious	Uncomfortable
Disillusioned	Helpless	Curious	Aroused	Exasperated
Bitter	Vengeful	Guilty	Insecure	Attraction
Satisfied	Enthusiastic	Revulsion	Anguished	Disoriented
Exhilarated	Hurt	Confident	Annoyed	Neglected
Uncomfortable	Regretful	Anticipating	Tender	Frustrated
Isolated	Trusting	Hurt	Rejected	Caring
Disliked	Delighted	Contempt	Disappointed	Alarmed
Optimistic	Confused	Brave	Humiliated	Hesitant
Dismayed	Lonely	Eager	Compassionate	Regretful
Guilty	Ambivalent	Lonely	Horrified	Stunned
Numb	Alienated	Weary	Self-conscious	Melancholy
Resentful	Calm	Comfortable	Irritated	Amazed

Even apparently negative feelings and emotions that are expressed and or dealt with constructively will unite and strengthen the team in the long term. This does require substantial self-awareness, self-confidence, and considerable interpersonal competence on the behalf of team members. It is also important that they time their use of emotion and feeling carefully. Premature and direct expression of strong emotions can be risky and can undermine the unity within a team, creating embarrassment or resentment. You also need to be careful of the cultural differences associated with expressions of emotion. For some cultures, emotions and feelings are important aspects of social development; think of the public grief and shame that is expected of Japanese executives who admit to failure or wrong-doing. Other cultures, meanwhile, might use humour as a means of lightening the atmosphere. But both of these approaches can be taboo to others. Be careful not to assume cultural stereotypes; whilst they may appear helpful, the nuances of everyone's identity and personal make-up mean that we are all different.

Reflection points

- What are the differences between emotions and feelings?
- What role do emotions and feelings play in our consciousness?
- What role do emotions and feelings play in how people communicate?
- Is the expression of all emotions appropriate in a work team?
- Can you choose your feelings?
- Can feelings be criticised?

Moro on social needs

As discussed in Chapter 3, team participation enables us to meet various social needs such as the need for inclusion, control, and affection. By inference we can extend this idea and say that good team participation gives us a sense of belonging, social identity, dignity, and respect. To a large extent, we define ourselves in terms of our identification and involvement with other people. Team participation is hence an effective way to actualise your personal and professional potential. If your team members feel that their social needs are met, they are more likely to commit to the team, which builds cohesion. For this to happen, both the team leader and the team as a whole need to attend to everyone's individual needs. Using your observation and intuition to observe or enquiring periodically how people are doing goes a long way. You can create a great sense of worth and value when you step in and show interest and concern towards individual team members.

When you are selecting a team or monitoring how well your team is working together, think about the needs that each member is seeking to satisfy through the work and within the team. If these needs are expressed and acknowledged and individual team members are themselves aware of their needs and the needs of others, you can expect even better results, particularly if the team leader and the team members have a common understanding of this from the beginning. Remember, individual needs in a team can vary greatly. The Scottish/U.S. social psychologist Gerard Egan has defined what he calls D-needs, M-needs, and B-needs in relation to interpersonal abilities of team members (Egan, 1976):

• D-needs stand for "deficiency" needs. If deficiency needs are not addressed they can hinder personal growth and hinder professional development due to team members' inability to function well within the team.
• M-needs stand for "maintenance" needs. These are the needs required for an individual to maintain emotional stability.
• B-needs stand for "being" needs. They manifest in the need for self-actualisation.

The mutual interest of individuals within their team, cohesion based on a shared mission, and the sense of belonging can all meet different M-needs and B-needs. However, people who have strong D-needs are easily intimidated by the emotional demands of teamwork. Egan described the relationship between the D-, M-, and B-needs and the expression of emotions in this way: People who are trying to meet D-needs often express emotions and feelings in an indirect and extreme manner. Their behaviour can appear irresponsible, unstable, unruly, and unpredictable. They either fear their feelings or use them as weapons. On the other hand, for a person who is trying to meet their M-needs, the expression of emotions and feelings is commonplace. Emotions and feelings are not suppressed but they can, however, be expressed in rather superficial ways. An M-person rarely becomes upset and is unlikely to display outbursts of emotion within the team; nor will this person show much passion. Individuals with B-needs can freely allow themselves to experience and express their emotions and feelings in assertive ways. People in this category do not deny the existence and significance of emotions and feelings, nor do they allow them to overly control their lives.

Emotions and feelings are the indicators of our needs (Figure 4.6). Therefore, their appropriate expression is important, as is the suitable response to them when they are expressed. As we saw in the Tuckman model, different emotions and feelings can be provoked at different developmental stages of the team's life-cycle and can greatly affect team performance. Feelings and emotions can either enhance or reduce the effectiveness of a team and its cohesion. Enhancement is more likely if the team culture is based on open communication and feedback.

A sound understanding of how to use emotions and feelings appropriately among team members makes the team better equipped to recognise the needs of individuals and to be able to meet them well. In order to promote a culture of open communication within your team, you need to recognise

Figure 4.6

Emotions and feelings are the indicators of our needs.

that emotions and feelings are a natural part of human make-up. Their expression must be permitted even though some people may initially find this uncomfortable. Showing true feelings with integrity—rather than suppressing them or favouring superficial expressions of emotion—is crucial when building up a team, ensuring clarity of communication and sound decision-making.

Using feelings or emotions as weapons to control or manipulate others will not cultivate good interpersonal communication within the team. Feelings and emotions are best dealt with as soon as they arise and before they build into hostility. You need to be prepared to meet both positive and negative emotions when they come up and to control both our own expression of feelings and emotions and our responses to others when they express theirs.

This is a capacity that can be learned through emotional assertiveness. When faced with an emotionally provocative situation, we may respond by aggression or avoidance; or we can choose to meet it with a sense of determination and the indication that we are willing and prepared to face these emotions in a level-headed and adult way. Once the initial intensity of the emotion has subsided, leaving open the possibility of discussing feelings and emotions in a constructive way is another useful response.

There are many things that can prevent open communication and the apt expression of feelings and emotions. Your individual ability and personality, your culture and upbringing will all have considerable impact on how well you communicate during moments of high-tension or emotion. Consequently, in diverse and multidisciplinary project teams you should anticipate a considerable variety of different emotional responses.

Reflection points

- How do you meet the needs of people through interaction with others?
- How do you deal with emotions in a relationship?
- What are D-, M-, and B-needs?

Different character types

Gerard Egan take his categories of D-, M-, and B-needs still further and he suggests that it is possible to categorise peoples' communication styles according to three main character types based on the D-, M-, and B-needs (Egan, 1976). These character types are the D-style, M-style, and B-style characters. Most people don't demonstrate a single style in all situations but sometimes show D-style, sometimes M-style, and sometimes B-style traits. However, where individuals show a tendency towards a given style, these can be described in the following way.

D-individuals tend to be introverted and trapped within themselves and in their own problems. They can find it difficult to follow the thread when communicating with others and can be reluctant to communicate openly. When they speak, it reflects their personal needs and not the needs of others or of the team. It can be difficult to converse with D-individuals and often the conversation will end as a one-way discourse where they dictate their own needs. D-individuals tend to attach themselves to certain roles and will also put others around them into predefined roles. They easily turn their relations into disputes when they are tempted to offer unsolicited advice to other members of the team who suffer from the self-absorbedness of these individuals.

M-individuals easily acquire communication skills but they often do not make use of them. If they do, they can often appear rigid or unnatural. These individuals are unsure what they want to give or receive through their interactions with others. They tell stories about themselves instead of engaging in sincere mutual conversation. M-individuals tend to look up to those who are good at communicating, without following their example within the team. They show up and listen to what is said but they find it difficult to respond constructively to what is going on. M-individuals are usually not very motivated but might do pretty well if they are kept on track within the team.

B-individuals work hard and take their role within the team seriously. They acquire communication skills fast and are able to show respect, empathy, and compassion in natural and credible ways. They respond to others empathetically without placing themselves in a superior role.

You may have witnessed a range of other character types in your experience of working in teams. People come in all shapes and sizes and we often have little idea of what others have experienced and what drives them to do what they do. But you can at least try your best and avoid prejudice and jumping to premature conclusions before you really get to know others.

Reflection points

- What constitutes a D-, M-, or B-individual?
- What do you think about this analysis of people in teams?
- What is your style?
- What is the style of others within your team?
- How do people learn from one another?

References

Bales, R. F. (1970). *Personality and interpersonal behavior.* New York: Rinehart and Winston.

Egan, G. (1976). *Interpersonal living.* Belmont, CA: Wadsworth Publishing Company.

Festinger, L. (1957). *A theory of cognitive dissonance.* Stanford, CA: Stanford University Press.

Festinger, L., Schachter, S., & Back, K. (1950). *Social pressures in informal groups: A study of human factors in housing.* Oxford, England: Harper.

Forsyth, D. R. (2019). *Group dynamics* (7th ed.). Boston: Cengage.

Lynch, So & Rose, (2006). Report from the Icelandic Red Cross.

Scholtes, P. R., Joiner, B. J., & Streibel, B. J. (2003). *The team handbook.* Waunakee, WI: Suttle-Strauss Inc.

Tuckman, B. W. (1965). "Developmental sequences in small groups" in *Psychological Bulletin*, 63, 384–399.

5 Communication competence

··

In the preceding chapters we have discussed a number of different aspects relating to team dynamics and team performance. In this chapter, we begin by taking a closer look at communication in teams and then move on to the individual development of communication competence and general team skills. This is very much a mixture of theory and practice and we include a number of group exercises that are aimed at developing your social intelligence and empathy towards others. As we delve deeper into interpersonal communication, we come to understand how even subtle behaviour impacts significantly on teamwork. Sensitivity towards the needs of others and the ability to participate in shared activities are important characteristics for healthy team functioning. As we have already discussed, some team members benefit from a high level of social intelligence, whereas others may struggle. If we are genuinely open to learning more about ourselves, we can use others to point out negative elements of our behaviour. These may be habits to which you are so accustomed that you may not recognise the unintended effects they can have on others with whom you work. The first stage is to acknowledge shortcomings in how you interact with others and as part of that process you need to decide what type of team person you want to be. The next stage is to put what you have decided into practice by developing skills, initially within the framework of a team environment that is safe and mutually supportive, and then in real-life situations with whoever is out there.

Social intelligence in teams

Social and emotional intelligence and the ability to show empathy are important factors in communication between individuals; particularly so for those who lead. Being out front typically involves you having to interact with a diverse range of people, and so as a leader, you need to have the depth of character to connect comfortably with a broad range of personality types in order to affect progress. For example, at any one time, a project environment may be characterised by situations in which workers and their unions may not be satisfied, owners may be demanding better profit margins, and various other stakeholders may represent a significant risk to future developments. These are situations that require level-headed leaders with a strong sense of self (not to be confused with selfishness) and highly developed social skills to find a balance between all the conflicting demands. When different individuals and groups are working with you in contentious situations, the main attributes they are looking for are integrity, respect, fairness, empathy, knowledge, flexibility, and that you will give their views proper consideration. As emphasised in *Project: Leadership* in this series, *transparency* is a key attribute for leaders.

In any organisation there can be different pressures on those who lead and those who are led. If you can diagnose disenchantment in team members (and any troublemakers) at an early stage, and react accordingly, you will avoid potentially damaging longer-term situations and be in a position to maintain an overall positive working atmosphere. Unfortunately, the *toxic work environment* is a well-recognised phenomenon and you'll need to be proactive in ensuring that you address any associated negative behaviour in a timely and decisive fashion. Where an unhealthy organisational culture has built up over a number of years, this can prove an arduous task.

In the context of project management, effective communication greatly increases the likelihood of achieving project objectives. The responsibilities of a project manager fall into three main categories (based on a classification by Meredith & Mantel, 2006). These are: (1) *responsibility upwards*, which is the responsibility towards those in higher power, i.e. executives who have decision-making power and define the frame of reference and objectives of a project; (2) *responsibility inwards*, which is the responsibility towards a project team itself; and (3) *responsibility outwards*, which involves responsibility towards those who have a vested interest in the outcome of a project, i.e. external stakeholders of one type or another. In this last case, specific user groups can often be formed to guarantee that the viewpoints of those that are to use the results of a project are considered. To take on each of these responsibilities, a project manager will need to ensure good and open communication and we'll explore the different aspects of what this involves in the sections that follow.

Reflection points

- How do you understand both social and emotional intelligence?
- Give examples of decisions that are inherently political in nature and what your approach would be in each case to find acceptable solutions.
- What strategies can a leader employ to tackle negative elements in an entrenched organisational culture?

Upwards communication in teams

In project work, it is the responsibility of a project manager to manage project resources, keep a project within timeframes and budget, and to ensure that management and the owners of a project receive detailed, consistent, and regular information about progress. A project owner is ultimately responsible for a project and, therefore, needs to make the (right) decisions about whether and how projects should be pursued. It is, therefore, essential that you keep your project owner well informed about the status of the project, including the cost, schedule, and prospects. You need to communicate clearly and efficiently with project owners as soon as a project seems to be changing its direction. This involves outlining the nature of the issues in whatever detail necessary, seeking parameters, and proposing possible actions for approval. The key in communicating upwards is to ensure that you demonstrate that you are on top of things. You want to avoid being caught on the hop by senior managers or project owners asking for information on issues about which you are unaware (Meredith & Mantel, 2006). In short, if there are larger problems of whatever type, convey these upwards, as early as possible.

These considerations are not just restricted to projects; they can equally apply to ongoing operational management and the issues that are encountered there. Imagine a water treatment division that starts to notice changes in the properties of grey (untreated surface) water, which then begin to impact on their ability to provide sufficient treated water. Rather than gradually turning into a critical situation as conditions worsen, early action should be taken and this can involve an appeal to decision-makers for the necessary resources to resolve the issue, if these are not covered by an existing contingency (see Figure 5.1).

Figure 5.1

Communicating upwards.

When team members show each other empathy it's a good indicator of mutual understanding. This lays the foundation for transparency within working relationships and provides for better decision-making. Showing empathy towards a project owner, for example, might involve you indicating your understanding of the financial or timing risks that an owner is taking and that their financial or time resources are limited. Once you've established trust and understanding, you'll find it faster and easier to agree actions that might otherwise have threatened your working arrangements. The owner should have an understanding of the constraints under which you are operating and be more willing to listen to what you have to say about addressing issues and achieving objectives. Of course, the same principle applies between managers and those involved in the day-to-day work who may have already accurately diagnosed any problems and understand the required solutions. It's easy to lose sight of or overlook what your subordinates are saying, which can lead to unnecessary problems, some of which may become terminal for the project.

Reflection points

- How should a project manager go about conveying an important message to project owners? What preparation should be involved and what should be avoided in communications?
- If the initial reaction of project owners to a project manager highlighting a festering issue is negative, what are the next steps that the manager might take?
- Are there differences in your answers if "project manager" is changed to "employee" and "project owners" is changed to "management" in the above questions?

Intra-team communication

This refers to communication within the team and the organisations and follows on from the above discussion (Figure 5.2). The communication channels between managers and employees, and vice versa, need to be always open and have sufficient bandwidth to carry the requisite information in both directions. This should also be the case for communication amongst managers and communication amongst project team members. You may find that pressure of work means that meetings are rushed, or that other less important items dominate the agenda, with the result that critical issues remain unresolved. In some organisations, organisational culture and politics mean the views of those higher up the hierarchical structure are considered to be sacrosanct and beyond reproach, and the views of those below are poorly respected. Alternatively, where incompatible personality types are asked to work in close proximity to each other, you may find tension increases and feelings may reach

Figure 5.2

Intra-team communication.

a boiling point. Measure the temperature and be ready to react proactively to early warning signs and find a mutually acceptable solution.

In project work, the role of project managers is a distinctive one as they are the direct line managers for the other team members (Meredith & Mantel, 2006). Consequently, you need to possess the competence to lead your peers to work with you and be able to use indirect power to encourage co-workers to collaborate towards achieving project goals. You'll often need to alter plans or working arrangements without causing undue disruption and you should encourage a positive working environment that supports each individual in the project team. The role of the project manager is therefore to bring out the best in each individual.

Team cohesion is important for internal communications. The success of highly cohesive teams reflects the fact that they are attuned to each other, contributing towards open team communication and mutual understanding between team members. Co-operation will be optimised when there is widespread understanding and acceptance of the backgrounds, expectations, and roles of individual team members.

The benefits of empathy in communication are clear, but exactly how can you make empathy a normal part of team culture? You can signal the importance of empathy in everything you do and possibly even formalise the idea in ethics guidelines. Worked examples that showcase empathy and the opportunity to practise the skill amongst the team through training exercises can all help. And you should lead by example in your daily dealings by demonstrating empathy in practice. Take time to monitor what is happening within the team and be ready to challenge or support any team members who are struggling with empathy.

Reflection points

- What is your experience of the following four forms of communication in work environments: (1) manager > employee; (2) employee > manager; (3) manager > manager; and (4) employee > employee?
- What factors can lead to important issues not being properly addressed at internal work meetings?
- Describe three different hypothetical examples of personality incompatibility in the workplace. What actions could be taken in each case to improve the situation?

Extra-team communication

Every team and organisation operate in a broader environment and part of this involves sending a steady stream of messages to individuals and groups outside the organisation which reflect the views of an organisation or of individuals within it (Figure 5.3). In the age of ubiquitous email, recording devices, and social media, organisations tend to be (sometimes justifiably) cautious about external communication and to have defined policies that cover how employees may disseminate information to the public. *Managing the message* is a hot topic in communication and media management and requires knowledge and understanding of the ways information can reach the public.

Figure 5.3

Team and organisation operates in a broader environment.

You can imagine how PR advisors might get very anxious knowing that an important client is about to face the press over a controversial issue. "There's no one who wants this thing over more than I do, I'd like my life back" is a now infamous media quote given by the then-CEO of BP, Tony Hayward, during the height of the 2010 *Deepwater Horizon* oil spill crisis, currently the largest in history. This message was given in the context of: (a) 11 rig workers having tragically lost their lives in the initial explosion; (b) tumbling share prices that were soon to near halve in value since the onset of the crisis; and (c) major environmental concerns as huge quantities of oil were escaping daily from the well into the Gulf of Mexico. Whatever good teamwork may have been happening at the time by BP crews intent on fixing the issue was overshadowed by this statement from their leader. Needless to say, the sentiment that this conveyed was picked up on by numerous commentators, including U.S. President Barack Obama, and Hayward was forced to resign shortly afterwards.

On a more positive note, large numbers of businesses are successful because they communicate the right message outwards. Whether it be a small local business volunteering to help out with community activities or a large corporation taking a lead in sustainable industry development, the overall message being given should be that those external to an organisation are being valued. It is important to realise that *everything that can be associated with an organisation matters in the public's eye*. In relation to an organisation, this includes: (a) any personal communications; (b) the quality and value of their products and/or services; (c) the appearance of all associable items, e.g. buildings upkeep, product displays, toilet cleanliness, and general hygiene; (d) the public behaviour of staff; (e) advertising standards; (f) business practices—including health and safety; (g) industrial relations; (h) community engagement and support—including employment opportunities; (i) environmental awareness; and (j) considerations relating to the past, present, and future of the organisation in question. Any of these can impact on an organisation's overall reputation. Vigilance and quick responses can be required to ensure that those with possibly malicious intentions are not capable of spreading disinformation or manipulating the public message across any of these areas for their own ends.

Most projects have many *stakeholders* external to the project owners and the project team, and communications outwards relates to communications with this group. Stakeholders, in this case, are individuals, groups, or organisations who are in some way involved in a project or have a "stake" or "vested interest" in the project or its outcome (PMBOK, 2018). Sometimes it is difficult to identify and define the stakeholders of a project. *Stakeholder analysis* can help you identify, analyse, and prioritise, on some coherent basis, usually according to how much impact they can have on a project. It is important to bear in mind that stakeholders can have both a negative and positive impact on a project and we return to this topic in *Project: Strategy*, also part of this book series.

As a project manager you may well be in charge of communicating with stakeholders that are external to a project. It is an important part of your role to ensure open communications with the stakeholders and understand their expectations and experiences. To this end, you'll need to employ different methods towards the stakeholders who are positive towards the project as opposed to those that are indifferent or negative. Expectation management is a key element and you will achieve the best results in this by listening and understanding the stakeholders' expectations and reacting in an appropriate manner. A key distinction between external stakeholders and internal stakeholders is the degree to which information can be exchanged as commercial and other considerations come into play.

An example of external stakeholders could be the proposed users of a product that is being created by a project team. Your aim in communicating with these users is to ensure that the project delivers the correct product and the users receive what they expected. Empathy helps to understand the users' desires, expectations, and needs, and helps them define these things for themselves. It is also important to prepare the users for receiving the products of the project and understand what they are receiving.

Reflection points

- What different communication channels do modern organisations use to connect with the public?
- Write a short account of where an organisation handled a public incident well.
- Write a short account of where an organisation handled a public incident badly.
- What is your most recent experience of external stakeholder engagement? In what way would you approach things differently the next time?

Social intelligence

Social intelligence involves reading social situations and responding to them in an understanding and considerate manner. You'll need to be aware of your own emotions, prejudice, and feelings when communicating and being able to distinguish these from those of others when listening. *Emotional intelligence* is "the ability to perceive emotions in self and others; to understand how emotions blend, unfold, and influence cognition and behavior; to use emotions to facilitate thinking; and to manage emotions in self and others" (Lopes & Salovey, 2008 in Forsyth, 2019: p. 275). Empathy, as a communication ability, involves being able to differentiate between your own emotions and the emotions of others and then attune to others when they express their own opinions, feelings, and emotions. This process opens up the communication and increases the trust between individuals. Increased trust leads to a more positive and effective work environment and a strong sense of empathy strengthens team cohesion.

Those that are good two-way communicators use their perception, insight, and shrewdness during interaction to achieve maximum influence. Having a good connection with your inner self helps you to disclose about yourself appropriately and, in that way, develop mutuality within a team. Insight into your own emotions does not necessarily lead to good communication, however. You also need to be able to read what is happening in the surrounding environment. Those that evaluate situations well use their broader insight to perceive, amongst other things, when others are becoming defensive or express something important in an indirect manner.

Being present at key times and paying attention to the opinions and stories of those around you shows them that you care for them and have their interests at heart. We can all be apathetic towards others at times, and you have probably experienced not being heard at one stage or another. To show attention to people who are expressing themselves, you need to listen to the content of what they are saying and let them feel that your attention is undivided. Imagine a group of students who are struggling to maintain interest in a rather lacklustre session from their teacher. Invite them to get up, move around, and change where they are sitting. You may find that this will not only re-energise them but it may also re-energise their teacher too. Most of us are sensitive to the attention, or lack of attention, that others may show us—which makes it surprising how often people are inconsiderate and insensitive in how they signal their disinterest and lack of attention to others. By giving attention to others, it is possible to influence them more, and those that receive the attention will become more open to the influence from the other person.

Reflection points

Body language. The purpose of this exercise is to interpret what messages are contained in our gestures and expressions. Imagine that you are in a meeting and that you are observing your peers doing the following (Table 5.1):

Table 5.1 Behaviours that might indicate unexpressed feelings and emotions

What is being expressed with these behaviours?		
• Nodding	• Twitching nose	• Inhaling rapidly
• Turning head quickly from side to side	• Raising one eyebrow	• Drilling heels into floor
	• Shrugging shoulders	• Swinging legs back and forth
• Smiling slightly	• Standing tall	
• Lower lip quivering	• Crossing arms at chest	• Sitting with arms and legs crossed
• Speaking at a high pitch	• Gesticulating violently	
• Speaking in monotones	• Holding on to something very tightly	• Squirming constantly
• Suddenly opening their eyes widely		• Leaning to one side
	• Shielding part of their body with their hands	• Finger tapping
• Looking down while speaking		• Glancing around rapidly
	• Breathing irregularly	• Turning pale

- What do you think their body language is saying if they express themselves in each of these ways?
- Can you think of more than one possible meaning for each type of behaviour?
- Compare your understanding of each body expression with others. In how many different ways is it possible to understand each type of behaviour?
- What conclusions can be drawn from different responses given by the team?

Non-verbal communication

Non-verbal communication (often called body language) can play a big role in conveying messages to others. Everything from an untidy workspace to turning up late for a scheduled meeting can carry an unintended message to others who may interpret it in different ways. In terms of face-to-face communication, body language plays a big role. Think about your posture and general bearing in contact situations like formal meetings so that you indicate that you are mentally as well as physically present. Egan (1976: p. 97) proposes the SOLER acronym to describe five key elements of good body position in communication: (1) The S reminds you to turn directly towards the Speaker—you are here because of them; (2) O stands for Open posture, which indicates that you are open for what the speaker has to say and are ready for direct communication; (3) L means Lean towards the other person to show them they have your attention; (4) E means maintaining good Eye contact, which is a good sign of greater intimacy; and (5) R reminds you to stay Relaxed and feel comfortable within yourself as it will be noticeable; if you do not the situation may become strained.

It is important to realise that your body is constantly expressing something. Surveys on the interpretation of peoples' physical expressions in non-verbal communications suggest that we find people who are physically still and stiff to be cold and serious. Those who are, on the other hand, active, conscious, and natural in their physical expressions are seen as relaxed, warm, and friendly. Only a few people within a group need to stop showing attention for the closeness between everyone to be lost.

Reflection points

- *The impact of body language on our understanding of words.* The purpose of this exercise is to give an idea of how much effect body language can affect the way we interpret the spoken word. Choose a member of your team, sit opposite to this person, and close your eyes. Talk for two to three minutes on a topic related to your project and keep your eyes closed the whole time. Then share your experience of your conversation.

What non-verbal messages did you miss, and in what way was this conversation lacking as a result?

- *Attention and revision.* This exercise aims to sharpen the recognition of bodily expressions as a communication tool. Select a member from your team and observe each other in silence for two minutes. Then close your eyes and describe your colleague's posture as you remember it. If you cannot give a good description after two minutes of observing it in silence, then open your eyes again and see what it was you missed. Close your eyes again and finish your description.
- *Effects of showing attention in a discussion between two or more people.* Select a partner from the group and a relevant topic and let your partner speak while you listen. You should try to keep your body language as neutral as possible, suggesting indifference. At a certain point, change your attitude and then show a lot of attention. Keep this going for a few minutes and then discuss together the different effects of attention and lack of attention from the perspectives of both participants. As a follow-up, gather the whole group together and repeat the exercise, speaking each in turn and changing attitudes as outlined above. Compare your observations at the end of this process (based on Egan, 1976: p. 101).

Physical and mental presence in teams

Your body language indicates to others whether or not you are showing them attention while they speak. It follows active listening, which is reflected in the posture and the body language of the listener. Facial expressions and gestures can indicate many things. Studies have shown that it is not only the choice of words by the speaker that determine the understanding of others of what they are saying. It has even been argued that words communicate only 7% of what is being expressed, while the nuances in the voice account for 38%, and facial and bodily expressions up to 55% (Mehrabian & Wiener, 1967). If facial expressions are inconsistent with the words, then the facial expressions often become the determining factor in the interpretation of what is being expressed.

Team members who are good communicators pay attention to all of this and respond to the overall communication; including the words, voice, and body language.

When on the receiving end of communication, it is important to monitor the correlation of words and body language. Non-verbal communication can help to highlight elements and bring life to interactions, confirm or negate the messages being conveyed in words, and can add implicit messages beyond what is said explicitly. Where there are language barriers of one type or another, body language can be very effective at conveying the right message, although you need to be careful about the interpretation of specific conscious gestures between different cultures.

Allowance also needs to be made for personality types. Some team members may communicate important information and emotions without much obvious physical expression, whereas others will be the opposite, adding drama to every sentence. Paying close attention to what is expressed through body language can help you to distinguish the real message being conveyed. For the listener, body language has two functions: firstly, it gives the impression that you are wholeheartedly present and ready for co-operation; and, secondly, it helps you to be an active listener. If you listen out for the meaning of the spoken words and their tone, while observing body language to check for a match, you'll have a sophisticated radar to detect the exact meaning from the communication, which may contradict what is being said in words.

We quickly identify the type of body language that is being expressed, but it does not necessarily follow that we will work on its interpretation. To encourage this, it is useful for the group to talk about the different forms of body language and teach each other to become better equipped to determine what different expressions indicate. Let's reiterate our previous words of caution. The action of someone silently bowing their head can indicate a number of things including: rejection, anger, desperation, forced acceptance, or something more mundane such as tiredness or a stiff neck, and there can be many nuances. Be careful not to become overly preoccupied with body language and nuances of tone or timbre. Over-analysing body language and non-verbal expression is a barrier to fast communication and may even disrupt how you communicate and work with each other.

Exercises

- *Listen to the nuances of body language and tone of voice.* Invite everyone in the team to each take five minutes to discuss what they like and dislike about their own behaviour. Those listening should observe and write down points about expressed body language and nuances in the tone or timbre of the voice and rate them for impact. You're not psychoanalysts so keep it simple: "You spoke very rapidly which gave the impression that you were nervous"; "You appeared calm during the conversation. Your hands were in your lap the whole time and you hardly moved your body, which made you come across as being a bit stiff and shy"; "You were sitting back with folded arms, perhaps even leaning to one side a bit, which made me feel that you might possibly have been disinterested". When the exercise is complete, you should switch roles and repeat the exercise. Share your experiences with one another.

Empathy I and II

Good listeners will listen attentively to what the other person has to say and will give them the opportunity to express themselves fully. They'll also work at giving a considered response to what they hear. This can either be in the form of questions, opinions, anecdotes, or suggestions, and should convey empathy.

Empathy is the process of trying to put oneself into the shoes of the person to whom you are talking to and seeing the world from their point of view, and in light of their experience, in order to gain a sense of their emotional reality. You need to share your understanding back to them so that they acknowledge (or challenge) the thoughts, behaviour, and emotions, and the foundations of these, and your interpretation of what you have understood. Essentially, empathy can be of three different types. We'll discuss the first two types in this chapter and save the third type for Chapter 7 (builds on Egan, 1976).

Empathy I involves sending a message to another person in order to let them feel that you have understood what they have said. At this level, you should be careful not to try and interpret or anticipate concerns that have not been expressed, or that may have been expressed but only in a non-direct or non-verbal way. This level also does not involve trying to figure out exactly what the person is saying, but rather to put yourself in the other's shoes and follow the overall message that they are verbally communicating. The aim of empathy I is to make it easier to create a connection between people as it involves making a conscious effort to understand each other and learn to trust each other. It also makes it easier for people to open up and address their own thoughts and concerns. It helps understanding the other person and enables them to relax and be themselves. Here's a scenario by way of illustration:

John says: When people in my team talk, I often fail to express myself and am frustrated by this. I think for so long in meetings about what I am going to say, that when I finally say something, the topic is not relevant anymore.
Susan uses empathy I when she replies by paraphrasing what John has said: So, you want to express your views to the team but you have to prepare it so well in your mind that you cannot express this until it is too late.

Empathy I can perhaps be better understood by comparing it with empathy II. Empathy II does not simply involve responding to what the other person says by reflecting back his or her message, but also to what is *being hinted at or suggested* and has *not been verbally communicated*, for example:

- *"When I hear you talk, I wonder if you are not also frustrated".*
  "As I listen to you, I wonder if you might not feel a little frustrated"
- *Having heard you say that … (empathy I) I think that if I were in your situation I would feel frustrated".*

The speculative aspect of showing empathy II is important as it is easy to back out if your interpretation and your assumption is incorrect. You are suggesting that the other is feeling or experiencing and it is safer to do it without making a direct statement by saying "You are …" as that can be confusing and patronising.

Take care when using empathy II, as it can generate a negative response if it is used too early in a relationship within a team. Its use requires familiarity and a trusted connection. Untimely use of empathy II can confuse people, frighten, or irritate them. No one wants to be the guinea pig for their team members' amateur analysis.

On the other hand, it can be very beneficial for individuals if they are lucky enough to work with colleagues who are good at using empathy II. It can help them to see themselves through other people's eyes and makes it easier to evaluate what effect their attitudes, behaviour, and conduct have, or does not have, on others. This allows them to understand themselves better and see how they might benefit from changing an aspect of their behaviour or their communication. The ancient Greeks venerated the idea of "knowing thyself" and this has long been thought to be very sound and prudent advice.

Once your team has become more comfortable with each other and are used to opening up about themselves, this is then an indication that it is possible to progress into empathy II. Here is an example scenario:

John says: I do think that I am particularly hard on myself. Yet, I don't remember having heard anything positive about me from others. They make demands of me, but I am never encouraged or shown affection. I feel that I am an outcast.

Susan replies, saying: When you talk about the fact that you think you are hard on yourself and never hear anything positive about you from others, I wonder whether the difficulty may stem from the fact that you don't fully accept yourself. I have often had the feeling that you are very hard on yourself.

The above example shows that empathy is not just a technique but also a natural human expression. Different individuals will use it in different ways. It also takes considerable practice to use empathy accurately (Figure 5.4).

Empathy is a useful emotion in communications at times when we may find it hard to express our understanding of the feelings, experiences, and behaviour of the person with whom we are communicating. The subtlety of the skill means there are a couple of things that you need to avoid. Firstly, beware of *clichés* as you will come across as unsympathetic and as patronising. For example, if John responded to Susan with: "Well, life isn't a bed of roses, it's a tough world out there". Secondly, you should also be careful not to respond immediately with a critical question related to what has been said. By asking a question such as "are you sure you're not overreacting?" you demonstrate that you haven't understood what (in our example) John is trying to express and you have shown yourself to be critical and unsympathetic to his mental state.

If you want to respond with a question, then make sure it is an open one, i.e. one that does not expect a yes-or-no answer, but encourages the speaker to express themselves in more detail. *Open questions* often start with "what", "how", "when", "who", "which" and it would be more appropriate if Susan were

Figure 5.4

Accurate empathy is important in communication.

to ask John: "How long have you felt like this?" A good communicator should also initially *avoid critical questions*, such as "why" or "what for". It can be difficult for someone who is trying to express their emotions and feelings to also have to justify themselves.

Practise asking *questions* that are *not solution-oriented*. The questions should be short as short questions have a tendency to be more open and are less likely to become elongated with unnecessary explanations. Solution-oriented questions are questions that demand actions such as: "What can you do about it?" "What should we do about it?" What can be done about this?" Avoid this form of question, at least initially, as they can: (1) make a person irritated if they have already tried different solutions and found them ineffective; (2) make them feel as if they are not in control of their destiny and are being forced into action; or (3) can have the effect that the person involved does not feel that they have to solve the issue themselves and can abrogate the responsibility onto you. Examples of open and short questions that are not critical or targeted at solutions might be:

- What happened?
- How is it now?
- Who is involved?
- What made you feel that way?
- What else do you think was a factor?
- How would you describe the situation?
- What is important?

There are a few other things that you should try to avoid when showing empathy level I and II. The following is based on a list from Gerad Egan (Egan, 1976).

As already mentioned, *avoid dropping into empathy II prematurely* as it is likely to be inappropriate and have the opposite effect to what is intended. Imagine if Susan had said to John, after only a short period of acquaintance: "You sound very down and I think you might have serious problems that you need to do something about". Taking this direct, accusative line with people that you are not too familiar with is quite likely to elicit a negative response.

When using empathy, take care to *avoid inaccuracies*, as your expression of empathy needs to be as clear as possible. If the recipient gets the feeling that you have not understood them correctly, they may try to correct you and, in doing so, they are likely to (partly or wholly) withdraw themselves from the discussion. An example of this might be if the speaker is trying to express themselves on something that is important to them but does not quite get the point across and you answer (or interject) by saying: "When you talk about this, it is obvious that you are not happy because of …." You have just signalled that you are tired of waiting for the other speaker to get to the point, but this type of rhetorical questioning may be an inaccurate reflection of the speaker's views and this can lead to misunderstandings and a desire on the part of the speaker to cease communication.

It is also important to *avoid pretending that you understand*. It can be difficult to understand what others are trying to express, even though you are giving them your full attention. This is particularly common when the speaker is not used to experiencing empathy in their daily communications. If the person is emotional or unclear, it may affect how clearly they express themselves and if they are excited or distracted, they may lose their focus, as may you. It is honest to admit that you have lost the thread of the conversation and need to get your bearings again, but also important to demonstrate effort in listening and apologise for not understanding, when appropriate. It is better to ask them to repeat themselves and then listen actively. This shows the speaker that you respect them and are interested in what they are saying. If you are unsure whether you have understood the person correctly, you should be cautious in answering and give them room to continue to express what they want to say.

Be careful that you don't fall into *parroting behaviour*, i.e. mechanical repetition of what the other person said. As strange as it may seem, you can see this behaviour sometimes in people who are otherwise very good at communicating or who should be specifically educated in the nature of good communication.

The goal of effective communication is to get to the core of the matter. When we show empathy I, we first react to what the speaker has been telling us directly by processing this information and generating our own thoughts. After that, we might make our own contribution. A good answer can get to the core of the matter of what the other person is saying very effectively.

It is poor etiquette to interrupt when others are speaking. Good communication requires that others have the opportunity to express their views and that we resist jumping from one subject to another. By giving others a good opportunity to express themselves, you give yourself time to think about the emotions and feelings that are being expressed and what is actually being said.

A moderate level of impulsiveness may be good, however, if you interrupt when you feel you have something that you need to say. Choose an appropriate way and moment to do this. The choice of language and tone, as well as your general demeanour, are important in this regard.

Conversations will be more effective if they happen on an equal footing in terms of language, tone, and demeanour. If you are talking to people who do not belong to your organisation or your profession, try to avoid *professional language* or jargon that is specific to your company and instead use *generalised language*. If there is a discrepancy in language, tone, or attitude, then you may distance those with whom you are speaking. Empathy involves "a normal conversation". Long speeches, monologues, and long answers should be avoided as this dilutes the interest of the audience. One way to encourage others to deal with their emotions is to express how you would feel in similar circumstances.

If a person feels threatened when talking about their feelings, it may be wise to focus on what they say explicitly with their words rather than give notice to their emotions.

Empathy is only one of many methods to form connections, but it is a very important method. However, if you use it in isolation from other methods and out of context of a normal conversation, then it can appear forced or pretentious. On the other hand, if you can successfully channel empathy and adopt the right techniques in interactions with others, then those around you will get the feeling that you are likeable and trustworthy. In groups where empathy is a dominant communication method, members experience a mutual understanding and trust towards each other.

Reflection points

- Observe the body language of your team members as well as document your own emotions, experience, and behaviour whilst the interaction lasts. Create sentences in the form of: "Now I am aware that… (referring to a piece of non-verbal expression of others or your own feelings or experiences)". This enables you to identify details in your communications and enable you to become more sensitive to the important signals in the communication process.
- Identify the feelings and emotions of others. Discernment and the ability to exercise empathy in our interactions with others are important competences. Listen to people talking and notice how emotions and feelings are expressed. Try to identify the exact feelings and emotions of the speaker in each case (Table 5.1).

Trust in teams

It can be difficult to conceive of other people's world view. Empathy requires skills that can be learnt and mastered, but more is needed to connect you to the person with whom you are interacting and to put yourself into their shoes, or frame of mind. You need to be comfortable to show affection, put your own issues aside, and make an effort to understand the experiences of another person. When someone gets a sense that they are properly understood, they will feel relief, ease, and trust. This can help them to come out of their comfort zone to express themselves, contributing to their increased development and maturity.

The foundations of proper communication are trust and credibility. Trust implies a belief that someone (or some people) will meet your expectations in the future. It is a basic building block for all human relationships, including team activities. If you and your colleagues fail to create a climate of trust, then the team is not likely to succeed. Trust has many forms of expression:

- *Confidentiality* such as not disclosing any material to others unless authorised to do so.
- *Reliability* to fulfil a promise and follow up on promises.
- *Consideration* when using authority.
- *Sympathy* in striving to understand the experience of another and making this known to them.

Trust, in all of its forms, is only possible if there exists a mutual recognition of values. The experience of trust leads to credibility and this is an essential trait for anyone whose role revolves around their communication ability (Figure 5.5).

It has been shown that businesses that are based on trust can increase profits, productivity, and employee satisfaction without having to increase their budget (e.g. Ciancutti & Steding, 2001). Trust is essential in any team

Figure 5.5

The experience of trust leads to credibility.

and cannot be built up without communication. It also needs to be earned and evolves with experience of co-operation, understanding, and knowledge of others.

People create credibility with their behaviour. The behaviour of an individual within a group determines whether the group will trust that individual. People will feel you are trustworthy when you maintain confidentiality and keep the promises that you made, as well as demonstrate honesty, openness, and sincerity. Credibility is also affected by factors such as showing warmth, enthusiasm, a willingness to co-operate, realism, optimism, and faith in the knowledge of the group.

Anyone who wants to be credible in team activities should develop their sense of empathy, demonstrate understanding of others, and use their social influences and power cautiously and with a clear intent that will benefit others. You should also remain open to the influences of others and avoid pretentiousness, selfishness, inattentiveness, and superficiality. It can be very damaging for someone's credibility in team situations if there is a perception that they are putting their own personal interests first at the expense of others or being underhanded in their dealings in some way. Individuals are trusted if they respect the needs and emotions of others and provide information and opinions in a way that benefits others. Being open and honest about your plans and intentions also increases credibility and creates goodwill. A group will have less trust in inactive team members than in active members. If you don't talk to the team about what you are doing, thinking, or feeling, your colleagues will have no sense of your activity.

Let's look at an example. Consultant, Peter, is hired to assist with the merger of two departments within a company. People are often scared of changes and insecure about what they will lead to, even though some may see new opportunities in these changes. As individuals often show considerable resistance to change, it is important to get them on board and build up their belief and trust in what the changes will lead to. Peter may use exercises such as those in the previous chapter to help build up team unity and a good spirit within the organisation. But he needs first to clear the air and get everyone to express themselves with honesty and integrity. The first step in mutual communication is listening, because without good listening there is an increased risk of misunderstandings. Throughout this process, Peter needs to recognise and understand discrepancies between body language and nuances of the voice, on the one hand, and what is being said, on the other. This perception allows him to recognise what is happening underneath the surface. If Peter is skilled at reading the employees' expressions and combining this with his detailed impression of what is said, then he will get a good grasp of the situation. The more experience Peter has, the clearer his understanding and the harder it is for individuals or groups to hide problems.

The exercises in this chapter help individuals to become more conscious of their feelings and what lies behind them, as well as practising active listening. This will help you to articulate your thoughts, understand and come to terms with feelings that you are not already aware of, and to express your feelings in an assertive manner.

Reflection points

- Listen to someone from your team talking and once you have identified his or her feelings try to articulate the experiences that underlie what they are saying by finishing the sentence:
  - "She is happy because   "
  - "He is experiencing rejection because…"
  - "She is uneasy because…"
  - "He is insecure because…"
  - "He feels relieved because…"

Check if you are getting this right by asking them for their feedback (builds on Egan, 1976).

References

Ciancutti, A. & Steding, T. (2001). *Built on trust: Gaining competitive advantage in any organization*. Chicago, IL: Contemporary Books.

Egan, G. (1976). *Interpersonal living*. Belmont, CA: Wadsworth Publishing Company.

Forsyth, D. R. (2019). *Group dynamics* (7th ed.). Boston, MA: Cengage.

Mehrabian, A. & Wiener, M. (1967). "Decoding of inconsistent communications" in *Journal of Personality and Social Psychology*, 6(1): 109–114.

Meredith, J. R. & Mantel, S. J. (2006). *Project management: A managerial approach*. Hoboken, NJ: John Wiley and Sons

PMBOK (2018). *Project management book of knowledge*. Philadelphia: Project Management Institute.

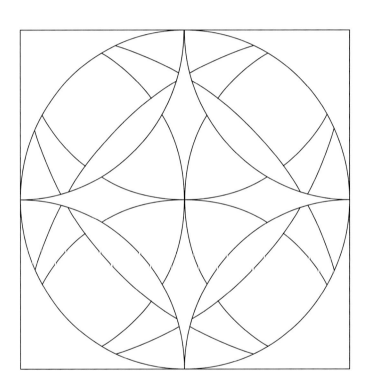

6 Authority and conformity in teams

· ·

Authority, integrity, and respect are important influences in management and communication. Effective application of authority and good communication, characterised by respect and integrity, are key elements of sound management. As a manager you need to understand what your authority looks like and use it in an organised and constructive way to meet your responsibilities. Authority exists in various forms and you may find it complicated and difficult to use at times. Sensible use involves fair and proportional action to resolve issues as well as encouragement and recognition of good work done. Misuse of authority, on the other hand, can be damaging, both to you and your team.

Authority in teams

Authority is commonly defined as the ability to enforce laws, influence behaviour, determine, and judge. Formal authority normally derives from an existing framework of responsibility, experience, and knowledge. According to French and Raven (1960; Forsyth, 2019), who studied teacher-pupil interactions in classroom situations, developing and maintaining control requires both *authority* and *power*. Authority is the right to make decisions that affect the choices that are made available to people; a right that will tend to go unchallenged provided people believe that the choices made on their behalf are reasonable. While authority is normally given to us, exercising our authority requires the power to make people comply. French and Raven described power as stemming from the five following sources:

- *Legitimate power* is based on a formal position of authority and social acceptance.
- *Reward power* is based on the right of some to offer or deny tangible or intangible rewards to others for doing what is expected of them.
- *Coercive power* is based on the threat of force to gain compliance from another.
- *Expert power* is based on possessing superior knowledge.
- *Referent power* is based on the affiliations to the groups and organisations.

Large projects will normally involve several distinct and different types of authority, each exhibiting different sources of power. The authority of a project owner, for example, will be of a different nature to the authority of a stakeholder, project manager, or members of a project team. It is useful in the initial stages of a project to map out who has what authority, the origin of the authority in each case, and the potential impact of that authority on the project. In the context of how you intend to use your authority, try to identify what your authority represents, where it comes from, and what *pros* and *cons* are associated with its use.

Formal authority—such as positional authority and legal authority—is based on rights assigned to an individual based on status. Police officers directing traffic, customs officials at airports, or teachers who dictate class lessons are all examples of formal authority; compliance with instructions or demands is backed, in each case, by specific powers. The authority of managers is fundamentally formal although it can also be based on their leadership ability to influence by using informal authority. Team members themselves need to agree collectively on the authority structure on the basis of which they are willing to comply, stay organised and successful. This usually involves agreement on the norms, values, and moral obligations adopted for the team.

When teams members are attracted to, respect, and identify with the person of authority, it gives that person an additional *informal authority based on personal attributes.* This authority is specific to the person on which it has been bestowed and can sometimes transcend their formally given status, or their legally bound authority. Within a team it is often the person who is the most popular, the one that others most want to please, or someone with particular personal charm or charisma to whom the team members give authority.

The authority and power of people with personal authority are based on the perception of their followers (Figure 6.1). Personal authority can be valuable in teams when it facilitates getting things done and keeping people engaged. Individuals with strong charisma can have a tremendous impact for

Figure 6.1

Authority is often based on the perception of people.

both good and bad so it makes sense to identify them and, where it suits the team's mission, encourage them, allow them to flourish, and get them on your side when you need to encourage other members to move in one direction or another. Power and influence are positive attributes, which can have a negative aspect to them; manipulative or dictatorial managers can exercise power over a team or teams that is unhealthy for the team and exposes the project and the organisation to risk. A good knowledge of boundaries and of what is appropriate in communications helps to identify any "red flags" in terms of an individual's behaviour and enables you to mitigate or decrease the importance of such individuals in groups and within organisations. This topic is further discussed in the *Project: Leadership* book in this series.

Reward-based authority is found in situations where those in authority have the power to give rewards or punishments to the people that they need to influence. These rewards can be in various forms such as money, benefits, increased status, or other acknowledgement, and access to tasks, roles, or parts of the project that might be desirable. High-level executives generally have the greatest reward-based authority although they remain answerable to the Board of Directors and to the owners. Alongside conventional payroll rewards, bonuses, and benefits, there are many other informal methods to reward people to celebrate achievements—with food, appreciation, and entertainment—for team members to relax, enjoy, and reflect on their success. Other non-financial rewards include flexible working hours, participation in attractive sub-projects, and the allocation of specific responsibility.

While all these various types of reward can be useful, remember that praise and constructive feedback are often the rewards that are most immediate, personal, effective, and cost-effective. Indeed, an absence of constructive feedback and praise can even lead people to start doubting themselves, feel unsure about what they are doing and, in extreme cases, leave their jobs. One of the most successful management training videos of the early 1990s, The Sid Story, introduced the idea of "planned spontaneous recognition". The idea is that as a team leader, every week or every month, or in advance of every project meeting, you should look for a behaviour that you want to encourage in your team. For example, it could be sharing knowledge or lessons learned, updating a risk register, showing empathy to a stakeholder … you choose what you want to reinforce.

The smart part of the concept is that if you observe the behaviour you then reward it with something small and personal—a thank you, a handshake, a home-made cake or even a badge! The reward needs to be something you give to the team member, or the team as a whole, rather than something from the company. If, on the other hand, you don't see any evidence of the behaviour you are looking for, then you don't say anything. Your team isn't aware of what you are looking for so there is no opportunity for them to gamify the whole thing and go through the motions (Edmonds, 2018).

Coercive authority is founded on the opportunity to threaten or penalise those who do not comply with requests or demands. Coercive authority sometimes takes the form of physical or psychological bullying—as happens when teams undermine members, speak behind their back, or unfairly criticise them. Individuals with little authority are actually more likely to resort to coercive power because that is the only power they have. The status of the individual on the receiving end of coercive authority influences its impact. If the person has a strong position, e.g. expert authority, the coercive impact is less. Stakeholders in projects sometimes hold strong coercive power, e.g. they can, for instance, threaten to stop doing business with a company if they are not satisfied with their undertakings. It is rarely an ethical form of influence and almost always self-defeating. It erodes trust and the coercive stakeholder is highly likely to find their behaviour is repaid in some way.

Expert authority in teams is based on the notion that those who obey the authority do so on the basis of a perception of superior knowledge and ability in the person with the authority. As with the case for personal authority, this depends on belief and perception from those identifying the authority, rather than any intrinsic fact. However, it is difficult to maintain expert authority without the knowledge or expertise to sustain the belief. In project teams, there may be many experts who each have (or should have) expert authority and it's down to you, the team leader, to check their credibility.

Information authority relies on having access to information and being in a position to use it. It can involve selectively distributing or withholding information, or even misrepresenting information. Project team leaders do usually hold substantial information authority, as they have been called actualise a mission based on information that they now possess. Team members can establish authority for themselves with the information they possess, either by revealing it or by intentionally keeping it to themselves. Experience that has been gained by a team member over a longer period of time can also give them authority and make them a *key figure* whose input is vital to the success of a project. This can provide the individual concerned with some leverage to influence what happens in the team or the project by offering or withholding access to the information. As with all these sources of power, however, clearly manipulative or self-serving behaviour is unlikely to endear yourself to the team or the organisation.

Finally, *commitment authority* is a less obvious form of authority that develops incrementally as someone encourages others to start committing to doing something on a small scale and gradually makes them extend their commitment. The initial commitment provides an opportunity to gradually secure increasing commitment. The bond between those making and receiving the request to commit becomes established in the mind of the receiver as he or she accepts increasing demands on their time or expertise. This "foot in the doorway" approach can be effective, but it does raise a number of ethical questions.

Reflection points

- What is the difference between power and influence?
- What gives people power?

- What examples can you give that reflect the different types of power that are discussed in this chapter?
- What else, beyond what we have discussed in this chapter, can give people power?
- How do you view the benefits and drawbacks of power?
- What ethical issues might arise in connection with using authority/power?

Obedience in teams

Teams, or certain aspects of teamwork, reflect compliance to authority. Occasionally project teams, or individual team members, find themselves taking orders that are ethically challenging or even morally dubious. This begs the question: Why do some individuals obey others? What makes people do things that are ethically ambiguous? Many studies have been conducted on the effects and application of power and obedience to people with authority. One of the most famous is Stanley Milgram's experiment at Yale University on how far people are willing to go to obey their superiors and what factors affect their obedience, including the influences of their peer group (Milgram, 1974). In the basic set-up, one participant was a "volunteer" who came forward as a result of advertising, another was a "researcher" who was responsible for the experiment, and the third person was a member of the research team who played "the role of a volunteer". The genuine volunteer was given the role of "Teacher" whilst the member of the research team playing the volunteer role was identified as a "Student". The "Teacher" was given instructions by the "Researcher", in a separate room to the "Student".

The "Teacher" was then asked to read a list of paired words, e.g. "blue box", "beautiful day", and so on, and the "Student" was required to memorise the list and then repeat the second of the paired words, when given the first word by the "Teacher". If the "Student" could not remember the word, then the "Teacher" was instructed to deliver an electric shock using a series of calibrated buttons. In fact, the buttons were fake and no "Students" were actually shocked. The "Teacher" was informed at the start of the experiment that the electric shock was not dangerous, merely painful. The machine had a total of 30 buttons, the first of which appeared to deliver a 15 volt shock, with subsequent buttons each increasing the voltage by 15 volts, and the final button labelled as giving a 450 volt shock. At each subsequent wrong answer, the "Student" was given a higher electrical shock. When the level had reached 300 volts, the "Student" was primed in advance to mimic protest by beating the wall and from 315 volts and upwards, to stop responding.

During the course of these experiments involving different participants, some questioned the situation after several smaller "shocks" had been administered, while most participants from the group of "Teachers" assumed that the experiment was completed when the "Student" went quiet at 315 volts. The "Researcher", however, indicated that "no" response constituted an "incorrect response" and urged the teachers to continue the experiment with increasingly strong instructions. No one who was involved with the experiment anticipated that anyone would give a 450 volt electric shock to another human being. They had posited that most of the participants would stop at 150 volts. The results, however, were totally unexpected. Sixty-five percent of the participants gave a 450 volt "shock" and none of them refused to continue before this had increased to 300 volts (Figure 6.2).

Various parameters were examined in the experiment to determine whether they affected the results. For example, the "Student" was sometimes asked to increase their level of protest; the "Teacher" was asked to move closer to the "Student" (on the other side of the dividing wall), and the "Researcher" announced to the "Teacher" that the "Student" had a heart problem. Different aspects of the environment were also modified, for example, decreasing the obvious level of supervision, making the level of expertise knowledge less visible, and examining group influences. The results of these changes were that—if the level of supervision was reduced, and if the volunteers did not respect the authority of the "Researcher"—the 65% obedience level fell to 20%. Changes to the physical environment were less effective. The greatest impact on the participants was when they were acting as a group in the "Teacher" role, and this led to the obedience level falling to 10%. All the situations were claimed by Milgram to be realistic; resembling genuine situations in which supervisors give subordinates orders. The emphasis throughout was on making it psychologically difficult for the "Teacher" to quit the experiment as they were given several levels of contingency orders which required them to continue even if they experienced misgivings.

The dominant reason participants gave for continuing was that, even though they felt they wanted to stop, they found they were unable to ignore the requirement to obey the "Researcher". Milgram's results can be interpreted

Figure 6.2

Milgram's experiment on obedience to superiors.

as indicating that obedience to a superior may often be a stronger compulsion than obeying your own convictions. Milgram's experiment also indicated that obedience to a superior was a greater coercive force than the burden that automatically follows the act of hurting another person. The resistance to the "Researcher's" instructions increased, however, as the "Teacher" moved closer to the "Student". The experiment also showed that respect for a superior has an important influence on how much power they have. Increased respect equates to increased power.

How truly representative is the experiment of human tendencies? Various authors have criticised or questioned several aspects of Milgram's study, its results, and conclusions. And others have carried out their own broadly similar experiments. A consensus view might be that the effects Milgram observed are real, but somewhat exaggerated due to the context of the experimental set-up.

In work life, teams are often put together with all employees being ostensibly equal. If the team does not respect the manager, then the level of obedience falls and a power struggle can ensue during which team members can dissipate a large amount of energy in trying to gain power and in their mental struggle with authority issues. This is fundamentally unproductive and it's important that authority and power are always clear in project teams. A laissez faire management and a lack of monitoring and control can result in lower compliance with directives and less overall success. The job of encouraging the continuation of good work and the avoidance of wasted work gets lost, with a consequent impact on both motivation and productivity. In making the project plan, therefore, it is important that you define the goals effectively: when should they be achieved? How should performance be evaluated, and by whom? And you need to follow this blueprint carefully throughout the life of a project.

Self-organising teams are teams that are sufficiently mature to be able to react themselves to changes in a project or their environment. They can do this by changing their approach, methods, focus, or whatever is needed to achieve set goals. If requirements change, the team takes note of it and adapts, usually by compliance to the expert authority of individual members or group consensus. When a team has become self-managing, monitoring has less value than it otherwise would and the most useful role you can assume is that of the external face of the team; someone fighting for its interests. In this context, where respect for expert knowledge and expert authority is paramount, project managers with expert knowledge are likely to have more power (and likely to be influential) than project managers without it. This would be typical in smaller engineering projects, for example, where one person can have a good grasp of the overall project requirements. Expertise in project management as a discipline in itself, on the other hand, can give a project manager expert authority that makes up for a lack of expertise in the technical subject matter of a project. Their team will, therefore, be content to obey their instructions, provided they do not conflict with their superior technical expertise.

Returning to theories of obedience, Milgram's experiment shows just how strong the effect of a presumed expert can be on individuals. Most team members are just regular people who are content to take orders, comply, and are likely to behave like the majority of the team. If the team unites in obeying their superior, individuals are likely to conform. However, if the team disobeys their superior the individual may choose either to follow the group or align with the leader. This is usually based on fear, rather than any rational reflection. Ask yourself whether your authority is effective in how the team achieves its goals, or if there is something going on in the team that prevents this. As we have discussed before, this means you'll need to communicate well with your team, have a good sense of how it is composed, and what is needed for it to work well.

Reflection points

- How do you use authority?
- When has authority been forced upon you?
- What are the power dynamics within your team?
- What types of behaviour are people likely to show only when within a team?
- What types of behaviour are people likely to show only when on their own?

Authority and vulnerability in teams

Obedience and submissiveness of individuals within teams are not necessarily reflective of personalities, but rather of the authority dynamics at play within the team. Authority figures can have a big impact on team members by, for example, manipulating the sources of power, monitoring interactions, or leading by example. One of the things that came to light in Milgram's study was that individuals who were lower down in the authority pyramid had a greater tendency to obey than those higher up in the hierarchy. This is not surprising and social conditioning to acceptance of authority is likely to be significant. It has also been shown that positive behaviour increases corresponding positive behaviour and *vice versa* in feedback loops, which is also not surprising. As a general observation, those who are higher in the authority pyramid, and have more power, tend to have more responsibility than those further down. Also, those who are lower down are keener to follow orders but also to avoid responsibility (Figure 6.3). In companies, this sometimes leads to a middle management that is not proactive and is resistant to accepting responsibility. This can be a top-down phenomenon, however, and may be encouraged when people in the lower levels see the upper levels as having authority and responsibility without accountability, which can lead to disenchantment and disengagement with their subordinate role.

Figure 6.3

People who are lower down are likely to follow orders and avoid responsibility.

In teams as a whole, there exists a continuum of authority structures ranging from a self-organised team (based, for instance, on democracy or meritocracy) to a dictatorial type of authority (autocracy), where the leader has sole power and tightly controls their team. In most cases, an experienced team leader will dynamically act on this continuum, sometimes use formal authority, sometimes delegation of responsibility and sometimes direct orders in order to make the team perform. This can also mean giving team members a certain level of authority or power as well as being held accountable for their work which incentivises and mobilises the team to take collective responsibility.

An extreme example of authority (with legislative basis in this case) is the authority that prison guards have over prisoners. This role of course differs from what we would expect to be going on in managerial teams, even though there are some important common elements. In this context, there are two classical studies that provide us with information on human behaviour, of team dynamics and influence. The first of these is the Stanford Prison Study carried out in the U.S. in 1971 by psychologist Phillip Zimbardo (e.g. Zimbardo *et al.*, 2000), and the second of these is the BBC Prison Study carried out in the UK in 2001 under the direction of psychologists Steve Reicher and Alex Haslam (Reicher & Haslam, 2006). Both these studies involved screening a wide range of public applicants in order to select 15 (BBC) and 24 (Stanford) "normal" men to perform roles as prison guards and prisoners with the ratio being five guards to ten prisoners in the first case and nine guards to nine prisoners in the second case (plus six standbys). After the men were assigned their respective roles, the "prisoners" were arrested and placed in a representative mock prison together with all the associated features such as cells, guard rooms, uniforms, keys, and surveillance. It was a deliberate policy in both studies to have a sharp contrast between the conditions of the guards and the prisoners with big differences in the quality of food and bedding, as well as features from real prisons such as roll calls and other predetermined routines. The primary aim of this research was to understand the relationship between extreme authoritative roles and subservient roles, and how each of these roles affects the human psyche and team behaviour. Despite sharing this primary aim, the studies themselves were each carried out in quite a different fashion and the results ended up being very different. Although scheduled to last for longer, the Stanford and BBC studies were halted prematurely after six and eight days, respectively, as each had gone far enough.

In the case of the Stanford Prison Study, the results of the experiment were unsettling in that a significant minority of the prison "guards" demonstrated sadistic tendencies in performing their duties; using arbitrary and psychologically damaging punishments that escalated over time. After an early revolt on Day 2, they came down heavily on the "prisoners" and used various psychological ploys to dehumanise them and break up any sense of group resistance. On the other side, the prisoners suffered various degrees of psychological trauma and quickly began accepting their new environment as their reality. They failed to show team camaraderie and each became isolated. It was clear by the time that the experiment ended on Day 6 that the guards' regime had won out and the more moderate "guards" were having trouble keeping the more aggressive guards in check, while the prisoners were becoming increasingly traumatised. At that stage the experiment had clearly crossed ethical boundaries.

In the BBC study, on the other hand, the treatment was not as extreme in the early stages, the ratio of "guards" to "prisoners" was less, and the "prisoners" gradually got the upper hand on the "guards" in terms of the mental battle. In the first few days, a system was set up whereby the "prisoner" who demonstrated the best behaviour was to be given special privileges so they could avoid the poor food and the worst elements of their environment. This situation, while it lasted, prevented a sense of proper team camaraderie from developing. As soon as the best-performing "prisoner" was chosen and an announcement was made that there would be no more "prisoner" promotions, the "prisoners" quickly consolidated as a team and became more determined to cause trouble for the guards. The "guards", for their part, were uncomfortable in their role, worried about external opinions at their use of their powers, and from early on did not function as a cohesive group. The "prisoners" took notice of this insecurity and division and they set about exploiting this and isolating the "guards". After various instances of resistance, a new "prisoner" was brought in who was an experienced trade unionist with tested negotiation skills. He was simply told he was going to be part of an experiment and the following excerpt, taken from the project website (BBC, 2018) describes his early impressions and actions:

> At first he is overwhelmed. Soon, though, he starts sizing up the situation. He watches. He asks. What are the Guards like? Are they united or

divided? Who is strong and who is weak? And what about the Prisoners? Where does power really lie?

He takes his time to assess the existing social reality. He doesn't act before he understands how things are, where the system is fragile, and hence what might be possible.

This new "prisoner" quickly spots an opportunity to improve conditions and approaches one of the softer "guards" to discuss possibilities. As he is working through this process, an incident occurs (keys are stolen by a rebellious and charismatic "prisoner") which leaves the "guards" in disarray and willing to accept an agreement involving more communal arrangements. The next stage involves a verbal battle between the new "prisoner" and the one who stole the keys for the support of the rest of the "prisoners" for this idea. The former stresses the importance of working together while the latter encourages individual acts of bravado and mischief. The new "prisoner" wins out in the end and a new agreement is formed between the guards and the prisoners with a list of new rules. This establishes a certain order, which is then deliberately destabilised by the researchers on Day 6 when the "guards" remove the new prisoner from the prison for "health reasons". This was done to see if the ordered system could be maintained even if its key advocate was removed. What followed was a rapid disintegration of the agreed structure and an increased level of disrespect for the "guards". The charismatic "prisoner" who had stolen the keys led this process.

As the "guard's" authority and cohesion was undermined, individual guards came under pressure with a high level of associated stress. Faced with growing harassment from the "prisoners", the "guards" increasingly failed to support each other, pursuing instead their own self-interest. This culminated in an incident where the "prisoners" gained access to the "guards'" room. By then, and despite a last ditch attempt by the "guards" to band together, the situation was lost and anarchy prevailed. The next development was that a core of four "prisoners" led by the "prisoner" who had stolen the keys looked to set up an authoritarian regime, with them in charge, an initiative that only met with subdued resistance from the others. By this stage (Day 8), however, the experiment was terminated on the advice of the ethical consultants.

Even though these experiments were somewhat artificial and not fully representative of real-life situations, the reality they created was internalised and very real to the participants. The individual and collective behaviour portrayed is reflective of what we hear of anecdotally in the real world. The following summary is based on the conclusions of the BBC study (BBC, 2018):

- Collective self-realisation has a strong psychological effect on team members.
- Team success is uplifting for team members and when faced with severe circumstance people in teams are less stressed and are less likely to allow adverse conditions to overwhelm them.

- Lack of team success, characterised by team performance that enables the team to achieve its goals, due to shortcomings in team spirit encourages despondency, stress, and burn-out.
- Collective psychological factors such as team identity, solidarity, and individual psychological factors (anxiety, depression, content) are all strongly correlated.
- Mental health is shaped by the quality of teamwork.
- Disempowering team members so that they can no longer actualise their personal values and beliefs leads to an acceptance of drastic alternatives in a desperate attempt to generate a sense of success.
- When a team is failing, team members are more prone to accept the authority of a strong leader who promises to make things work.
- This combination of failure and promise encourages team members to become more authoritarian.
- Our latent behavioural characteristics come to the surface when we are either in positions of power or vulnerable.

These social experiments help to illustrate how authority and power, vulnerability, team cohesion, and unity may evolve in extreme situations. We might not expect the same degree of disfunctionalism to appear in a project team in an organisation yet the pressures and the tendencies that led to anarchy in the research environment are just as real.

Reflection points

- How was power manifested in the two studies described?
- How has power been manifested in a project you were involved in?
- What is the difference between formal and informal power?

Power in teams

Power or the ability to get others to follow your requests and demands can take many forms. In some situations, making demands of others clearly leads to tension, conflict, and confrontation; while, in other cases, the reverse will be true. In management situations there can be up to four different parties affected by the exercise of power: namely those exercising the power, those on the receiving end, those who witness it directly, and those who are given a secondhand account of what is happening. For example, consider a situation in which a manager chooses to make an example of an employee by reprimanding him or her in front of others in order to have a deterrent effect on both employees who are present and indirectly, employees who are not present but will learn about the incident from their co-workers. The manager's actions can have many different consequences and the story of what has happened will spread throughout the company via the grapevine—the informal chats, rumours, and gossip.

The three-stage model developed by the American psychologist Herbert Kelman (1958) and outlined in Table 6.1 explains how authority and power are accepted and complied with by those on the receiving end.

The three stages shown in Table 6.1—compliance, identification, and internalisation—include descriptions of the social adaptations made by team members in each case. Evidently, compliance differs from internalisation, for instance, as much higher managerial oversight is needed to keep team members compliant. At the identification stage, team members may be more questioning of the authority than at the internalisation stage. Where team members have totally internalised the external authority, they lack the critical distance which is essential for healthy organisational improvement, effective problem identification and problem solving, and to avoid issues such as groupthink, where the team's need for cohesion outweighs all other factors and which encourages very poor decision-making.

Resistance to instructions or requests can arise for many reasons and those in authority can be challenged in ways ranging from the mild to the extreme. In choosing whether or not to resist the demands of those in power, an individual will firstly consider whether they agree in principle with the demands; secondly, if they can cope with the demands being made; and thirdly, if these demands are fair in comparison to those made to others. Perceived unfairness in the use of power can generate opposition and teams that feel affected may align under common cause and form a strong *social oppositional force*. Teams can become non-compliant if sufficient resistance builds up and managers can be left in untenable situations in the face of opposition power. The classical case is what happened in the Pacific in 1789 on board the ship, *HMS Bounty*, when a mutiny formed that left Captain William Bligh and those of the crew supporting him, cast adrift on a small boat that Bligh eventually navigated to safety.

Take time to think about the variety of effects that the application of different types of power can have on your teams and look for strategies that are most likely to motivate the team to perform their mission. Coercive power, for

Table 6.1 Kelman's theory about 3 stages of adherence to authority

Compliance	Team members obey the demands of authority but do not agree with them. If the person in authority does not monitor their subsequent behaviour, then they are likely to drift into non-compliance.
Identification	Team members begin to obey the demands of those in power, as they aspire to become like them, or want to gain their attention. Team members endeavour to model the behaviour of the person in power.
Internalisation	Team members follow the instructions and mirror the expectations of those in power since these resonate with their own personal values, convictions, and objectives. They obey even though they are not being monitored.

example, is rarely likely to lead to sustainable success, as coercion can cause a negative reaction leading to inactivity or sullen and silent disobedience. Your team's reactions to what you ask of them depend on what you request, how you do so, and whether this is fair, sensible, and meaningful. Using reasonable persuasion and leading by example is more likely to make people respect and empathise with you rather than more hard-hitting approaches. Such methods could be perceived as threatening, humiliating, and unjust. Using power through bullying will be corrosive for your team if it doesn't actually land you in legally hot water. You'll need to practise and develop approaches to your authority and communication methods that lead to maximum performance and make people content.

The psychologists Dacher Keltner, Deborah Gruenfeld, and Cameron Anderson created a theory of power, and lack of power, called the *Approach/ Inhibition Theory of Power*. According to their theory, reactions and attitudes of individuals change depending on how much power that person has (Keltner *et al.*, 2003). The theory outlines two types of tendencies in human reactions to changes in the environment. The first type of reaction are *approach-related tendencies*, characterised by activity, empowerment, looking for rewards and opportunities, increased power and motivation. The second type of reaction are *inhibition-related tendencies*, characterised by defensiveness, threats and risk aversion, caution, lack of motivation, and overall reduced activity. The theory predicts that those who have more power have a more positive view towards change than those who possess less power. Those with little power often have a more negative view of change as they are more likely to see it as a threat. Those who possess power are more likely to be encouraged to take action. Knowledge of this theory can help you to predict the reactions of those affected by your intended changes.

Reflection points

- How do you think you can develop a culture of supportive respect?
- What impact is force likely to have on people?
- When does power become violence?
- What is violence?
- What is the relationship between level of power and desire for change?

The will to rule

We all differ greatly when it comes to our need to control people and situations. Some of us desire power whereas others shun it. There are also differences in how people with authority use that power. Power-driven individuals are more likely to pursue power and achieve higher positions within teams and organisations. They are also more likely to misuse their power and are more prone to the belief that different rules apply to them, i.e. that they are more important than those who have less power or status. This was the central theme of George Orwell's classic allegorical novel, *Animal Farm*, published in 1945. Those who seek out authority are also more likely to increase the distance between themselves and those they manage, they are more likely to underestimate their subordinates, and they believe that their subordinates are not trustworthy, i.e. that they need much supervision (Zander, 1985; Forsyth, 2019).

Power seekers often desire power for the sake of authority and the status it gives them, rather than pursuing it for the benefit of the team, organisation, or society. They often put in considerable effort in maintaining their power. Unfortunately, those of them who are unable to handle it well tend to create tension and stress within the team and disputes become likely. This manifests in all sorts of ways: undermining of the team members by the manager; deflection of blame for negative results; an unwillingness of the manager to realise that the team is willing to co-operate, and perhaps even irrational decisions that demotivate or sideline some or all of the team. So the attitude of an individual to power and how they are likely to handle and use that power is an important factor in selecting managers for different roles. It is also important for the would-be manager to understand the nature and extent of the power they will have and how this may vary over time. Do they have the power to recruit or replace new people for their team? Do they have the authority to offer incentives or reward on behalf of a company (Figure 6.4)?

These are all things that a manager needs to know about when they start their work. The modern professional environment is largely characterised by rapid communications, increased bureaucracy, and automation, and these factors combined can significantly reduce the amount of leeway in projects. This has tended to reduce the tolerance and resilience within projects for the unusual or the undefined. These factors, amongst others, have resulted in increased pressure on managers in some cases, which makes it important that they have the right tools to respond to both the expected and unexpected,

Figure 6.4

Positions come with different levels of authority.

both technical and non-technical issues. That puts the onus on managers to be effective communicators; able to make themselves clearly understood and able to understand those who work on the projects that they manage.

Reflection points

- What is power seeking?
- What are those who seek power most likely to do in relation to those who do not seek power in an organisation?
- How are relations between superiors and subordinates manifested?
- What characterises a good relationship between a superior and a subordinate?
- What characterises a bad relationship between a superior and a subordinate?

Integrity in teams

People with *integrity* are those that have shown consistency in their actions, adhere to sound moral and ethical standards, and live according to healthy values. People are more likely to be perceived by others as having integrity if their values have been tested by prior events and their subsequent actions were honourable, i.e. their status as persons of integrity has been earned. Individuals with acknowledged integrity can have a strong degree of influence over groups, particularly those whose members come from differing backgrounds, who are not well known to each other, or have had negative experiences in the past and are generally sceptical. In projects, for example, stakeholders who hold opposing views will respond better to each other if they believe that the project leader is a person of integrity who is not unduly swayed by any particular side.

You need to be able to read the expressions and emotions of team members and stakeholders, and this can be easier if you approach your project with a transparent aura of integrity. Others should be more open and willing to express their true feelings, and communication will be much more effective if the right level of mutual respect is shown. It is important for the team itself to show integrity, as well as respect and empathy in their communications. Look for workshops and other development opportunities where you can encourage them to practise these qualities. If a team has these qualities, it can also make it harder for outside entities that may have a negative agenda to influence team members—e.g. through feeding them propaganda, disinformation, or other forms of coercion. While the importance of these elements remains undiminished, the communication process itself has become more diverse (and complex) in recent years. The use of email, SMS, and video messaging means that a manager may now spend less time in face-to-face situations than in the past. You need to adapt to these new communication methods accordingly, while still conveying the same sense of integrity, respect, and empathy. Keep your eye on the flow of information between team members and external parties as rapid communications mean that sensitive, false, or otherwise damaging information can now travel around the world almost instantaneously. Proactive measures, guidelines, and education are far more effective than reactive response in mitigating the damage of any incidents. Of course anything of this kind can also damage the perceived integrity of individuals and organisations.

Try developing the habit and the skill of asking for clarification when you are in doubt to help avoid misunderstandings. You might ask: "Have I understood you correctly when you say…?" In order to ensure good information exchange and better decision-making, team members need to be free to air their views in an open and supportive environment and the manager will, of course, set the tone for this. One aspect of showing integrity in communication is by responding quickly to needs or circumstances that arise within a group instead of delaying. Another aspect is being careful to avoid dragging personal matters into communications within a team, and to keep the focus on what is currently happening rather than bringing up a series of unrelated issues from the past (see Figure 6.5).

We often refer to our "role" while defending ourselves against accusations and excusing our behaviour. Be careful not to abuse your role by using it to excuse inappropriate behaviour that is damaging to the integrity of your position. Professionalism carries with it expectations in regard to values and actions. The integrity of a judge, for example, is critical to their role and they

Figure 6.5

Everyone has something that they want to keep only for themselves.

must be aware of this at all times in their communications and actions. The same general principle applies to managers in project teams.

Reflection points

- How does integrity manifest in teams?
- What is the best way to ensure integrity in communications?
- What are people likely to hide behind their mask?

Sincerity in teams

Sincere and transparent communication enables a deeper relationship to form between a manager and colleagues or other stakeholders. Where necessary, you should be able to step out of your role and become an active listener to the problems of others. Regardless of whether these problems are closely related, loosely related, or unrelated to the work at hand, they can have an overbearing effect on people and therefore need to be aired and dealt with. Being sincere means being free from pretence, deceit, or hypocrisy, and this is a necessary precursor to developing trust in a relationship. Any of your team should be able to express their feelings directly to you, and you, in turn, need to be honest about what you can do given the circumstances under which you have to operate. Avoiding misunderstandings is very important in this process and direct but measured communication may be required to get a message across.

A sincere and transparent communicator is able to respond normally to other people when they are approached without warning and are unprepared. Your spontaneous reactions are indicative of your proper consideration of others and that you do not need to spend time crafting responses. You can develop this capability through practice and training in listening equally to your inner feelings at the same time as you are listening to the person with whom you are interacting. A sincere communicator is focused on what is happening around them, their responsibilities, and their expression towards other people. Express yourself without any hindrance, which means that you do not continually need to evaluate and ponder what you say before you speak. Take the circumstances into account each time and choose your words carefully. As is the case for an athlete, good performance is a mixture of innate ability and training. Together, these give you the ability to respond correctly and intuitively, even when you are suddenly required to do so.

Those who are sincere are less likely to be defensive. When they express themselves, they do it in an empathetic but assertive manner towards the person with whom they are communicating. You should have a sense of where your weaknesses and strengths lie in communicating with others. When someone expresses a negative attitude towards you, try to understand what that person is thinking, how they feel, and what lies behind the view that they expressed; rather than your natural reaction, which may be to become defensive and reciprocate the negativity. People who are sincere communicators feel good about themselves without being smug and self-centred. If you continually spend time engaged in self-defence, you will struggle to identify with your team. Managers who are sincere are true to themselves and their stated and real values will be the same. This means that there is consistency between what you think, say, and do. Consistency also means that you show consideration in your communications and are careful about expressing your thoughts and feelings with others. Think about how you can be agile in how you communicate and be ready to bite your tongue in order to show consideration to those who are expressing their feelings and thoughts to you. You shouldn't be afraid to expose yourself emotionally in your communication, where this is appropriate. For example, if you are dissatisfied with the progress of a project, or specific aspects of a project, express your concerns to the right person instead of remaining silent and expecting them to know what you are thinking.

Reflection points

- What is the difference between integrity and sincerity?
- Practise responding spontaneously and sincerely to each other by expressing the emotion that you are experiencing at that moment.
- What emotions are appropriate to express within your team?
- What emotions are not appropriate to express within your team?

Respect in teams

Self-respect and respect for others are positive emotions that are important in all communications. You need to be comfortable within yourself to earn the respect of team members and to show them respect. Respect improves the reliability of communication between individuals. It makes it possible for everyone to be able to work together, constructively and in harmony. Respect is generally either expressed in words (particularly *tone of voice*) or body language but may also involve remaining silent and not disturbing someone. Even if you feel respect, the ability to demonstrate this to others in communication is not automatic or self-evident and hence you should practise this quality to become good at it. To show respect you need to *be present* and *listen attentively* in order to follow the concerns of others, help them with any issues they have, and support them in achieving their goals.

Punctuality is another way of showing respect. It sends the message that you are ready for co-operation and are committed to the work. Everyone will overlook occasional lateness for reasons beyond your control but being continually late or tolerating lateness from team members will generate resentment and will not add to a sense of teamwork.

Working successfully with others involves mutual respect and a willing to commit to co-operation (Figure 6.6). Show interest in sharing ideas, listen to

Figure 6.6

Working successfully with others involves mutual respect and commitment.

the opinions of others, and be open to criticism of your views or work. If you want to earn respect from your co-workers, then you need to listen to them and give them an opportunity to express themselves freely. You need to be willing to work on your own communication methods and skills, review your connections with others, build up relationships, and change your communication styles if necessary.

Co-operation depends on sustained good relations. If a team member is negative and lacks interest, look at what communication has taken place within the team and whether someone within the group has said or done something that might have initiated this behaviour. Try to find the root of the problem and determine whether it stems from events within the team or outside of it. Make sure you are ready to react to circumstances in a timely manner and don't be afraid of confrontation if necessary, however, be careful to acknowledge the views and needs of others. Encourage the whole team to deal openly with any difficult circumstances when they arise. You can do this by asking open questions either individually or collectively, i.e. questions that do not only require "yes" or "no" answers. An open and assertive approach respects team members and encourages them to explore their own feelings, helps identify the root of the problem, and naturally leads them towards solutions.

Reflection points

- What is respect?
- How does respect show in teamwork?
- How do you show another person respect?
- What types of behaviour show disrespect?
- What is the difference between being inconsiderate and being disrespectful?

Caution in team communication

Being cautious in communications and actions means taking care to avoid risk or mistakes, such as divulging too much information, showing insensitivity in delicate situations, misunderstanding what others are trying to communicate, or acting prematurely on incomplete information. It can be very hard to undo or retract something once said (particularly if it has an electronic record associated with it)! You need to develop protocols that you can clearly outline to your team. This will take practice and as with many things, a manager will set the tone for their team.

Team members will routinely receive a variable mixture of criticism and praise from a manager and you need to apply caution in how you approach this. Avoid picking one or more of the same individuals and either constantly berating or constantly praising them in front of others. This will either be construed as bullying or as favouritism, and neither approach is likely to lead to better team spirit and productivity. Remember to take the views of your whole team into consideration so that no one feels isolated or victimised. Criticism, in particular, is best given constructively and on a one-to-one basis, but you should learn to give negative feedback effectively in a group setting. Avoid personalising issues and speak in matter-of-fact tones; relate facts without excessive emotion.

We have already discussed active listening and empathy and these are the best methods to express respect towards co-workers. They help us to understand each other and to demonstrate we understand what encourages and discourages those around us. This work can take time and everyone in the team needs to show patience. It may be a challenge in pressurised situations but if you don't take the time to give attention to the needs of others then there is likely to be even greater pressure further down the line as previously hidden problems surface and your team lacks the resilience to deal with them.

Different managers interpret how to take a proactive communication approach in different ways, and sometimes this may appear counter-intuitive. For example, one manager may go out of their way to show friendship and support to team members as a way of pre-empting any unhappiness. On the other hand, another may be cautious in forming relationships with team members as they see themselves as needing to retain distance, because they may be called upon to perform certain unpleasant tasks like failing or firing someone.

Depending on your approach, proactivity can therefore involve both closeness and distance in your communication with others. A closer approach requires additional caution, as it may not be appropriate to show other team members the same warmth as you would do in a friendship, especially not early on in the teamwork. It is easy to misinterpret such behaviour, which may come across as superficial and even needy.

Reflection points

- Practice caution in your team by asking about the needs of others, whilst being considerate.
- In pairs, experiment with your comfort zone by expressing yourself on a subject that matters to you and allowing your partner to support you in expressing it. Let each other know if caution was or was not shown and describe this in more detail.
- In pairs, describe to each other the reactions of a listener that provide support and those that do not.

References

BBC (2018). www.bbcprisonstudy.org (accessed 28 June 2018).

Edmonds, S. C. (2018). https://www.drivingresultsthroughculture.com/2010/08/02/catch-people-doing-things-right/ (accessed 28 June 2018).

Forsyth, D. R. (2019). *Group dynamics* (7th ed.). Boston, MA: Cengage Learning.

French, J. P. R. , Jr. & Raven, B. (1960). "The bases of social power" in D. Cartwright & A. Zander (Eds.), *Group dynamics* (pp. 607–623), New York: Harper and Row.

Kelman, H. (1958). "Compliance, identification, and internalization: Three processes of attitude change" in *Journal of Conflict Resolution*, 1, 51–60.

Keltner, D., Gruenfeld, D. H., & Anderson, C. (2003). "Power, approach, and inhibition" in *Psychological Review*, 110, 265–284

Milgram, S.(1974). *Obedience to authority*. New York: Harper & Row.

Reicher, S. D. & Haslam, S. A. (2006). "On the agency of individuals and groups: Lessons from the BBC Prison Study" in T. Postmes & J. Jetten (Eds.), *Individuality and the group: Advances in social identity* (pp. 237–257). London: Sage.

Zander, A. (1985). *The purposes of groups and organizations*. San Francisco: Jossey-Bass.

Zimbardo, P. G., Maslach, C., & Haney, C. (2000). "Reflections on the Stanford Prison Experiment: Genesis, transformations, consequences" in T. Blass (Ed.), *Obedience to authority: Current perspectives on the Milgram paradigm* (pp. 193–237). Mahwah, NJ: Erlbaum

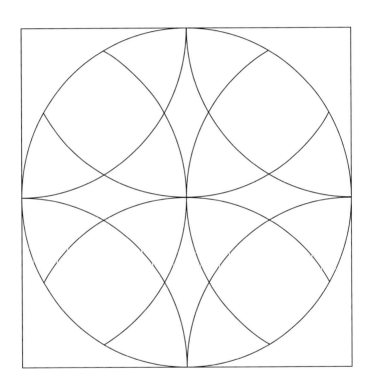

7 Decision-making in teams

● ●

Good decision-making is an essential element of team success and a key part of the discipline of management. Experienced managers have long recognised the importance of good communication to understand problems and decide what to do. All members contribute to the discussion through constructive criticism, discussing ideas and potential solutions. A well-orchestrated team of informed individuals will generally have a better chance of making a good decision than a person who is working alone and unaided. Such a team should be better suited to select, evaluate, judge, and problem solve especially when this involves many areas of detailed knowledge and there are many permutations to think through for each option that can be taken. This chapter discusses all these aspects as well as empathy and reciprocity in communication.

Team decisions

The strategy that a team uses to make decisions can have a major impact on the progress and quality of the decision. In general, as we have outlined, the quality of decisions may improve if there is a team rather than an individual behind it, with the proviso that the team has the requisite capability. Broadly speaking, the combined knowledge of a team is more than that of individuals and there is more security in implementing a team decision because of the consequent support this will give it. When you are leading a project team, it is important to understand and manage the expectations of project owners and stakeholders and to approach decision-making in such a way that it optimises the team's strengths.

It is not entirely a given that a team of people make better decisions than individuals. The performance of a group is dependent upon several factors including the nature of the task or project. Teams tend to take more time to reach agreement and short-lived opportunities may be missed while waiting to arrive at a consensus. An experienced team member, for example, may spot a real bargain for materials and equipment that will be needed later in a project. By the time consent to purchase is given by a team, however, the opportunity may have been lost. Tasks and projects that rely on the subjective views of a number of individuals may also prove difficult if a team decision needs to be made. This can lead to polarised positions, prolonged stand-offs, and unsatisfactory compromises. Teams may also fail due to factors like "groupthink", biased influences, and when decisions are based on limited knowledge and experience.

Decision-making is one of the primary purposes of many teams and so it needs to be done well. This means your decision-making team has the right mix of people who are qualified, experienced, and with the right background for the task. Appropriate qualifications, talent, skills, resources, and a good knowledge of the subject at hand are all prerequisites. Let's explore four key aspects behind sound decision-making in teams (Figure 7.1).

The first aspect involves *information*: What is the problem? What do we need to know? Why do we know it? In answering these questions, it is crucial for the team to have:

- Ambition to find the best, most relevant information for the case.
- Ability to identify what resources are required.
- Ability to identify all potential stakeholders and interested parties; both supporters and blockers.
- Clear approach to gather and distribute the information among the team members.

The second aspect is that a group has *proper discussion* and even debate before solutions are determined. A team that gives itself time to analyse and consider different options will make better decisions. A good discussion and airing of opinions gives the opportunity to share information and can uncover more knowledge than the group was believed to possess. Having contemplated the given information, individuals within the group can engage in collective cross-examination, provide additional information, and engage in reflection, which stimulates others to follow suit. The result is a well-rounded and often novel grounding for a solution. A common shortcoming of team

Figure 7.1

Decision-making is one of the primary purposes of many teams.

decision-making, however, is that meetings fail to distinguish and prioritise core issues so that valuable time is wasted debating insignificant details. This can either be accidental or deliberate on the part of team members who are working to their own personal agenda.

The third aspect of good team decision-making is that the members of the team should have a *common understanding* of the nature of the decision that they are intending to make. Consequently, professional team decision-making should thus follow a specific process which provides information and items relevant to the decision and frames the entire activity. There are a number of methods for decision-making in a group and the value is largely contextual and situational (see Table 7.1).

The fourth aspect of a team decision-making is the *implementation* of the decision.

The fifth step of the process is to *assess the quality* of the decision: Was it a good decision? Was it necessary? Was the outcome good? What do we learn from this decision-making process?

Reflection points

- What decisions have you taken as a group?
- How can a group influence the quality of decisions?
- What methods can be used to make decisions in a group?

Pitfalls when teams make decisions

There are a number of potential pitfalls when making a team decision. Here are ten of the most important to get you started:

1 The team may avoid making a decision or take responsibility.
2 Information not supporting a particular view may be deliberately kept away from a team by someone (inside or outside the team) who has an agenda.
3 Distributed responsibility and lack of personal accountability may encourage the team into more risky decisions than responsible individuals would do on their own.
4 The main focus of the decision-making process may shift from finding the best solution to finding one that is agreeable.
5 A decision may be aimed at meeting minimum requirements rather than being ambitious.
6 Too much time and energy are spent on gathering and disseminating information, much of which ends up as being irrelevant to actual decision-making.
7 The team as a whole may not sufficiently represent the requisite background, knowledge, and experience and/or lacks key information.

Table 7.1 The most common methods for decision-making within groups (Biech, 2001)

Method	Disadvantages	Advantages
The leader alone decides	• May not consider the knowledge within the team • Limits responsibility for and ownership of the decision • Disagreements with the decision can generate frustration and hinder effectiveness	• Effective when a leader has all the information • Takes the least amount of time of all the methods
Individuals within the team contribute but the leader decides	• Leader puts forward the criteria for the decision which can increase the likelihood of misinterpretation • Little opportunity for group creativity or the search for new ideas • The decision may lack the support of the whole group	• There is no need to collaborate with the whole group • Does not require much time from group members
Team input but leader decides	• Takes more time and effort • Can create unproductive competition between team members • Leader may only hear what group members think he or she wants to hear • Can lead to "groupthink"	• Benefits from team discussions and multiple opinions • Group members can play with each other's ideas
Democratic decision	• A decision based on a majority can leave the minority group unsatisfied or resentful • Does not necessarily use all of the natural resources of the group	• Good for fast decision-making when a unanimous agreement is not needed • Shuts out unnecessary discussions
Minority within the team decides	• Not a joint obligation • Unresolved disagreement can have a subsequent and unforeseen negative effect	• Useful when it is not necessary to involve the whole group • Provides opportunities for role division • Opportunities to use specialists
The team decides unanimously	• Hard to reach	• Can be necessary when there is a lot at stake
Team consensus	• Takes a lot of time and mental energy • Time pressure needs to be minimum • Risks cautious and conservative decisions	• Creates original quality decision when at its best • Attracts obligations from all of group members • Uses all of the group's natural resources • Strengthens the decision-making ability of the group for the future

8   The group may become polarised with little chance of constructive dialogue between two (or more) sides.
9   The team members' poor communication skills may compromise the discussion and the final decision.
10 The team may gradually shift the focus of the decision from the interest of the project towards the self-interest of its members.

If a good culture of communication exists within a team it is more likely to make a solid decision (Figure 7.2). Exploring data, framing it into reliable information, and reflecting on that information with the full knowledge the team possesses will enable the team, through a constructive discussion, to form a community of inquiry. The Icelandic National Assembly of 2009, which was a large national dialogue organised in light of the financial crisis in Iceland, and which involved 300 volunteers and 1200 socially representative participants, provides a good example of just such a community. A variety of methods were employed to enable all the participants at the meeting to express themselves. For example, tables of nine participants each were provided with paper to write down their opinions on a selected topic before being asked, each in turn, to explain these opinions to the rest of the table. This process was repeated across multiple topics around the numerous tables, and it soon became evident that the discussion of individual topics using this approach resulted in group interactions and a greater maturity of opinion. The opinions were organised into themes before the participants were invited to vote on the decisions.

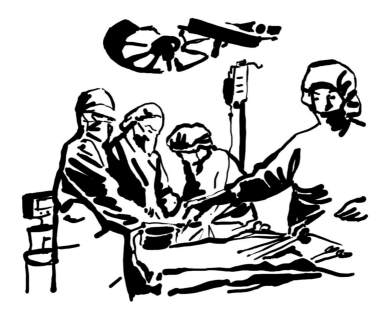

Figure 7.2

Good culture of communication makes helps solid decision-making.

Exercises

- What are the disadvantages of making decisions in a group?
- What examples can you give of poor decision-making in a group?
- What characterises good conversational culture?
- How would you apply the method used at the Icelandic National Assembly in 2009 to your own project work?

Groupthink in teams

Groupthink is one of the most-commonly recognised risks associated with decision-making in teams. This term describes a process whereby conformist thinking and the absence of critical voices leads to poor collective decision-making. It came to prominence after the American psychology professor, Irving Janis, wrote a paper on the reasons for poor decision-making in groups (Janis, 1972). His famous example was the U.S. Bay of Pigs Invasion in 1961 to overthrow Cuban leader, Fidel Castro, which turned out to be a fiasco. The CIA-led plan had been hatched during the Eisenhower Administration in the context of the Cold War and was given final approval by U.S. Military Command during the Kennedy Administration. Shortly after it was initiated, the offensive experienced several major setbacks and was defeated, which was a major embarrassment for U.S. hegemony. It also led directly to the very serious Cuban Missile Crisis in the following year, which saw a very tense standoff between the Russian and American naval fleets (Forsyth, 2019).

In analysing the Day of Pigs decision, Janis found that team dynamics worked to stifle dissenting voices, and critics were not given a sufficient platform to air their views. In this conformist environment, the result was that the group as a whole remained blind to potential drawbacks, which turned out to be crucial in the end. By the time the Cuban Missile Crisis occurred, the U.S. Executives had improved their decision-making procedures so that all dissenting voices were given air time. Better decisions were made and the threat of nuclear war with Russia was averted.

While various authors in recent years have criticised Janis's work as incomplete, the concept of groupthink has become well established and has been signalled as a causal factor in a number of recent high profile financial crashes. In Iceland, for example, the years leading up to the 2008 Financial Crash saw the development of very close links between the Government and Central Bank, on the one hand, and banking and business interests, on the other hand. As with other examples where groupthink is prevalent, the pressure to conform was high, people surrounded themselves with like-minded individuals and became unwilling to listen to dissenting voices. There are a number of additional causative factors that allow groupthink to take hold. The views of a powerful and charismatic figure (or sub-group) can come to dominate the team and they may incidentally influence or deliberately manipulate others. Drugs, alcohol, and other moral challenges can be exacerbating factors in groupthink.

Groupthink happens when a team creates a norm, which consequently overrides any criticism, and starts to make decisions on the basis of the group's needs rather than on the basis of information at hand (Ott *et al.*, 2008). Team members become too interlinked, and their unconscious need to gain unity within the team prevents them from seeing things in a sober way or airing their opinions if they do. They become afraid to stand out and common sense gives way to herd mentality. This pathological condition reduces the quality of team processing and decisions. Eight main characteristics of groupthink are outlined in Table 7.2.

In general, groupthink fosters a pervasive tendency to conform and this creates a very strong consensus and sense of unity of purpose with the team. Beliefs, feelings, a sense of justice, and reasoning are suppressed as team members seek to defend their own interests and avoid team fragmentation. The problem may also stem from a lack of insight or determination as well as insecurity about their own skills, knowledge, or ability to object. Going against the flow takes courage and can result in expulsion from the team.

Table 7.2 Reasons and characteristics of groupthink (partly based on Janis, 1971)

	Reason	Characteristics
Invulnerability	Overvaluation of the group or the project	Certainty of victory, overly optimistic, arrogant
Rationalise bad decisions	Simplified vision of the work; lack of criticism; the group assumes the result	The team members justify their actions, they cannot change older decisions
Ethical requirements	Blind belief in the ethical superiority of the group	Refuse to face ethical consequences of their actions
Stereotypes	Immovable opinions	Have unshakable opinions
Pressure for uniformity	Uniformity becomes the smoothest way to proceed	Opposing opinions are badly viewed
Suppressed emotions	Fear of expressing criticism in front of the group	Opinion sharing happens outside of the group, comments passed on to the superior by bypassing the group
Unanimity	Great cohesion	Everyone agrees with the first speaker if no one says anything, i.e. silence equals agreement
Direct pressure from "mind-guards"	Attempt to prevent lack of uniformity within the team and protect the leader and team members from uncomfortable information	Information avoided, lost, forgotten, or judged inappropriately

Groupthink can lead to poor decisions as it will most often only allow for a few options to be evaluated, or even just one option. Important information is kept away from the team, detailed data is not sought, objectives are undefined, and/or risk assessment is not performed. Teams can also spend time on details losing sight of their main objective. Signs that groupthink has occurred is apparent when people find it difficult to subsequently explain or justify a team decision. Another warning sign is uniformity amongst team members. Being a part of the team becomes more important than the subject at hand. Differences of opinion are not recorded because no one wants to disturb the peace or upset their teammates and colleagues. Cohesion and groupthink are most likely in a group whose members fear group rejection and are eager to belong, being willing to lower their critical faculties in the process.

Returning to the example of Iceland in the years leading up to the financial crash in 2008, there are many questions with regards to the decision-making of the banking teams: Did groupthink cause conformity? Did groupthink result in information not being acted upon? Did groupthink lead to government officials becoming incompetent, or were they kept in the dark by the banks and various financial institutions? Were these government officials under pressure to see nothing wrong? The executive teams in charge of these banks, as well as the various different employee groups, can be said to have overvalued themselves, becoming blind to their own shortcomings and external risks. Overconfidence, arrogance, and an alarming degree of risk underestimation was displayed. Some had their eyes open and recognised the risks that were being taken, but they were still happy to go along with the flow so long as it was profitable.

Exercises

- What is groupthink?
- Name some examples of groupthink.
- What characterises groupthink?
- Can groupthink lead to good decision-making in a group?
- How can groupthink lead to poor decision-making in a group?

Poor decisions in teams

The main reason for groupthink is excess conformity within the team (Janis, 1972; 1983). A team that does not show this conformity when it makes a wrong decision may have some other reason for its poor outcome. The composition of the team, the nature of the challenges that it faces, time constraints, financial pressures, and lack of communicational ability are all important factors. It is easy to envisage poor decision-making in a team that does not have enough time to weigh up different options fully; or does not have the resources to gather the necessary information; or suffers from poor communication.

In order to learn from the past mistakes of teams, you need to understand why a team made a wrong decision, and it may be necessary to recreate the environment in which the decision was made in its entirety. For example, a particular piece of information, that may be obvious in hindsight, may not have been available to the decision-making group. If other factors are discounted in this process, and no other clear reasons for poor decision-making are found, then it is likely that groupthink was a defining factor.

Groupthink can be generated as a result of defects in team or organisational structure. If certain teams are isolated from other activities this may block the normal flow of information and communication. This is a challenge that team leaders should consider and ask themselves: How does our management style, our communication style, our presentation of issues impact the decision-making of our teams? Research shows that teams in which the leader uses a *closed leadership style* are more biased and members are more inclined to mimic the opinion of the leader. This is more likely to happen if the leader offers his or her opinion before the team discussions which will, quite naturally, influence other team members. Leaders who are overly focused on their own power and on securing a particular set of results can influence (or bully) a team in a variety of ways. The net result, however, is broadly similar in that the team becomes less effective, regardless of the level of team cohesion. Focusing more on *process* than just on results is also likely to have a positive impact on the quality of the discussion and consequently enable better decisions.

There is also a danger of groupthink where conditions are challenging, tension exists, or where time to decide is short. All of this can trigger stress, which can threaten professionalism, logical thinking, and precision. In such circumstances, teams tend to make quick decisions, exaggerate positive consequences of those decisions, overlook main points, be seduced by details, and fail to request the information they need. When a team is under time pressure and in a constrained situation, it is more likely to be rushed into decisions and to ignore those that disagree. Those members of the team who agree stick together and are less willing to hear other opinions and reach a general consensus.

In unexpected situations which require immediate response, firm decisions, and where there is no time to seek certainty, teams may defer to a strong authority as, for example, when rescue teams get caught in difficult situations requiring immediate, life or death decisions. Unfortunately, these are occasionally bad decisions that would never have been made under normal circumstances. The goodwill and honest objectives of the decision-makers in this type of scenario are usually not doubted and, instead, mistakes are explained on the basis of circumstances at the time.

In some cases, though, the incentivisation of the key player in decision-making is an area that should come under scrutiny, as various hidden personal motives can exist of which others in a team are unaware of. If someone personally gains as a result of a particular outcome, then their judgement may be biased and should be called into question. Also, when personal accountability is lacking, teams may potentially tend towards a riskier but more rewarding option for team members themselves. In such a situation, it may be difficult to find people who take up the opposing case, as all involved may be happy with the personally favourable outcome. Where this happens, it takes a courageous decision-maker and possibly even external insights to point out the mistakes that are being made. The consequences may only become obvious as details of the decision emerge but even then it may be impossible to establish who knew what and when and who decided and why.

Exercises

- What examples of groupthink can you find within your organisation? What situations are likely to create groupthink?
- What factors, other than those that have been mentioned in this chapter, can lead to groupthink?

Effective decision-making in teams

There are various ways to prevent groupthink and avoid poor decision-making and these also depend on the nature of the situation. In safety critical contexts (policing, medical care, military operations and so on), training in protocols, leadership, and effective communication using simulation is effective in building a zero errors culture. In the heat of the moment a decision by fire fighters courageously to enter an unstable burning building is very human and understandable. However, this decision, however laudable the motives may be, if taken recklessly, endanger lives. An experienced team with a more dispassionate overall view of the situation would decide not to enter in a large group and adopt a different approach. In any difficult situations, leadership, cool appraisal, and effective communication are critical aspects of clear decision-making; and are often best done by a reliably informed and experienced team that is physically removed from the centre of action.

An open leadership style and balanced opinions are two means to bring out the best in a team and to avoid groupthink. As team leader this will often require you to step back from a proactive role and instead facilitate an open and free discussion, encourage co-operation, critical thinking, and keep your own views to yourself until others have had time to express theirs. Listen carefully to everything and everyone without prejudging. It may even be a good idea to nominate at least one *Devil's advocate* in your team who has the task of maintaining a critical viewpoint and stimulating creative discussion. The team may find it healthy and refreshing to meet occasionally without its leader so that they can learn to form their own views before presenting the outcome of their deliberations when you re-join the team. You can then participate in the subsequent discussion, seek more information, ask for clarification, and offer your reflections on the team's concerns.

As the deliberations progress further, encourage the team to engage in a fair and constructive criticism of all the ideas being discussed and make sure they explore the issues from an ethical viewpoint (Figure 7.3). You may find our books *Project Ethics* (Jonasson & Ingason, 2012) and *Project: Leadership* (Jonasson & Ingason, 2018) are helpful in this undertaking. Any critical discussion should demand a careful consideration of *definitions* (what?), *reasons* (why?), *assumptions* (what is a given and what is not?), *inferences* (what are the consequences?), *truth* (is it true? What is the evidence?), *examples* and *counter-examples*. In ethical terms this means exploring what are intended (and unintended) consequences of our decision? And to what principles do we genuinely adhere? Exploring the full range of "what if…?" scenarios is often time well-spent for any issues that are significantly large-scale and complex to warrant it.

External experts can provide a fresh perspective based on their knowledge and experience. So, think about drawing on the expertise of other people within the organisation who are not directly involved in your project or consider funding some time for an external consultant to offer their input. This could be on the basis of an audit of your findings or a process-review of your approach to problem-solving and decision-making. Finding a well-qualified, external reviewer can be a challenge. Make sure you pick someone on the basis of their proven track-record or from recommendations from colleagues

Figure 7.3

Encourage the team to engage in a fair and constructive criticism.

Table 7.3 Methods that prevent groupthink (partly based on Janis, 1972)

Methods	Objectives
Creative thinking	To avoid following the patterns of the past (unless they can be shown to work)
Ethical thinking	To mirror all aspects of the decision based on the principles of virtue, utility, duty, rights, and care
Critical evaluation	To encourage critical thinking
Not mentioning priorities	To stimulate the research spirit of the team
External evaluation groups	To not allow the team to be isolated or constrained in its thinking
Conversation outside of formal meetings	To gain more perspectives
Presentation from an external individual who has knowledge of the subject	To encourage criticism and increase information
Use a "devil's advocate"	To get everything out in the open, in particular those issues the group avoids discussing
Be careful to avoid assumptions about others' intentions	To meet others with an open mind
Arrange sub-committees that meet and then come together in a main committee	To obtain more points of view and deepen the discussion
"Last chance dialogue"—meeting that exposes all doubts	To identify pitfalls and focus on what matters

you trust. You need someone with the technical experience and the social skills who can challenge your work and who won't simply tell you what you want to hear. Table 7.3 provides some useful methods that you can use to foster sound decision-making in teams.

Ideally, these approaches should be normal work procedures, but they are not always followed and they are particularly relevant in this context. Without a structured and well-rounded approach of some kind, there is a danger that you'd end up with homogenous decisions which are unsound, unwise, or even plain wrong. Project management is largely about dealing with decision-making, negotiations, and compliance and making sure that a team uses the appropriate work methods. The project manager is responsible for ensuring that decisions are taken in the right way within the team and that its decisions are reflective of the issues and the circumstances in question.

Exercises

- What situations reduce the likelihood of groupthink?
- What methods can be used to reduce groupthink?
- What else, beyond what we've discussed in this chapter, could reduce the likelihood of groupthink occurring?

Using empathy III in teams

Obstacles to teamwork and ineffective team decision-making are often caused by misconceptions, inaccuracies, and a lack of mutual understanding. In earlier chapters we have discussed the means to deal with this by using empathy I and Empathy II. It is now time to introduce empathy III.

Empathy III is designed to enable you to work efficiently against misunderstanding and to clarify perspectives. It is a great way to shed a light on things that are unclear. Individuals who can make good use of empathy III in their communications are more able to move the team forward, towards success. If the whole team is skilled in Empathy III, it opens up the possibility of an open and honest discussion where opinions, feelings, and emotions are appropriately expressed and each individual is supported in advancing their communication competence within the team. Empathy III means that individuals in the team, and the team as a whole, will begin to function as mirrors for each other. Empathy III gives you, as an individual, and the individuals that you work with, a chance to view yourselves more objectively and often in a different light.

As confidence in the use of communication skills increases within the team, and individuals get to know each other better, they will also start to be able to share feedback on one another. This mutual feedback matures the team communication and leads to greater depth in the interpersonal relations. The goal is to increase sensitivity and the ability to translate awareness into words that others can understand and learn from. When they have reached this level, the whole team should have acquired the skills of attention, listening, and sensitivity through empathy I, II, and III, which all are important for effective communication.

In our discussion on empathy I and II, we looked at the value of one individual supporting and mirroring another. Empathy III involves expanding the level of empathy to further enhance mutual understanding. Before illustrating its use, let us first discuss a couple of methods that can be used to deepen the level of communication (based on Egan, 1976). We introduced the first two—empathy I and empathy II—earlier in the book.

The first method is for the listener to use empathy I by *summarising* all that has been said. The listener collates what they have heard and briefly repeats it to *capture the essence* of what was said. The emphasis is on the whole picture rather than on specifics. The words and phrasing should be as close as possible to those used by the person who spoke and you should place particular emphasis on the feelings and emotions. This process can help to clear up misunderstandings on both sides, to assuage concerns, and to provide support. Hearing a summary reflected back to them by another person can also help the original speaker focus their thoughts and may prompt them to form an idea or solution that they had previously not thought of.

The second method is for the listener to use empathy II by speculatively interpreting what the other person said and carefully suggesting what might be his or her suggestion, opinion, feeling, or emotion. Such an overall *interpretation* of what was said is designed to give the person who was talking a chance to hear their thoughts from a different perspective.

The third method is for the listener to *rephrase* what the person has just stated or hinted at. This differs from empathy I and II as now the listener expands sensitively or goes further in his or her interpretation. The listener answers the person by rephrasing what they have said in a non-judgemental manner. This can give the speaker a new perspective on what they have been trying to express and a more accurate understanding deeper into their state of mind. If successful, then it can even enable the other person to see themselves in a new light.

The fourth method is more indirect and involves sensitively responding to someone by *pointing out the tendencies* that they expressed in terms of attitudes, opinions, and behaviour. These tendencies can relate to emotion (e.g. boredom, fear, joy, excitement, and so on), behaviour (e.g. dominance, concern, fear of relationships, co-operation, tendency to blame others), experience (e.g. being a victim, being respected, made to look foolish, being considered threatening, being a success or failure), or some combination of these. You need to be careful when experimenting with this approach because the person with whom you are speaking to can easily experience your commentary as an attack on themselves. Make sure you are as precise as you can be by referencing information that the person, him- or herself, has given and think about your use of language. For example, using wording such as: "If I understand you correctly, you were afraid to co-operate in that way as it would have made you look foolish?" This communication method is based on there being a mutual understanding and that the parties involved are ready for reciprocity of one kind or another.

The fifth method involves *helping the speaker to draw conclusions* from what they have expressed (Figure 7.4). This requires a high degree of precision, consideration, and proper timing. If the conclusions that you draw run counter to the expectations of the other person, or are conveyed in an inappropriate way, there is a danger that the original speaker might interpret them as either an attack or as an attempt on your part to ingratiate yourself. You may identify something (e.g. a solution, an omission, a mistake) based on what was expressed, but you need to carefully consider how to highlight this. A nuanced and subtle approach is almost always your best strategy, although in cases where you are very confident that you have a high degree of mutual rapport with the person to whom you are speaking, you may be able to take a more direct or even blunt approach to get to the heart of the matter.

The sixth method involves trying to move the conversation from what is less important to what is *more important*. If the other person is vague and indirect when talking about a subject that seems to matter a great deal to them, then you may detect this and respond by steering the discussion towards what is of most importance. This involves taking the initiative to respond directly, in a determined and open manner, about what really matters to the speaker

Figure 7.4

Helping the speaker to draw conclusions from what they have expressed.

in order to get more out of the discussion. Ask yourself: "What lies behind this discussion?" or "What needs to be revealed?" You'll need good judgement and discretion to respond in the right way and it may take some practice to get this approach right. Depending on the nature of the dialogue, the issue of importance may be relatively trivial or very serious. If sufficiently serious, then you may be better off encouraging the person to seek the help of a professional coach or counsellor.

Thus, empathy III is all about expressing your feelings and/or emotions with regards to what the other person has said and explaining why you feel that way. The best way to do this is by saying: "When I hear that you are happy with your decision, then *I feel glad because* I now see that you are making progress". Use your own feeling and emotions too.

Empathy I, II, and III involve clarifying and mirroring what a person has said; using interpretation rather than repetition, so that they understand that they are being supported; as well as seeing their predicament in a new light. These methods can help a team focus their thoughts and develop ideas or solutions that they had not previously considered. In the process, what was said half-heartedly may be made more convincing. What was expressed in an unclear manner may become defined and put forward in a more determined fashion, and what has been expressed in a superficial manner may be re-evaluated in more depth.

Exercises

- Review empathy I and II; what do they involve?
- What is empathy III?

- In pairs of two—alternately speak and listen to each other with the listener in each case rephrasing what the other person expressed, without losing its meaning.
- Repeat the process and have the listener point out tendencies in what was expressed.
- Repeat the process and have the listener draw conclusions from what was expressed.
- Repeat the process and help the other person to understand what aspects are more or less important in what they expressed.

Mutuality in team communication

Rewarding one positive action with another positive action is the basis of mutuality in relationships. It involves both giving and receiving, and the ability to do both is a very important attribute for team members. Good communication within a team happens when there is meaningful and effective two-way interaction between different members. It is best when this is balanced and, even if someone in your team may be good at using empathy III, it may not be advisable that they unwittingly take on the role of team therapist. The drawback is that they are then likely to become somewhat isolated from the team as a whole, and their normal role and the natural development of the team may suffer as a result. They are one of the team, and should consider themselves as such, and should not be required to take on this role. If they do, the relationship of that individual with the group becomes a therapeutic relationship and the group starts to seek out help instead of building two-way communication among its members in the normal way.

Reciprocity is a key aspect of many different types of interactions between people. It can become an issue in teams if individuals are perceived as only capable of either giving or receiving, and do not reward others in the same way as they have been rewarded. It is an important aspect of third level empathy and a number of different characteristics that have a reciprocal nature are listed below:

- Mutual trust.
- Mutual inquiry.
- Mutual growth.
- Mutual honesty.
- Mutual exploration.
- Mutual co-operation.
- Mutual decision-making.

Since reciprocity is a key factor in communication ability, groups who work on developing their communication need to understand that most types of interaction are only ever of limited use unless they are mutual. A team can be a learning community in which everyone has something to offer. The group as a whole cannot demonstrate empathy III unless its members are motivated to explore the experiences of and with each other in a deeper manner.

Remember, good self-awareness and empathy with your own emotions and feelings greatly increases your ability to gain an understanding of others. When experimenting with your team, test how you tend to react to opposition, criticism, and conflict in communications. This should highlight any sensitivities you have and dealing with these in a non-adversarial environment can help to strengthen you, making you better prepared to interact with others in an empathic way. The objectives of empathy should be kept in mind at all times—that is to try to *understand* the other individual better, as well as trying to understand yourself without attempting to "psychoanalyse" either party.

The dialogue example shown below involves an exchange between two team members and illustrates empathy III in action. It was captured during a student workshop that was part of the Master of Project Management (MPM) at the Reykjavik University. At this stage, team members have become reasonably capable of using empathy and can immediately detect if an individual within the team is not working as expected and if any irritation surfaces between individuals. The team discusses the matters that arise in a sensitive, mature, and empathic manner and this works to relieve any tension:

Jane: "Jon, can I talk to you briefly? I need to discuss something that I've noticed".

Jon: "No problem, what is it?"

Jane: I have a feeling that you are not committing enough time to the work of the project team these days, and that there is something bothering you. You seem absent-minded, frequently show up late, are on the phone a lot, and sometimes are easily annoyed by others. Am I right or wrong about this?

Jon: You're absolutely right Jane. I have been extremely busy in my day job, while also feeling that this project is not for me, and the endless stress of combining the two is getting on my nerves. If I have been withdrawn lately, then I am sorry, it has nothing to do with you or the other team members. I will try to improve on this, and please give me a sign if you think that I am becoming irritable. I hadn't realised that I was affecting others and it is not fair towards any of you who are all in similar situations. It is still a great team to work with and I want the project to go well for us.

An interaction of this kind is conscious, but at the same time team members are doing each other a favour by pointing out what could be improved. In his response, Jon also shows empathy as well as reciprocity as he is concerned about the effect his behaviour is having on others. Such conversations indicate that the group is mature and they help to improve the efficiency of the team. Both Jane and Jon have expressed their feelings and are therefore more aware and focused. Now Gudrun joins the conversation and talks to Jon:

Gudrun: As I understand it, Jon, your day job is very demanding but is also rewarding. The project we are working on does not give you as much satisfaction, and you feel that it takes time and energy that you would rather have for your job. You still want to work on this project but are struggling to focus because of the stress. Don't forget that many of us, including me, are in the same boat although I am sure things will be less stressful once this project is completed.

Gudrun tries to go deeper into what Jon has just expressed and gives him the opportunity to see his predicament as others see it. Such interaction can increase self-awareness and communication. In this way, third level empathy provides an opportunity to understand what lies behind the words of others.

Exercises

- What makes communications interactive and open?
- What encourages third level empathy?
- What discourages third level empathy?
- Practice similar kinds of communication to those found in the example.

Conviction in teams

Conviction is a strong belief in something. The *power of conviction* is the ability to achieve consensus on specific objectives by convincing others of their value. To do this, you can use your reasoning to help others understand and agree with your objectives and/or by appealing to people's emotions so that they will support the objectives in question. The power of conviction can be a very important aspect of ensuring that personal or group goals are achieved and to encourage others to participate. You'll need to be convincing to succeed. Think about how to promote the advantages, demonstrate clarity and determination, lead by example, avoid errors and oversights, and be consistent and firm in your beliefs and your approach.

Being convincing is both a personal skill and method (Figure 7.5). In terms of preparation, start by defining your objectives, have a clear idea of the results you're aiming for, and understand what constitutes success and failure. You'll also need to assess how much relevant knowledge associated with a subject both you and the team have and to establish a plan to monitor progress. Detail can be very important, so make sure you have studied the facts from other individual cases and rehearsed your arguments based on these, with an awareness of the opposing evidence. When dealing with anyone having a sense,

Figure 7.5

Being convincing is both a personal skill and method.

beforehand, of their attitudes, interests, and connections, without assuming or pre-judging, can help you pitch your case. When presenting, state your case calmly and confidently, be prepared to field a wide range of questions, and remember to thank the people at the meeting for their participation and contribution. Following on from your meeting, you should be able to cultivate relationships with the stakeholders, building your knowledge and learning from experience.

To be convincing requires a sound rationale for opinions and decisions, a demonstration of emotional involvement, and an appropriate response to the situation as it unfolds. It is important to maintain confidentiality and to earn the trust of others by listening actively to their views. The power of conviction involves capturing a group's interest and encouraging them to join you in a quest that you believe has a realistic chance of having a positive outcome. In order to maintain trust, it is also important to use your authority and influence in a sensible and productive manner and to be transparent in the way you disclose relevant information. Behaviour such as unfair criticism and not listening to others or respecting their contributions is likely to be counter-productive. Those who: (a) do not encourage others; (b) are withdrawn; (c) are pessimistic; and (d) are unable to maintain the focus and attention of a group; fail to be convincing. You'll also struggle to be convincing if you only take into consideration the views of a majority, or of whomever happens to be in a position of authority, while ignoring the views of others.

Exercises

- What is conviction?
- What is the power of conviction?
- What makes people convincing in communication?
- What might be the limitations of strong conviction in communications?

References

Biech, E. (Ed.). (2001). *The Pfeiffer book of successful team-building tools*. Chicago: John Wiley & Sons.

Egan, G. (1976). *Interpersonal living*. Belmont, CA: Wadsworth Publishing Company.

Forsyth, D. R. (2019). *Group dynamics* (7th ed.). Boston, MA: Cengage.

Janis, I. L. (1972). *Victims of groupthink*. Boston, MA: Houghton Mifflin.

Janis, I. L. (1983). "Groupthink" in H. H. Blumberg, A. P. Hare, V. Kent & M. F. Davis (Eds.), *Small groups and social interaction* (volume 2, pp. 39–46). New York: Wiley. Originally published 1971 in *Psychology today*.

Jonasson, H. I. & Ingason, H. T. (2012). *Project ethics*. London: Gower/Routledge.

Jonasson, H. I. & Ingason, H. T. (2018). *Project: leadership*. London: Routledge.

Ott, J. S., Parkes, S. J., & Simpson, R. B. (2008). *Classic readings in organizational behaviour*. Belmont, CA: Thomson Wadsworth.

8 Assertive leadership in teams

· ·

In the preceding chapters we have touched upon the impact of authority and power on teams. In this chapter we delve further into the nature of team leadership, and how this affects the ability of the team to communicate and perform effectively. There is an assortment of commonly held beliefs and theories on what constitutes leadership and its impact on team performance. Even though you as a leader may have formal managerial authority over your team, it is mainly your ability to use your informal influence that is your best source of power to get things done. The quality of your interaction with your team as well as circumstances also play a major role. So how should you act as a leader in a team? As a director—using commands and coercion or, as a facilitator, positively attending towards the needs of team members? Is leadership based on having power *over* people, or having power *with* people? Whichever your view, there is a mutual relationship between those who lead and those who are being led. Your leadership competence will eventually be based on your ability to influence other team members for mutual success. Even though you may empower others, you remain nevertheless ultimately responsible for the way that power is used. You can find further insights into the subject of power and influence in the book *Project: Leadership* in this series, where we give a comprehensive account of the scope and depth of the topic.

The leadership role

A leader is someone who has recognisable—be it formal or informal—authority over others and who should, at least in theory, have the power to compel others to get things done. In project management the leadership role is one of the first to be filled when a team is formed. The leader then becomes the focal point of the project and usually has a say in choosing the team. In very small and short-lived projects no specific leader may be assigned. For larger projects, however, someone with leadership authority is needed to manage and co-ordinate operations, as well as provide the experience, credibility, and resilience to navigate a complex and often politicised decision-making process.

If you look at the nature of projects being undertaken and the organisational charts in many organisations, you'll usually find specific projects that cut across a number of departments. These departments can also seek assistance from a project resource pool—perhaps a project management office (PMO)—to manage, guide, and execute projects or programmes. One advantage of this centralised function is that when multiple departments or work areas are involved in the same project, you benefit from an unbiased leader who helps sustain the team and ensures that the various interests of different parties do not impede the overall progress of a project.

Having a leader in place clearly shows others where the responsibility lies, as well as provides a central point for gathering disparate information. In addition, the rulings of an effective leader can avoid teams getting bogged down in intractable disagreement.

If your team is unhappy with you, they may undermine your authority, which in serious cases means you need to step down as leader or be replaced. An alternative is to have a rotating leadership structure with individuals taking turns as a leader for specified periods before passing on the baton of responsibility. It is quite normal for team members to judge the role and performance of their leader closely and, if they look to you as a true leader, they may even exaggerate your importance in the work of a team. There are also cases where a strong team member or sub-group can, for whatever reason, overtly or covertly oppose a leader, and try to influence others to share their views. A number of factors, including beliefs, personal dislikes, and rival ambitions can drive this. Overall, there is no doubting that leaders have a strong influence on teams, and it has repeatedly been shown that team members are encouraged to apply themselves more diligently and deliver better results in the presence of a purposeful and influential leader.

Reflection points

- What is the role of the leader in a team?
- How do teams without a leader operate? What leads to people wanting to have a leader to follow?
- What influences do the nature of different projects and cultures have on the need for leaders?

Leadership skills

Your leadership skills are what enable you to organise, manage, co-ordinate, support, and encourage the team in pursuit of their project outcomes. They also reflect your ability to get others to achieve more than they themselves believe that they can achieve. Leadership skills involve being able to read others and to influence complex communication processes within teams, as well as having the determination to encourage others in a team to succeed and achieve the objectives that have been set. *Leading by example* is a strong way to demonstrate your leadership ability, although exactly how you do this will vary from project to project.

There is a two-way relationship between a leader and other team members, and a leader can openly communicate with and influence team members, and vice versa. Leaders oversee *resource sharing* as team members agree to work together, sharing their time, energy, and talents for mutual benefit. Leaders have *transformational* influence when they enhance the interest, confidence, and satisfaction of team members by uniting them with a larger purpose and through that, have a positive impact on their attitudes, values, and needs. Leadership skills are also based on *co-operation*, when you recognise the importance of others and are willing to work with them in an open and productive manner, and *adaptability*, where you lead a process that helps the team to adapt to situations without losing sight of specific goals. Depending on the nature of a project and its associated team, your required leadership skills will vary. For example, a complex software development project and the performance of a sporting team in a competition involve very different leadership roles.

There are two basic models of leadership that are commonly referred to and these are *task-oriented leadership* and *relationship-oriented leadership* (Figure 8.1). A *task leader* focuses on the objectives of a project and the operational goals

Figure 8.1

Are you a task or relations oriented leader?

of a team. To achieve success, a task leader sets goals and defines the criteria for any outcomes. They allocate specific roles to team members, making them responsible and determining work procedures. It is also a task leader's role to propose solutions and manage follow-up. Efficiency and the contribution of a team matters a lot to a task leader. A *relationship leader*, on the other hand, mainly focuses on relationships and communication within a team. This role involves stimulating team spirit, supporting and encouraging team members, reducing disputes between individuals, and establishing mutual understanding. Although leaders may have different styles and techniques, the two basic functions they have is to co-ordinate the work that a team has to perform and address the communication needs of a team. There are indications of gender differences in the methods of leaders. It is often believed that women are more comfortable as relationship leaders whilst men more so as task leaders. However, research indicates that women in leadership roles tend to be both relationship-oriented and task-oriented whilst men are just task-oriented.

Exercises

- What is reciprocity in the context of the leadership role in teams?
- What does resource-sharing mean in the context of the leadership role in teams?
- What is transformation in the context of the leadership role in teams?
- What is collaboration in the context of the leadership role in teams?
- What is adaptability in the context of the leadership role in teams?

Who leads?

Leadership can come in many guises. While someone may be in a position of authority and power, they may still show weak leadership and prove ineffective as a result. Others, on the other hand, may have no formal authority but yet are looked up to by others, and have the ability to make others follow them.

The relative roles of nature, nurture, and context in determining whether someone becomes a leader is a debate that has run since antiquity, and scholars remain divided on this topic. There has been a widely held belief that people have innate leadership capabilities. The Greek philosopher Aristotle, for example, argued that people were either born as leaders or as followers, and this view is still widespread across different cultures. It is a view that has been linked to that of hereditary leadership ability and used to justify systems such as patrilineal authority (descent through male line), which was prevalent in many societies, and remains so in some. Those in power in these situations, of course, promulgate this viewpoint as it is in their interest, even though it lacks any strong scientific basis.

Innate tendencies or traits in individuals can be seen in a wide variety of groups such as school gangs, work teams, juries, and rescue teams. Individuals will assert themselves in different ways and may work towards a leadership role either opportunistically or incrementally. Their authority, in this case, comes when their role is accepted by others, at least until they do something that is widely disagreeable, or are unable to deal well with stressful situations. This authority may be official or unofficial. In the latter case, it may be a strong team member to whom others look up and follow, even though, on paper, everyone may have equal authority. The motivation to become a leader, if it exists, can vary widely and may be altruistic or selfish, with variations in between.

Nurture is also clearly a factor in deciding who becomes a leader in certain kinds of situations, with an example being the public school system in the UK that has produced a disproportionally high percentage of political, civil service, and business leaders. In addition to these factors, former British Prime Minister Benjamin Disraeli once wryly observed that: "history is made by those that show up". While this quote can be interpreted in a number of ways, it has a ring of truth in the sense that the mere fact of turning up for events and committing yourself can gradually lead to gaining an important role in decision-making, and perhaps becoming a leader—either by accident or design. Other examples of context as a deciding factor in who becomes a leader are when a situation suddenly becomes favourable to a particular leadership candidate, or when influential individuals or groups sponsor someone who has the required attributes for leadership according to their interests. In the modern era, equality, democracy, and meritocracy are more prevalent in deciding who gains authority, although kleptocracy, nepotism, and various forms of discrimination continue to exist.

Leadership theory offers many different arguments as to what makes some people and not others, good (or great) leaders. In the 19th century, for instance, much emphasis was placed on "greatness" in leadership, and male military heroes such as Napoleon, Julius Caesar, and Alexander the Great were frequently cited as model examples. This approach is encapsulated in the *Great Man Theory* popularised by historian Thomas Carlyle, which can be summed up in the phrase: "leaders are born, not made". A related theory is the *Trait Theory* proposed by Francis Galton in his book *Hereditary Genius* (1869), which also talked about people being born with certain inherent personality traits that explained their later role as leading figures. While taking account of physical traits that can influence leadership (e.g. gender, age, height, weight, strength, looks, or ethnicity), a number of key personality traits are related to leadership capability such as drive, communication ability, and ingenuity, and these are discussed in more detail in the next section.

Not long after the views of Carlyle and Galton on heroic greatness and genius were published, prominent thinkers of the time such as Herbert Spencer wrote opposing views that diminished the notion of being "born to rule". During this time, Russian novelist Leo Tolstoy put forward a different view that can be referred to as the *Zeitgeist Theory*. This emphasises context as a key deciding factor in leadership and argues that individuals achieve leader status because circumstances and the spirit of the times are on their side. Inherent ability has little to do with it. *Situational theory* argues that there is no single "best" style of leadership and that effective leadership in any given situation is related to the specific tasks that need to be undertaken and the nature of the team that will carry out those tasks. Team nature includes team size, existing team relationships, team maturity, and complexity. Leadership works best when it meshes with the development stage of a team (Hersey & Blanchard, 1977). Related theory is the *interactional theory* which basically asserts that no potential capacity or trait of an individual operates in isolation. It describes the traits for leadership as stemming from a combination of superior will, initiative, knowledge, and capacity. The standing of someone as part of a team, including a leader, is not related to their personal capacities and traits in the abstract, but rather how their *special qualities* relate to other team members in the pursuit of given goals in a particular environment. In saying this, it is not the possession of these special qualities that is important for individual standing, as such, but rather how others *perceive* you to have those qualities (e.g. Gibb, 1950).

Modern leadership theory and the general consensus appears to be that while certain traits are desirable, the particular circumstances in each case are important and that people can gain leadership ability if they work hard at achieving (Zaccaro *et al.*, 2004; Nye, 2008; Forsyth, 2019).

Whatever the source of leadership authority, there are some desirable traits that are of value for leadership, and we have listed some of these below:

- *Self-determination:* competence of having the energy, mental strength, and perseverance to reach goals and objectives.
- *Self-confidence:* competence to be comfortable with your abilities and signalling this to others.
- *Communication skills:* competence to convey a message effectively through speech, writing, and discussion and to respond empathically to others.
- *Assertiveness:* competence to set boundaries and confront others when needed.
- *Resourcefulness:* competence to contribute, support, and facilitate others.
- *Honesty and integrity:* competence to behave in a consistent way and being true to yourself and others.
- *Creativity:* competence to realise novel ideas and solutions.
- *Intelligence:* competence to think through problems using reasoning and abstract thought as well as to read the emotions of others and respond accordingly.

The following characteristics may also help you to become a good team leader:

- Open, sociable, personal, expressive, and interested in working with others.
- Likeable, warm, and generous.
- Conscientious, responsible, results-driven, reliable, and organised.

- Self-control and emotionally stable under pressure while remaining determined.
- Intellectually capable, with appropriate knowledge and possessing good manners.

Teams can benefit from having leaders who are more intelligent and/or have greater expertise and experience than other team members, as team members will believe this gives them better direction as a whole. But you should largely have a shared mindset with the rest of your team, in terms of motivation, attitudes, values, and understanding. Teams need leaders they can understand and with whom they can bond, rather than leaders who have advanced management skills and stand out from the group in terms of their overall approach.

If you are choosing a team leader from within a new team, the most outgoing team member may seem like the obvious candidate. But more introverted individuals may possess better leadership capacity, even if they appear more withdrawn and show a lower level of participation and little interest in the team and its achievements. Talking and delivering are two separate things, however, and you'll need to adapt to your team leader's preferred style (introvert or extrovert) as will he or she need to adapt this style to the needs of the team.

It isn't simply personality traits and achievements that determine who is the best candidate for a leadership role (Figure 8.2). Age, gender, ethnicity, race, cultural background, education, religious and political affiliations, social status, family background, and other group memberships will also influence the decision. Fortunately, the growing understanding of the value of diversity in teams and the dangers of prejudice and stereotyping should help avoid bias

Figure 8.2

What determines who is the best candidate for a leadership role?

in the selection. Teams often rely on the knowledge that comes with success, experience, and age, and provide leadership on the basis of these. If team members assume that age denotes wisdom, experience, and ability, they are more likely to favour leaders who are older rather than younger. On the other hand, younger leaders may offer a fresh outlook and approach to projects and it's important for the continued development of your organisation's project management capability that you provide plenty of opportunities for young, up-and-coming employees to experience being the leader.

Despite the increasing emphasis on diversity and gender balance, there remain very large differences in the experience of female project leaders between countries. Recent International Labour Organisation (ILO) statistics showed that women hold almost 60% of all management positions in Jamaica, while the equivalent in Pakistan is around 3% (both in the year 2008). The figures for the UK are midway at around 35% (2012). According to the ILO, women tend to be concentrated in positions relating to HR, PR & Communications, and Finance & Administration, as opposed to Research & Product Development, Sales and Operations, and General Management. This latter grouping is more associated with the eventual rise to CEO level and so "area of activity" appears to be an important factor in future career development.

Reflection points

- What qualities are likely to characterise leaders in groups?
- Who is the leader of your team?
- How did the leader in your team get the leadership role?
- What is the difference between male and female leadership?

Successful leadership in teams

Let's take a moment to look at the theories to explain why some leaders succeed while others fail. *Participative leadership theories* are those that suggest that the ideal leadership approach is one that takes the input of others into account. Different perspectives on participation are evident in the three main leadership methods (Lewin *et al.*, 1939). Firstly, team leadership can be *authoritarian*, i.e. where a leader makes all the decisions themselves and uses only a small amount of information from other group members. Secondly, team leadership can be *democratic* where other group members are allowed to participate in the decision-making process, although a leader remains responsible. Thirdly, a *laissez-faire* leadership method is one in which a leader interferes very little and more or less leaves the group to make decisions for themselves. The success associated with each approach can vary depending on the nature of the situation. While democratic methods can be very effective, it may also take a long time to reach agreement, and sometimes an authoritarian approach can be more successful. With an experienced and creative team who are also sensitive to interference, a laissez-faire approach may work best.

Another category of leadership theories are *transformational leadership theories*, with descriptions first introduced by the American historian James MacGregor Burns (1918–2014) (Burns, 1978) and then developed by the British scholar Bernard M. Bass (Bass, 1985; 1990). These focus on the connections between leaders and followers and how the latter are inspired and motivated by the former. Leaders, in this case, normally want each team member to fulfil their true potential and are typically very ambitious in terms of how they visualise overall success. This leadership style requires charisma, vision, high moral and ethical standards, and being an example for others to follow. A leader will typically have a zealous approach and their enthusiasm and positivity can prove infectious to others. Project work often begins with a bold shared vision and this is then followed by a strategy of implementation and an action plan. Delegation of responsibility involves bringing the best out in individuals and monitoring and encouragement are important aspects of this, as is joint problem solving.

Bass developed *Bass' Transformational Leadership Theory* that defines transformational leadership in terms of how a leader affects followers who are expected to show trust, admiration, and respect. Transformation may occur when leaders increase awareness among their followers of the importance and value attached to an undertaking, convince followers to act more out of group interest rather than self-interest, and activate the higher needs of their followers. Four factors characterise transformational leaders (the 4I's): (1) they have *idealised influence* by showing conviction and emphasise the importance of mutual trust and proper evaluation in decision-making; (2) they provide *inspirational motivation* with a clear future vision; set goals, speak with enthusiasm, use encouragement, and demonstrate commitment; (3) they provide *intellectual stimulation* to group members by questioning the values of received opinions and encourage their colleagues to search for new approaches, try new methods, and to express themselves openly; and (4) they show *individual consideration* for individuals within the team, find out about their needs, respect their desires, encourage them to use their skills, and guide, teach, and train where appropriate. According to Bass, anyone who combines all these four elements will achieve success in any team and in all cultures (Bass, 1990).

The *Contingency Theory of Effectiveness* (or *Fiedler contingency model*) of the Austrian/American Fred E. Fiedler (1922–2017) was popular in the 1960s (Fiedler, 1964). Fiedler researched teams that worked to achieve set goals under the guidance of a leader. His main conclusion was that there was no such thing as an "ideal" leader in the broad sense. In order for a team leader to be effective in their role, there should be a match between the style and capability of the leader and the nature of the situations a team is faced with, i.e. one is contingent on the other, and the dynamics change as situations change. This model moves away from the idea that leader effectiveness is simply related to personality traits and also looks at leaders as being either task-oriented or relationship-oriented, or somewhere in between. In this case, emphasis is placed on *situational control*, and only those leaders who can demonstrate this can be confident that others will follow their orders or suggestions. Fiedler considered situational control to be a critical factor and broke it down into the following three components:

- *Leader-member relations* refers to the degree of mutual trust, respect, and confidence between the leader and team members; if good then the leader will have to spend less time on controlling behaviour and conflict within the team, and vice versa.
- *Task structure* describes how clear the work activity of a team is and the extent to which it is structured and unambiguous.
- *Position power* refers to the power that the leader has through the ability to reward or punish.

A key variable of Fiedler's model is that of *least preferred co-worker* (LPC). This is based on the entire previous experience of a leader and how they rate their least preferred co-worker under several binary categories that have numerical scales (e.g. unfriendly = 1 to friendly = 8, guarded = 1 to open = 8, and so on). Leaders who receive a low-LPC score across the different categories are considered to be task-oriented, while those with a high-LPC score are considered to be relationship-oriented. Situations are "favourable" when leader-member relations are good, tasks are highly structured, and the leader has high position power, and "unfavourable" in the opposite case. Fiedler's conclusion was that low-LPC leaders (task-oriented) perform best in situations that are either extremely favourable or unfavourable, whereas high-LPC leaders (relationship oriented) perform best in situations that are intermediately favourable. According to Nye (2008), there is a wide variety of contexts in the application of power and you'll need to be acutely aware of aspects such as: culture, distribution of power resources, followers' needs and demands, time urgency, and information flows. This implies that effective and appropriate leadership requires multiple approaches and flexibility to meet the demands of dynamic situations (Forsyth, 2019).

There are various other theories that are based on the idea that leaders are either relationship-oriented or task-oriented, or somewhere in between. One example is the so-called Blake Mouton Managerial (or Leadership) Grid, which was designed by management theorists Jane Mouton (1930–1987) and Robert Blake (1918–2004) in 1964 (Blake & Mouton, 1964). They believed that leadership style was based on how leaders answer the following two basic questions: *How important is the performance of the team? How important is the wellbeing of the team?* A true team leader in this case shows both concern for individual members of their team and team performance (or production).

The Leader-Member Exchange Theory (LMX) gives insights into the relationship that exists between the leader and each team member. According to this theory, a leader has a special relationship with each team member and this relationship can be different from the leader's relationship with the team as a whole. The idea is that there is a natural tendency for group members to form subgroups that can be called inner and outer groups. The *in-group* consists of those that are more closely linked with the leader. They normally have more interesting roles such as that of advisors, administrators, or assistants and may have a higher degree of competence. They are more engaged and show more commitment and loyalty. They may have limited scope to be critical of a leader and are more likely to toe the line. They are also more likely to have a greater chance of being rewarded. The *out-group*, on the other hand, is formed of those who are less linked with the leader and who contribute less. They can be disaffected as they are more likely to be given less interesting and more mundane tasks to carry out and may have a lower degree of competence. There may then be team members who: (1) may aspire to join the inner group and work hard at gaining access; (2) are happy to remain in their peripheral position; or (3) may be looking for an opportunity to leave the team. It is in your best interests to ensure that everyone becomes part of the in-group as this maximises success (Forsyth, 2019).

In an ideal world, a good leader should ensure that their role is relevant to the present and future, and in tune with the spirit of the times. You should respect good traditions, but also make changes where necessary. You should be alert to peoples' situations and experiences and be aware of any ethical issues that may arise. In order to influence others, you should be someone with drive, good motivational skills and infectious enthusiasm, as well as capable of showing others empathy and understanding. You should be constructive in the sense of building up individual and community awareness and pride, and you should encourage sustainable development. You should also strive to see different cultures in a positive way and encourage relationship-building.

Reflection points

- To what extent is your group relationship-oriented?
- To what extent is your group task-oriented?
- How does the concept of least preferred co-worker relate to your experience of working in groups?
- What roles can a leader serve in a group?

Confrontation in teams

Confrontation involves a challenge on the part of one individual (or group of individuals) within the team to another individual (or group of individuals) to examine both their behaviour critically, and the impact of this behaviour on others. Convention commonly sees confrontation as a hostile discussion that occurs when one person is unhappy with the behaviour of another. The behaviour may be conscious or unconscious and the confrontation aims to

Figure 8.3

Confrontation is a delicate matter that needs to be prepared for with care.

highlight this dissatisfaction and to seek resolution, usually in the form of an apology and a commitment to change. Confrontation is, however, a delicate matter that needs to be dealt with and prepared for with care (Figure 8.3). If you manage it sensitively but assertively, it can have a positive and constructive effect on both parties and lead to improved future relations.

Sooner or later, you will be faced with the need to deal with unconstructive or disruptive behaviour, reprimand your co-workers, or generally deal with difficult characters. These involve confrontations of one sort or another, ranging from a mild reminder to a serious rebuke, and you'll need to learn and practise various approaches. Make sure you react promptly once you become aware of an issue and guide the person or people involved to a meeting at a suitable location of their choosing, such as their office. Once there, open with a brief even-tempered explanation of the issue as you see it and then invite those who are at the centre of the issue to air their views while listening actively. Where necessary you may also interject with open questions in order that everything is out in the open and clearly understood. For more difficult cases, it is worth considering having at least one other trusted person to witness the meeting so that what is said and done is documented. This could even be a professional mediator. Once the other side of a story has been heard, you need to consider what was said and act decisively by explaining with sincerity and controlled emotion how you view the issue and the effect it has had on others. This may be enough to alleviate the situation in many cases, with both parties having resolved their differences and showing greater awareness for the future. However, you may experience cases where difficult follow-up action needs to be taken such as imposing a penalty or even dismissal. Taking a proactive approach will help to prevent a situation getting out of control and stop issues from festering. You'll want to keep a positive and trusting outlook and avoid paranoia but you should be aware of the potential for things to be going on behind your back and the danger of bad feelings being spread.

There are a number of books that identify a range of difficult personality types and give recommendations on how best to deal with them. An early example was Robert Bramson's *Coping with Difficult People* (1981) in which he described the following range of difficult personalities:

- *Hostile aggressives* are those who bully and overwhelm others and who act without any consideration for others, using anger as a means of communication.
- *Complainers* are those who are unhappy no matter what and have no consideration for the plight of others nor are willing to take responsibility to improve situations.
- *Silent and unresponsives* are those who are consistently uncommunicative and no one knows what they actually think.
- *Super-agreeables* are personable, outgoing, and often enjoyable people who do not deliver on what they promise, or at least not in the way that was required.
- *Negativists* are those who are convinced that no new idea or approach will ever work and are very good at dampening optimism.
- *Know-it-all experts* are those who are superior in their own view (who may actually know a lot or very little) and who let everyone else know this, being either condescending, imposing, or pompous in the process.
- *Indecisives* are those who let events decide, rather than making timely decisions, and who do not finish things.

Most of us may recognise our own behaviour on occasion falling into one of these categories but truly difficult people have a clear tendency towards one or more of the negative behaviours outlined. They can be considered as being *stereotypically difficult*. Other difficult character stereotypes include:

- *The secret sniper* who sabotages co-workers while remaining hidden.
- The e*xploiter* who uses the work of others without acknowledgement for their own advancement.
- The *bulldozer* who carries on working hard in a particular way regardless of consideration of the views and actions of others.
- The *balloon* who frequently has big ideas which then blow up and come to nothing.
- The *slacker* who is lazy and relies on others to do the work for them.
- The *gossip* who cannot be trusted to keep any important information confidential.

It may be difficult to identify negative characteristics at an interview but they can come to the surface subsequently or they may undergo a transformation of character for the worst, sometimes under the influence of others. In dealing with these individuals, it is important to maintain the work output of the team as a whole and to avoid the spread of negative approaches such as bullying and laziness amongst other team members.

Confrontation requires a level of assuredness, preparedness, consideration, and determination. Careless confrontation that is apathetic, insincere, or poorly managed will damage communication with the person involved. In a confrontation, you are asking someone to take a serious look at their behaviour and the consequences of that behaviour. There may be many reasons behind this behaviour and you need to tread carefully and with sensitivity. Berenson *et al.* (1968) describe five types of confrontation:

1   *Didactic confrontation* assumes the receiver lacks important information or has misunderstood certain information. The aim is to try to help him or her to better understand things and to point out how their lack of information or misunderstanding is affecting the *confronter* and possibly others.
2   *Experiential (or caring) confrontation* is when the confronter informs the receiver that their opinions of themselves are not consistent with their self-perceptions, and that these differences need to be somehow resolved.
3   *Weakness confrontation* is when a receiver's weaknesses and limitations are pointed out to them. This is a delicate process requiring a lot of consideration and can be positive and constructive if done well, but negative and destructive if done badly.
4   *Strength confrontation* is when a receiver has their strengths pointed out to them by a confronter, including positive characteristics in the receiver's personality that they are not aware of, or do not use as they should, possibly due to lack of confidence.
5   *Encouragement to action* is where a receiver gets support from the confronter to try to overcome a lack of resolve to take action on an issue, rather than reacting passively—this can involve putting forward a range of solutions to what the individual is dealing with and encouragement to take the necessary steps.

In the context of confrontation, we might ask: Why do we perceive situations differently? There may be several reasons for this not least that situations are rarely black and white so conflicting perceptions, interpretations, or opinions are understandable. *Discrepancy* describes a behaviour in which we think or perceive of something differently from how we express it, while in *distortion* individuals avoid facing facts and produce convoluted and often wildly exaggerated interpretations in an effort to match reality to their preferred version of it. It is not uncommon for someone to see the environment in light of what they want or need to see instead of what is real. *Games, tricks, selective hearing,* and *smoke screens* are things that people often apply in order to protect themselves. We can adopt roles, pretend to be different people than we are, and use tricks and deception to avoid others finding out the truth (Egan, 1976). These mental games may often involve:

- *Red herrings*: Unrelated topics designed to distract a confronter off.
- A *straw man argument*, in which an opponent's views are deliberately misrepresented.
- *Circular arguments*: Arguments that start with a conclusion and for which no firm basis is ever established.
- *Moving the goalposts*: Replacing pre-existing criteria with new criteria that are less robust to support your argument.
- *Ad-hominem attacks*: Attacking the arguer rather than the argument.
- *Cherry picking*: Choosing information that suits your argument while ignoring other incompatible information.
- *False analogies*: Comparing one situation to another when they are quite different and not comparable.
- *Post hoc ergo propter hoc*: Assuming that event Y must be related to event X because event Y came after event X.
- *Thought-terminating clichés*: Something that when said or thought brings consideration to a close and no further questioning is undertaken (a *mantra* is an example).
- *Hasty generalisations*: Speedy conclusions based on insufficient evidence.
- *Jesuitical reasoning*: Subtle and clever reasoning used to distract from an otherwise weak argument.
- *Kettle logic*: Using multiple inconsistent arguments to defend a position.
- *False attribution*: Implying something is related to something else when it is not. Other fallacies mentioned above are variants of this.

Exercises

- What are the main types of confrontations?
- Try to use different types of confrontations in your conversation.
- Share examples with your colleagues where there was inconsistency in what you thought and what you said. Tell each other about examples where you, e.g. embellished the picture of yourselves to others to make yourselves look better.
- Share examples with your colleagues of when you have experienced tricks and deception during discussions, negotiations, or confrontations.

Entitlement for confrontation

Confrontation requires empathy and needs to be direct, encouraging, and constructive if it is to be done successfully. Team members need to earn the right to confront others in the team and this isn't something that simply comes with being a team member. Only those members of the team who are active and fully engaged within the team have this right. You need to make sure that there is a good relationship between the people involved; mutual respect and understanding and that everyone has a shared desire for improvements. Individuals who initiate confrontation need to have a good connection with their inner selves and be prepared for how challenged team member(s) may react. They need to be able to show determination and must respond well to confrontation themselves.

Responses to a confrontation can vary greatly. The challenged person will quite naturally have a certain sense of themselves and their own behaviour. When suggestions are put forward by a confronter on the behaviour of a receiver, then the receiver in question can be forced to reconsider their ideas about themselves. This can be difficult. A common reaction is for conscious and subconscious defence mechanisms to kick in and these can manifest themselves in various ways. Listed below are several common types of negative defence responses identified by Egan (1976: pp. 188–189):

- *Indifference*: Answers tersely, for example, "maybe", while, in reality, disregarding the message.
- *Misrepresentation*: Not acknowledging what really matters in the message.
- *Disrespect*: Shows the confronter disdain or contempt and counterattack by, for example, by doubting the integrity of the confronter.
- *Conviction*: Tries to get the confronter to change his/her mind by appealing to their intelligence or blaming circumstances.
- *Doubting the importance*: Belittles the weakness that is being pointed out.
- *Denial*: Does not accept the message or any observations that have been made.
- *Getting support*: Replies by referring to the support of others such as: "This is not what my friends say".
- *Superficial agreement*: Say they agree and accept hands down what the confronter has said, while, in reality, have little interest in change and hopes to avoid further confrontation.

From the point of view of a receiver, constructive responses to confrontation involve thinking on your feet and seeking further information. If an individual is confronted in a fair and responsible way, then the onus is on him or her to answer the confronter with equal sincerity, openness, and in the same direct manner as was shown to them. The first thing that needs to be checked by a receiver is that they have understood the confronter correctly. Often, a receiver has to be patient and self-disciplined in order to delve deeper and understand what the confronter is actually implying, especially in the case of something that is uncomfortable to talk about. This is exactly when there is the greatest risk that you will automatically revert to defence mode.

Confrontation can be challenging for both the confronter and the receiver and requires a considerable range of skills. It is advisable to practise confrontational skills with competent people who are willing and open to test themselves in both roles and become more attuned to the responses of others. In such a setting, the receiver may also ask others if they agree with the views of the confronter. When a receiver is sure that he or she understands what is being said, then it is good to use others to dissect it as thoroughly as possible and to practise appropriate responses. This method enables each team member to explore in detail what others think and, most importantly, what they themselves, as receivers, think deep down about the assertions or statements. If, in the view of the receiver, the observations of the confronter are reasonable, justified, and useful, then it might be worthwhile to consider them and to change behaviour accordingly. It is easier said than done to adopt new behaviours and it takes time to adopt new behavioural patterns. For more on this topic read *Project: Leadership* in this same series.

Constructive confrontation in communication is useful for both the confronter and the receiver and works best when it is used sensitively, and benefits both parties equally. As a confronter, it is necessary to have a clear view of what the intention of the challenge is before initiating it and ask yourself questions like: How will the message be interpreted by a receiver? Will it be perceived as an attack? The effect of confrontation in communications is questionable, on the other hand, if a confronter has either no intention to understand the receiver better or is unwilling to help the receiver to understand them better.

Having constructive impact on others requires that we are willing to *confront ourselves* by taking a critical look at ourselves. Healthy self-criticism is crucial if you want to tackle things in your own behaviour and take the responsibility of needed behavioural changes to heart. Individuals who can challenge themselves in a confrontation can later seek confirmation from other team members and gain their support to become more aware of behavioural patterns and solicit encouragement for change.

Confrontation can be *transformational* if it is executed and responded to in the right manner. It can help team members to express their opinions openly for greater team engagement and sound decision-making. The challenger should show politeness and care and the receiver should aim to understand the message correctly, check if defence mechanisms might negatively influence the discussion, and use the feedback given in a constructive way. Managers need to learn the skill both of confronting team members and of responding to their confrontations.

Reflection points

- What preconditions are necessary before confrontation is used?
- What should be avoided in a confrontation?
- How is it possible to confront oneself?
- Why is accuracy required in confrontation?

Assertiveness in teams

Self-assertions, self-determination, knowing how to be heard, and avoiding being walked on or taken for granted are all important elements in team communications. If done with consideration and skill, these elements can have a strong positive impact on communications. As other team members are encouraged to look under the surface and uncover things this will enable both you and the team to understand where you are coming from. Many things that lie beneath the surface can impact team performance. Confrontation aims to have team members dive under the surface and reveal underlying frustrations, opinions, and feelings.

Assertiveness is all about taking a decisive position in regard to others and making them aware of it. Individuals who use assertiveness as a communication method draw attention to themselves and demand that other people take notice of them. The following is an example of a verbal exchange from a typical committee meeting that illustrates this well:

Chairman: "So, I would like to sum up by saying that we are all agreed that (some action) is the best way to proceed and that we wish (some people) success in making this happen".

Assertive member: "Excuse me, chairman, but I would like to state for the record that I do not agree with this action and my reasons for this have already been clearly presented at the meeting here tonight".

The advantage of this approach is that it is both clear and direct without being judgemental. If someone crosses the line, or ignores your views, then you need to deal with that situation. As in the example, it can be important to demonstrate assertiveness while the issue is active and in front of others. If the member had complained to the chairman in private afterwards, it would not have had the same effect and others might never have become aware of their opposition and assumed that everyone had agreed with the decision.

Assertiveness involves listening and observing, and then responding (Figure 8.4). It can be used to solve problems; create and maintain discipline; develop respect; and for a variety of other purposes, including when seeking advice as needed, discussing responsibilities and duties with colleagues and so on. Decisiveness is being true to yourself. It is crucial for effective leadership and enhances credibility and determination in communication as *Yes means yes and no means no*. Where stakes are high it is important that those around you see you adopt a responsible stand and decisiveness is key.

In the handling of any dispute, decisiveness involves discussing matters face-to-face, acknowledging the problem, and encouraging the other person to describe the problem as they see it. Agreeing on the nature of the problem is an important step in providing some form of a lasting solution. When negotiating a settlement maintain an engaged but neutral tone, refer to what the other person has said, build on their ideas for a solution,

Figure 8.4

Assertiveness involves listening and observing and then responding.

and describe the outcome that you hope for. You'll need to agree on a joint action plan which clearly states who does what, when, and how. In the case of personal problems, it is even more important to listen to the concerns of the other person, acknowledge what they have to say, and confirm an understanding of what they have said. Depending on the nature of someone's role, they will have a particular set of responsibilities, obligations, and desires that will drive their sense of assertiveness and decisiveness. In all this, you want to avoid procrastination but make sure you allow ample time to listen to others in an engaged and open manner before determining a future course of action.

Exercise

- Work in pairs of two. One person should deliberately cross the line while communicating with the other person, e.g. aim to get something from them that is inappropriate. The person who receives the query should demonstrate how to react with decisiveness to this approach by following the process below:
  (a) Describing the *behaviour* of the other person ("When you…")
  (b) Describing the *feelings* that arose ("I felt…")
  (c) Describing *why* those feelings arose ("…because…").

Offering opinions or solutions

Being able to react well to others and give considered opinions are important skills for team managers. You may have some natural abilities in these areas but you'll still need practice and possibly even training to become truly proficient. There are various things that you'll want to consider in this context:

when should you offer your opinions to others?; how should you tell others about your thoughts and feelings that are relevant to them?; and how should you react to their reactions?

Opinions may be given by interested or disinterested parties and are given either as neutral viewpoints or with the view of influencing the behaviour and actions of another. As such, the approach taken in communicating opinions will vary. If you want your opinions to register with the receiver, you must give them in the right way. Only offer an opinion when it is needed and keep it within the boundaries of your role. Good co-operation in teamwork typically involves all team members being open-minded and receptive to the opinions of others from the outset. This means that opinions on issues need regular airing and the environment of regular team meetings provides a great structure to do this. Begin with an agenda outlining a series of topics that you or other team members introduce and explain. Once introduced, leave each topic open for discussion and encourage the team to seek a wide range of opinions. Invite the participants to introduce new topics (if they are deemed relevant) under the closing section of a meeting, as any other business. If structured and managed carefully, team meetings can be a very effective means of having a fully representative range of opinions aired. These can be observations, interpretations, positive reports, criticisms, compliments for a job well done, or reprimands.

It is important that everyone is familiar with a situation and understands the context before they give an opinion. Take time to reflect whether it is appropriate to give an opinion. It should always be clear why you are offering an opinion beyond a simple desire to hear your own voice. A constructive exchange of opinions will not happen unless the receiver is willing to listen, and that they are satisfied that they are being shown respect and care. There are times when it is *not* appropriate to give an opinion: (1) if you are not well informed about what lies behind a situation or the behaviour of another person; (2) if you don't care about the other person or have finished working with them and are not being constructive; (3) if you are criticising someone over something that is beyond their control, or if they (or you) lack confidence; and (4) if your opinion is not helpful to others or the progress of work, or if the time and place is inappropriate, then it should also be left unsaid. In relation to timing, avoid giving an opinion when you or the other person are emotional. Practice makes perfect when it comes to giving opinions. Try practising in private and rehearse what you intend to say. Working in a team development session is a perfect setting for practice of this kind.

When conditions are appropriate to give your opinion, keep the following points in mind: (1) be clear, precise, descriptive, and professional—avoid complicating your language with metaphors or long speeches; (2) show respect and empathy; (3) provide the opinion as close as possible to the time after the incident occurred to which an opinion relates; (4) avoid exaggeration and stereotypes, as well as passing premature judgement; (5) if you pass judgement on others, they are likely reciprocate, and the opportunity for a constructive dialogue may be lost if this is not handled well on all sides; (6) avoid giving opinions on behalf of others (e.g. "We think…") unless given the formal role of delivering the views of a team. Unless a group is too large, or there is little time, it is better that people speak for themselves as it encourages everyone to think for and express themselves. When giving an opinion, use a phrase that begins with "I…" and not with a question. For example: "I have a problem with completing the agenda when you show up late for meetings" rather than "When are you going to stop being late?"

Opinions are typically in the form of judgements, statements, or views and vary depending on their basis. A professional opinion, for example, will be very differently constructed from an uninformed opinion and may have legal repercussions, while other types of opinion include off-the-record opinions, non-biased opinions, biased opinions, initial opinions, scientific opinions, and so on. Make sure you support any strong opinions by facts and rehearse all the different arguments to avoid being caught out by those with opposing views. Opinions are typically subjective and it is natural to have differing opinions about many things. As long as people are clear about the basis of their opinions, are able to express them appropriately, and are also willing to listen to the views of others, then this should lead to constructive communication. Some people have trouble accepting positive opinions of themselves or their work and you'll need to work out how to approach them the right way so that they come around to accepting it. For example, if someone has a tendency to change the subject when being praised, you may have to repeat or reinforce the compliment before it is accepted.

As someone expressing an opinion you should also be able to receive an opinion from others; be it positive or negative. At times, such as when you are caught off guard and unprepared, this may not be easy, and you may experience automatic, physiological stress reactions such as tensing of muscles, involuntary negative facial expressions, and breathing that becomes faster and shallower. Take a few deep breaths, it will help you to think clearly and allow any immediate irritation to subside. Then, instead of interrupting and disrupting the thoughts of the other person, listen and perhaps ask open-ended questions periodically to get more information. Everyone has the right to get a clear opinion and it is natural to ask questions such as: What makes you think that I am pushy?

Once you have been given an opinion acknowledge it and re-word what you have heard in his or your own words to indicate that you have received and understood it. Focus on and recognise good and valid points, accept what is definitely right, and be open to what may be right. By doing so, you acknowledge the point of view of the person who is giving the opinion and show that you are trying to understand your own reaction to it. Recognising the perspective of the other does not necessarily mean that you will change your behaviour or attitude. It is possible to accept a portion of the feedback given by someone else but to reject other aspects. For example, you may accept that you have been too late with something but disagree that this was due to any irresponsibility. Take a little time to process what has been conveyed to you. You don't have to respond immediately; you can seek the opinion of others and request time to think about what has been said; reserving your response for a later meeting, if need be.

Clear and well-stated positive opinions from respected individuals carry a lot of weight and can provide a great lift to team members who may suffer from low self-esteem. We all benefit from a reminder of our good qualities, from time to time—both those that are obvious and those that may be unconscious. A common reason for low self-esteem is that individuals do not realise the qualities that they inherently possess. The act of team members sharing their opinions on each other's strengths can be a rewarding experience and create a good atmosphere. Opinion giving can also be invigorating—preventing the team from stagnating and participants from losing interest as a result of a lack of emotional or intellectual challenge.

Exercises

- Identify three qualities in yourself and three qualities in others in the group.
- Make as objective a description of these qualities as you can by describing in what way they are positive and state what their effects are.
- Tell the others what you think about your own strengths.
- Tell the others what you think of their strengths.
- Do you have strengths that others do not identify, or do others point out strengths to you that you did not know about?

Brainstorming in teams

Those who lead teams use their communication skills to mobilise and motivate others to work. This work may often be carried out in teams in which people do not know each other well. It makes sense to start a new project by having an open and in-depth discussion about the problems that lie ahead and how to approach and resolve them. *Brainstorming* is a great way of doing this as it enables team members to multiply ideas that you can then collect, analyse and, if useful, adopt to ensure success (Figure 8.4).

Invite one person to facilitate the discussion. He or she should encourage the team to focus by sticking to one problem at a time and beware of letting the conversation diverge. The facilitator may also ensure the team stays aware of the bigger picture and avoids getting bogged down in detail of one particular aspect of a problem. In their role, the facilitator should encourage participants to come up with new, original, and clever ideas that relate to the problem at hand. They should take care to prevent the discussion from becoming hijacked by a few individuals and provide guidance rather than criticising or rejecting ideas out of hand (see Figure 8.5).

Figure 8.5

Team can benefit from a well-orchestrated brainstorming.

It is worth laying some ground rules in order to help ensure the flow of ideas.

1   Everyone should be encouraged to make comments on all the issues that come up, no matter how weird and crazy they are.
2   The evaluation of ideas should be postponed until the brainstorming is over. During this time, all ideas are valuable.
3   Look for as many ideas as possible. The more relevant and original ideas you have, the greater the likelihood that the best solution will be chosen, and the stronger one is able to argue in favour of this choice.
4   Team members should try to develop ideas based on those of others, as well as try to develop and improve other's original ideas (cross-cueing).

Experience shows that teams who become practised at brainstorming learn to improve each other's contributions, so that an idea offered by one individual is readily developed by others. Often, an idea that may seem, at first, absurd becomes a good solution after a little polishing.

Sometimes, ideas are thrown around randomly at a brainstorming meeting. This may work in smaller informal groups but is likely to become chaotic in larger groups. More commonly, participants are given a specific time (say 5–10 minutes) and asked to write down their ideas on different topics or issues, and these ideas are then collected. The facilitator then asks each participant what ideas they have written down. If an idea has already been put forward and the team member does not have any further ideas, then they are free to say "pass". The facilitator may go around the circle as many times as is needed to gather ideas.

Brainstorming has both pros and cons. You may be able to generate hundreds of suggestions on how to solve the problem that is being discussed, but it is unlikely that they are all good and realistic. There may be a temptation for individuals who are not genuinely engaged with the group to hold back and this can constrain the dynamic and the quantity and quality of ideas you generate. The following actions can improve brainstorming:

1   Explain the problem to participants including any constraints.
2   Define the conditions that need to be met for the solution to the problem.
3   Ensure that the team focuses during the brainstorming the whole time and isn't waylaid by irrelevant issues.
4   Encourage positivity.

As the aim is to encourage active participation with a positive attitude, the facilitator should observe the level of participation and encourage those who are less talkative to speak out. Brainstorming can be fun and encourages the group to own and work with ideas that have been put forward. Remember to write down all the ideas that surface so that you don't overlook any in the subsequent discussion.

Reflection points

- What is effective brainstorming?
- How is brainstorming useful in communications?
- What are the advantages of brainstorming?
- What are the disadvantages of brainstorming?

References

Bass, B. M. (1985). *Leadership and performance beyond expectation.* New York: Free Press.
Bass, B. M. (1990). "From transactional to transformational leadership: Learning to share the vision" in *Organizational Dynamics,* (Winter), 19–31.
Berenson, B. G., Mitchell, K. M., & Laney, R. C. (1968). "Level of therapist functioning, types of confrontation and type of patient" in *J. Clin. Psychol.,* 24, 111–113.
Blake, R. & Mouton, J. (1964). *The managerial grid: The key to leadership excellence.* Houston: Gulf Publishing Company.
Bramson, R. (1981). *Coping with difficult people.* New York: Doubleday.
Burns, J. M. (1978). *Leadership.* New York: Harper and Row.
Egan, G. (1976). *Interpersonal living.* Belmont, CA: Wadsworth Publishing Company.
Fiedler, F. E. (1964). "A contingency model of leadership effectiveness" in *Advances in Experimental Social Psychology,* 1, 150–190.
Forsyth, D. R. (2019). *Group dynamics* (7th ed.). Boston: Cengage .
Galton, F. (2005) [1869]. *Hereditary genius.* New York: Cosimo Books.
Gibb, C. A. (1950). "The research background of an interactional theory of leadership" *Australian Journal of Psychology,* 2, 19–42.

Hersey, P. & Blanchard, K. H. (1977). *Management of organizational behavior.* Englewood Cliffs, NJ: Prentice Hall.

Lewin, K., Lippitt, R., & White, R. (1939). "Patterns of aggressive behaviour in experimentally created 'social climates'" in *Journal of Social Psychology*, 10, 271–299.

Nye, J. S. (2008). *The powers to lead.* Oxford: Oxford University Press.

Zaccaro, S. J., Kemp, C., & Bader, P. (2004). "Leader traits and attributes" in J. Antonakis, A. T. Cianciolo, & R. J. Sternberg (Eds.), *The nature of leadership* (pp. 101–124). Thousand Oaks, CA: Sage.

9 Successful teams in context

∙∙

Team dynamics and team communications can greatly affect individuals and impact whether they are motivated or discouraged to participate and perform fully. Participation in a team may encourage you to perform much better than you would if on your own; or, in another set of circumstances, you may become more complacent, less motivated, and reliant on the work of others. So, what is the link between personal ambition and team performance? How are they optimised? Is it better to work alone or as part of a team? What is a successful team in terms of interpersonal relations? In this final chapter, we deal with these questions, as well as look at the environment of a team and its influence on teamwork. At the end of the chapter we look at effective communication in teams to revisit material that has already been discussed in the book and place it in an overall context. As we have stated throughout, the ultimate goal is to have open, honest, efficient, and mutually supportive communications within teams to bring out the best in teamwork.

Motivation in teams

Motivation relates to the driving forces behind how we all behave. We have touched on this area at various times in the preceding chapters. It is often characterised as simply the seeking of reward and the avoidance of punishment, although these are not the only factors at play. The relationship between personal motivation, application, and success, on the one hand; and team dynamics, on the other hand, is a complex area with a number of dynamics and outcomes at play. What is apparent is that some teams motivate team members, while others seem to discourage them, and we will look at the reasons for this in greater detail in this chapter.

Some individuals operate best when they have clear, measurable goals, either set by themselves or by others, that are regularly monitored. Others are primarily motivated by financial reward or social recognition. Others still are innately motivated to see projects realised that are close to their heart. Most of us are motivated to some extent by a mix of all three of the above.

Figure 9.1

Your expectations have an impact on your performance.

Constructive feedback and recognition are also important aspects for motivating people to perform to the best of their ability.

Your expectations of work and projects have a major impact on your performance (Figure 9.1). It is quite normal to ask yourself at the beginning of any new project: What do I get out of this? Does this have a purpose? Am I capable of this? Depending on the answers to these questions, you may find yourself encouraged or discouraged. Two elements are common, in some form or other, to most of the motivational theories. These are the need to see that your work will lead to reward and the expectation that you are capable of finishing the work. Your personal and technical competence can matter a lot here, as you normally need both motivation and ability to succeed. We can broadly summarise this relationship as follows:

Ability + Motivation = Success

Different expectations and the mix of different skills amongst team members mean that team leaders will often need to provide direction and organisation to get their team to perform as a unit. It is useful to begin this process by inviting the team to define their values, mission, vision, goals and objectives, and then work on the basis of these definitions and discuss the different roles within this framework. The level of team involvement and decision-making in this process will depend on the maturity of the team, the time available for self-organisation and, in some cases such as technically challenging or dangerous environments, the team leader may need to be more prescriptive in their approach.

Another way to encourage or discourage people to complete tasks is what has been called *behavioural conditioning*. This method, which is often applied in the training of animals, is based on using positive behavioural reinforcement (rewards) and negative behavioural reinforcement ("punishment") to train behaviour and instil discipline. Individuals are then rewarded for desirable behaviour and punished for undesirable behaviour. It is important to realise that the method only works if the people with whom it is being applied understand the relationship between their behaviour and the positive and negative reinforcement that is applied. They should also feel that praise, reward, and any sanctions are appropriate and fair. You need to be careful to treat your team like adults; you're not training a pet or teaching children. If you treat team members as either of those things then they will respond with anger or by reciprocating as petulant teenagers.

You may ask yourself: What is a sufficient reward? And what is an appropriate "punishment"? Psychology is a major factor here and it is entirely natural that people look at how others are treated and relate that to how they perceive themselves to be treated. In doing this, they are looking to ensure that they are not losing out and at least have as good a reward or equally bad punishment as everyone else. In simple terms, it can be said that behavioural reinforcement is good when it is coherent with what is required to achieve success. Appropriate "punishment", in this context, may involve delaying rewards, reprimanding someone in an honest conversation, or temporarily removing a project from someone with the promise that they can get it back if they improve. People need to know in advance what actions lead to rewards and what actions lead to punishment, and to see that this is managed in a fair and consistent manner. The criteria for good behavioural reinforcement includes the following:

- Explain what is expected and by when in terms of overall targets.
- Make it clear whether all parties will receive rewards, what criteria are associated with these, and when they will be received.
- Make sure these rewards are transparent, fair, and proportionate.
- Make it clear when the group as a whole will receive a reward for a job well done, not only individuals within it.
- Explain what happens if what is expected is not done correctly or on time.
- Provide regular feedback both on what was done well and what needs improvement.
- Everyone should understand when a response is appropriate and sufficient.

Paid work and voluntary work are likely to have different motivational conditions associated with them and enabling volunteers to perform requires an engaging project, skilled leadership, and a good team structure to set up the right environment. Particular motivational difficulties in this case can arise if the work becomes too time-consuming, too complex, or too dull.

Motivation can also be spontaneous, intrinsic, or intuitive and stem from the act of performing a task. The work itself is its own reward and encourages you to keep going and complete goals successfully. For example, surgeons who specialise in particular areas of medicine that are extremely challenging are often motivated by the need to continually learn and stretch their competence. This phenomenon is clearly less likely to occur among people who do repetitive work where there is little intellectual challenge, novelty, or progression, and among people who feel that their contribution is of little value. *Job enrichment* is an approach that can help generate intrinsic motivation. This involves adapting work to the needs, interests, and ambitions of the person doing the work for increased contentment at work.

Reflection points

- How are ambition, ability, and performance/achievement connected?
- How do teams affect the capabilities and ambitions of people?
- What are the criteria for behavioural strengthening in teams?
- What is spontaneous motivation?
- What does the term "effective teamwork" mean in your team?
- What experience do you have of job enrichment?

Social facilitation in teamwork

In an experiment in 1898, the American psychologist Norman Triplett studied why cyclists achieved better times in competitions than during training. When he looked at individuals who practised either alone or in teams, he saw that their performance grew in the presence of other cyclists and spectators. He called this effect *social facilitation* (Triplett, 1898). This is one of the reasons why athletes are more likely to beat personal records at sporting events, rather than when they are exercising alone, even accounting for the effect of better sports facilities at these events and physical factors like reduced drag due to wake effects.

In 1965, the Polish-American psychologist Robert B. Zajonc added to the knowledge of social facilitation by showing that it matters whether the tasks being performed are easy or complicated. His results indicated that it is easier for people to perform simple tasks in the presence of other competitors and crowds such as lifting weights, cycling, and swimming. If, on the other hand, the task is complex, then the presence of others can be discouraging or distracting, e.g. when an inexperienced student has to solve a maths puzzle or knit a complex knot in front of others. In this latter case, close proximity to others can increase the stress for an individual and hamper their thought processes, and the notion of social facilitation can become social inhibition (Zajonc, 1965) (see Figure 9.2).

Such results should be borne in mind by leaders when they are trying to get a team to solve complex tasks. It can be productive to create space for people to do their work sometimes on an individual basis and at other times as part of a small work team. It is also helpful to break the task into multiple work phases and thus make the project more manageable and easier to process. Theories based on studies of the effects of social facilitation on teamwork often seek explanations for this effect in relation to how human beings are

Figure 9.2

Teams can both facilitate and inhibit people.

social creatures and react in a particular and fairly predictable manner when they are around others. Physiological arousal, evaluation concerns, and impact on concentration and focus are three areas where the presence of others can impact performance. There can also be cases where individuals consciously underperform so as not to stand out from their peers for various reasons, i.e. *self-inhibition* in the presence of others (Forsyth, 2019).

Social facilitation or social inhibition occurs when an individual is affected by strong physiological responses while performing a task in the presence of an audience (*audience effect*) or competitors (*co-actor effect*). These responses can either have a positive facilitative effect or negative inhibitive effect on performance. In the former case, tasks would typically be simple tasks, but also include more complex tasks that someone is an expert at or have become autonomous. In the latter case, these would be tasks where there is typically greater complexity, requiring greater conscious thought, or where things are still being learnt (Weiss & Miller, 1971). These responses were also shown to be present by Schmitt *et al.* (1986) in experiments where the audience were blindfolded, wore earplugs, and did not say a word. Another theory is the *evaluation apprehension theory*. According to this theory, people work harder if and when they feel that others are assessing their performance. In team situations, this can create a driving force that results in better performance in familiar and simple tasks but has a discouraging effect for more complex tasks. A further theory suggests that it is mainly people's understanding of apprehension that was the source of social facilitation effects rather than the *mere presence* of others (Cottrell, 1972).

Reflection points

- What is social facilitation?
- How does social facilitation appear in your team?
- What is social inhibition?
- How does social inhibition appear in your group?
- What kind of work do you find easier to do in a group?
- What kind of work do you find more difficult to do in a group?

Self-presentation and distractions in teamwork

The *self-presentation theory* can be explained by using the analogy of the theatre as a representation of everyday life. Here, the emphasis is on how people perform in the presence of others, and it is noted how people react differently whether they are in a situation that is metaphorically *front-stage* (in front of a formal audience), *back-stage* (on their own or among close associates), or *off-stage* (with an informal audience). Important aspects here include: *setting*–primarily relates to the nature of an audience and the immediate environment; *appearance*–e.g. clothes and props denoting status; *manner*–how a performer plays their role and what an audience expects for that reason; and *front*–impression given to the audience. Not surprisingly, research suggests that individuals with high self-esteem tend to perform better when being observed, while those who doubt their own abilities tend to perform better in private (Goffman, 1959; Sanna, 1992).

The *distraction-conflict theory* says that when people work in a team, their attention is no longer focused on just the work that is to be done, but also on others in the team. Having others around causes people to become more aware of them and make social comparisons. The feeling is that evaluation is mutual and an individual can become distracted if they perceive others to be better at performing similar tasks. Although quite likely, it is not a given that this phenomenon will affect performance in a negative way. For example, the impact may be that this fight for attention increases motivation, which may then increase success in performing tasks as long as they are simple and familiar (Baron, 1986; Sanders, 1981).

Managers can use these results to trigger reactions in people that lead to success in team activities. For example, they may set it as a work rule that people who are working on more complex technical tasks are allowed to prepare in private instead of under the scrutiny of the team. This simple work rule can help individuals and the whole team to achieve success. Research on what is most effective and convenient in overall team performance show that there are both advantages and disadvantages associated with team engagement. It is good in the sense that it is helpful to arrange your thoughts by talking to others and to get useful tips from them. It can, however, be detrimental if the task requires specialist knowledge and concentration and the presence of others proves to be distracting. For example, others may have unrealistic expectations, make disruptive comments, or ask irrelevant questions. It is evident that individuals perform better in front of others when they have acquired the technology, gained the skills to perform a task, and are confident enough not to be distracted (Forsyth, 2019).

Reflection points

- How does the knowledge that others are evaluating you affect your performance? How does self-evaluation affect your performance?
- How does your attention on the group affect the projects that you are working on?
- What method do you find most successful when preparing for an exam?

Social loafing in teamwork

Social loafing in teams happens when an individual team member makes less of an effort in performing straightforward tasks than they would if he or she were on their own or in smaller groups. This loss of motivation happens for a variety of reasons and normally requires that the team is sufficiently large for responsibility to be diluted and both good and poor performance hidden from view (Forsyth, 2019). In this context, more time can be spent on non-productive activities such as idle thought or chat and unnecessary communication. Steiner (1972) proposed a model that relates to declining productivity in groups as follows:

Actual productivity = Potential best productivity
−Losses due to faulty group processes

Decline of team performance can take place even though team members are highly qualified and able and have all the necessary resources for the project. It appears as if the influence of loafing on the part of one or more team members infects the rest of the team which then interferes with its performance. If the team leader realises this, then they can have an influence on the productivity loss by being alert to the forces that have a dissuasive effect.

There is also a link between team size and performance. Performance does not necessarily increase proportionally to the increased size of a team. Larger teams involve greater diversity, more views, and thus increased likelihood of conflict, as well as less clarity in responsibility, social comparison, and reliance on others. More energy goes into monitoring and co-ordination, and there is also the risk of *slacking*, as well as the formation of subgroups or cliques in some situations.

The earliest studies on this phenomenon are from the first decades of the 20th century. For example, the French agricultural engineer, Max

Ringelmann, carried out a famous study on the effects of different group sizes on performance, both amongst humans and animals (Ringelmann, 1913; Forsyth, 2019). He found in the cases that were studied that individuals contributed less in a group and more when they worked alone. One experiment involved looking into how much power individuals applied in pulling a rope, both alone and as part of a group. It was found that the combined power of individuals did not increase in proportion to the increase of the group size, as one might have expected. Hence, we speak of a so-called *Ringelmann effect* that describes how much unit productivity decreases, as group size gets bigger. Ringelmann's findings connected two key factors that affect the productivity and contributions of people in a team. On one hand, there is a lack of coordination, which means that it is not possible to combine the work contribution of participants. Rope pulling is a good example of work that requires co-ordination but it is natural that people have a tendency to pull at different times. On the other hand, people come to rely on the efforts of their fellows, and this means that their individual performance level is reduced (Forsyth, 2019). With further studies, it has been shown that a lack of co-ordination is probably not a very big part of reduced productivity of individuals in teams. The main reason seems to be that *increased reliance* is placed on fellow group members when working in a group. Social loafing is widespread and found amongst both men and women of all ages and in different cultures (Forsyth, 2019). One can conclude that it is not self-evident that individuals will work well together as a team and that everyone will do their best. This is what a team leader needs to manage and it is their role to bring the team together, promote team spirit, and smooth the path to achieving good results.

In terms of minimising loafing, there is no such thing as an ideal number of participants that are most suitable for teamwork (Figure 9.3). This number largely depends on the nature of the work. A general rule of thumb, however, is that if the team members number more than five, then it will be harder to activate the team and clique formations are more likely, and the management of meetings will be more difficult. The solution may involve creating subgroups where people get more responsibility and the overall project work is divided into a series of discrete tasks.

It has been argued that the size of project teams should not be less than two and not more than 25 and that successful teams generally have fewer than ten members (Burn, 2004). In larger teams, some negative effects are that interactions become more complex, it is more difficult to reach agreement, and the workload will be uneven. Smaller teams have shown to work better together if individual participation is higher and workload and stress is more evenly distributed.

As already mentioned, the optimum size of a project team depends on the nature of the project or task. Disadvantages of having a team that is too small include that its members will potentially not cope with the full scope of the project, resulting in excessive workload and stress. If there are too many people in a team, there is a danger that resources will be wasted and co-ordination and management will be more difficult.

Figure 9.3

There is no such thing as an ideal number of team participants.

The British management theorist Meredith Belbin (2007) placed great emphasis on having diversity within an oversight team. He argues that the foundation of good co-operation is that people know the different roles in a team and understand their own role within the overall context. It is desirable that there is a good balance in the team and that the main roles have good representation in team discussions. Belbin's general conclusion is that six is a good number for a team, although as low as four may suffice in many situations. In these smaller teams, it is possible to appoint people that cover the nine essential roles that he identified, i.e. some people will need to perform more than one role. These roles are:

1   *Co-ordinator*—e.g. chairperson.
2   *Shaper*—process driver focused on "winning".
3   *Plant*—creative ideas person.
4   *Monitor-Evaluator*—objective and analytical problem solver.
5   *Implementer*—dependable person that turns ideas into action.
6   *Resource Investigator*—instigator and networker that provides early momentum.
7   *Team Worker*—low-key facilitator performing essential background role.
8   *Completer-Finisher*—a perfectionist willing to take the time and effort to produce things to a high standard.
9   *Specialist*—an individual dedicated to the pursuit of knowledge in a particular area who can advise and teach those around them.

It is relatively easy to manage and co-ordinate the activities of a team of six or less people. Communication is simple and the workload can be equal (Figure 9.4).

Figure 9.4

It is relatively easy to co-ordinate a team of six or less people.

There is less chance of social loafing if individuals believe that their contribution makes a difference and that they are valued. If that's the case, individuals are likely to put in a greater effort and it is less likely that they will be free riders that contribute little to the work of a team. Similarly, a person puts in more effort if they think they are indispensable to a team because their contribution is somehow special. There is, however, also a certain risk in team activities that people feel that they are contributing too much to a team compared to other equally qualified individuals that are present. There can be one or more individuals in teams that can be described as *workhorses* and it may take them some time to realise that this is the case (if at all) and that others are coasting on the back of their hard work. If people become aware of such a situation, they can become angry and demotivated, and will normally seek a resolution to what they perceive as an unfair situation. They see that they are being tricked into contributing more than the others. This phenomenon, while it lasts, has been called the *sucker effect*.

There is a greater risk of loafer and workhorse subgroups forming if teams are assembled to work on unpaid projects that are added to other existing projects. An example of this is when student teams are expected to work on a project that is borrowed from an organisation. The students are operating on different terms from those within an organisation and they have to apply themselves to both their studies and the project work. In this context, it is not uncommon that disputes can arise that can be difficult to resolve. It is therefore necessary at the beginning of team activities to raise these issues and any others that can affect the performance of a team.

Teams that set clear and challenging targets achieve better results than teams that do not have goals. Having a clear direction and future vision matters a lot in convincing workers to pull the wagon in the same direction. Numerous studies support this and show that clear objectives are linked with many positive consequences for the work process, such as increased productivity, better organisation, better monitoring of quality, and increased team cohesion. Other factors that can reduce social loafing include: (a) if projects are exciting and challenging; (b) if a team member believes that poor performance of the team will affect him/her personally; (c) if good performance is rewarded; (d) if the whole team is rewarded; (e) if there is a willingness to assist other team members who may not have the prior skills but who have the will to make an effort and learn; (f) if team members feel that the work of their team is important; and (g) if ambitions are high and the goals are desirable and realistic.

Reflection points

- What is your experience of social loafing?
- How does the model of Steiner, discussed above, manifest itself in your team?
- How does the *Ringelmann effect* manifest itself in your team?
- What is the contribution that you and others make in joint tasks within your team?

Team composition

The composition of a team can be vital to its success, as Belbin and others have noted (Figure 9.5). As well as having people fill the various roles, it is also important to have a harmonious environment. Most projects require teamwork and teamwork can be complicated at times with a wide range of potential conflict points. Good teamwork can appear so natural and smooth it is often unnoticed, while poor teamwork can make even the simplest of tasks seemingly impossible.

The American psychologist Thomas North Whitehead (1938) observed employees who worked on making electrical components. He showed, quantitatively, how much of a difference to productivity there is when individual team members disrupt teamwork. The efficiency of a team of five increased from making 50 items on average per hour to 70 items on average per hour when two team members that caused communication problems

Figure 9.5

The composition of a team can be vital to its success.

were exchanged for two new team members who did not cause communication problems. The American social psychologist Ivan Steiner (1972, 1976) compared achievements of teams in projects with the baking of a cake. It is important to follow a recipe and have the right ingredients. Having good ingredients, however, does not ensure that the cake will be a success if the proportions are wrong. In the same way, having talented group members does not guarantee the performance of a group, as the group also needs to be properly composed.

Communication skills and the abilities necessary to solve disputes are important qualities that members of successful teams possess. In teams where diverse abilities and skills are present, there is naturally a potential for higher performance, especially when those team members that are less productive may be influenced by the stimulation and ambition of others in the group. They may aspire to be like the most prolific team members and plough their own productive furrow, or, more modestly, provide important background support work, both resulting in better results. Mixed teams often find it easier to cope with changes related to work conditions, as there is more width in the talents and qualities present, and flexibility is greater. Greater diversity can also increase the chances of a group finding more varied solutions to problems and increase creativity and innovation. In mixed teams there can, however, also be a lack of cohesion, as each group member perceives others as different from themselves. In this case, diversity can naturally increase disputes within groups (Jackson *et al.*, 1995; Williams & O'Reilly, 1998).

Teams can be diverse or homogeneous in a variety of ways: Examples include professional background, age, gender, experience, education, and how long individuals have been members of a team. These affect teams in different ways. How long individuals have been members of a team seems to matter significantly. Homogeneity within a team on the basis of length of membership seems to go hand in hand with participants achieving better connection and better communication, and group efficiency grows in response. Studies of diversity with regard to the background of team members show that increased variability in terms of specialisation and education can lead both to increased conflict and increased efficiency of a team. Other studies show that the effect of age distribution on the efficiency of a team is not great, but it has been observed that increased variability in the age profile of a team goes hand in hand with increased absenteeism and turnover of personnel (Burn, 2004).

Without venturing into what specific advantages there are of a good gender mix in teams, it is widely accepted that balance is important. There can be negative effects on productivity if the ratio is very uneven in either direction. Difficulties seem to arise in particular when there is only one woman or one man in a group. Such individuals can often be overruled by the others in a group and become a victim of stereotyping when the other members expect that they behave in a certain way. One observation about gender indicates that coaching has a positive effect on teamwork, leading to improved performance, and that women are more likely than men to make an effort to learn from past experience in projects.

Gender stereotyping is not productive in team activities (e.g. Harris & Sherblom, 2005). The view that men behave more as leaders and women more as subordinates is deeply rooted in some cultures but has been shown to have no basis in reality when women have had the opportunity to progress their careers and take on leadership roles. It is generally recognised that women are more sensitive than men to indirect communication and more active as managers when it is important to encourage people, stimulate communication, and listen out for the opinion of others.

Mixed groups are often well suited to finding solutions to problems and enhancing innovation and originality. Project teams can, for example, have many participants involved in the project in different ways, although this can require close management. Sometimes a team leader may manage a team that never even comes together because of geographical distance; relying on methods like video conferencing to replace face-to-face meetings. Where this is the case, important body language and signalling cannot be used to the same degree and greater care may be needed to ensure that messages are conveyed accurately and efficiently. In face-to-face communication, it is common for things to be clarified in informal discussions between group members at breaks or subsequent to meetings and this can be a very important aspect of communication that has no direct equivalent in distance communication. In addition, group members may be from different countries and speak different languages. The different interests of these individuals, allied with language and cultural barriers, can have the effect of reducing concern and enthusiasm. These are factors you need to be aware of as team leader. Clarity of thought, decisive leadership, and good communication are therefore important. Simple guidelines can also be important such as showing respect for the different time zones that others are working in.

It can be difficult to be part of a team where harmony is lacking. It is the role of those who select a team and the team leader to identify goals and have all members committed to achieving them. Once a team is formed, a leader needs to ensure that roles are suitably designated and disputes and disagreements are dealt with in an efficient and productive manner. As part of their role, the leader must be able to recognise the characteristics of individuals, understand human nature, and be able to work with what they are given. They also need to be aware of their environment and circumstances such as the loss of team members and plan for a range of eventualities. In the preceding chapters, many aspects that impact these areas have been discussed and the reader is encouraged to refer back to the specific examples given.

Reflection points

1   How is your team composed?
2   What effect does diversity have on team success?
3   What effect do cultural differences have on the success of teams?
4   What encourages you in performing your team role?
5   How do you evaluate your performance in the work of the team?

Successful teams

Different teams can be easier or harder to evaluate in terms of their success depending on the role they fulfil. For example, you can evaluate the performance of a sports team (that can be seen as a form of a project team) on the basis of how they fare in competitions, and you can see what separates good teams from bad teams. Other project teams, on the other hand, can be more difficult to assess, although simple concepts such as the project management *Iron Triangle* with its three different elements of time, cost, and quality are a useful evaluation tool. But it is more complex to evaluate performance in aspects such as team communication and co-operation. We suggest a basic framework below, which offers a starting point for assessment.

1   Clear values, mission, and vision.
2   Realistic understanding of the team's strengths, weaknesses, opportunities, and threats.
3   Clear goals, objectives, and well-defined assigned tasks.
4   Well-defined roles.
5   Plans for improvements and appropriate change management.
6   Clear and concise communication.

7   Constructive and positive behaviour.
8   Mutual engagement and even participation.
9   Well-defined rules of conduct.
10   Up-to-date awareness of progress (or lack thereof).
11   Strong communicational strategy with all stakeholders and interested parties.
12   Reliable project sponsor that backs up the team.
13   Professionalism.

You can discuss performance and capability using the various headings outlined above during *joint review meetings*. Experts in organisational development have highlighted the importance of teamwork in transformational processes. While working as a team can be contraindicated at times, research shows that it has many advantages over other arrangements. Employees' communication capability increases and their overall knowledge of work processes improves when working in teams. This leads in turn to increased initiative, participation, and activity. Employee satisfaction and productivity tend to go up, and absence from work and staff turnover down. Changes in teams do affect performance and you should expect more marked improvement if you can create an integrated programme for change (as opposed to ad hoc and apparently unconnected changes) whilst ensuring continuity of output. Changes seem to have more effect on performance if they affect the whole team rather than just one or two individuals.

Operational systems and team arrangements alone will not be enough to ensure increased performance. Potentially good teams can be very inefficient if there is a prevailing atmosphere that does not encourage productivity. If you are trying to tackle this, it is more effective to carry out a review of operational goals and increase the level of active team participation rather than to undertake superficial actions that are supposed to "improve morale" within the team. There can be significant shortcomings in the team environment that you can easily overlook, such as a lack of appropriate support to implement new work practices, or wages and benefit levels which fall woefully short of reflecting the performance and contribution of the team. Be careful not to assign blame too easily as lack of resources or poor HR are usually outside the team's control. There are plenty of organisations where senior managers are unaware of, ignore, or simply don't recognise publicly the value that teams bring to the project *at every level*.

Reflection points

- What methods can be used to evaluate results in teamwork?
- What factors can define the success of teamwork?
- What is the difference between success and development?
- What is development in the context of organisations?
- What is change management?

Team environment

All teams have to deal with contextual realities that can be defined as the "team environment". At all levels within the team environment there are factors that can have strong effects on behaviour and performance (see Figure 9.6). At the base level are individuals that are part of a team, which is part of an organisation, which is part of a broader society (stakeholders and interested parties), and then beyond that is the natural environment. These different levels have different corresponding environments that influence teams in different ways.

The immediate team environment affects both individuals within teams and teams as a whole, albeit in different ways. The effects can be both positive and encouraging, or negative and discouraging—to the point of preventing teams from achieving their goals. Examples of immediate environmental factors that may affect the work of teams and cause stress are temperature, noise, hazards of various kinds, and atmosphere (Forsyth, 2019).

It is clear that *temperature, air quality*, and *weather conditions* can greatly affect teams (Figure 9.7). The ideal temperature for working indoors is between 19 to 28 degrees Celsius, but humidity also matters. Outdoors, clothing has a crucial impact on how comfortable it is to work with the prevailing temperature. If it is too hot or too cold this will affect performance and team members are likely to try to avoid exposure to adverse temperature or weather conditions, for example, by rushing to finish a task in order to be able to return to a more comfortable environment. Excessive heat causes tiredness and discomfort. Too much heat and too much cold also reduce levels of communication and co-operation within a team. In the most severe cases, this can cause exhaustion and other health problems.

The impact of *noise* can be very different from one individual to another. Teams seem to be able to adapt to working in noise for short periods, but long-term noise has a lasting impact on their performance. The main effect of noise on teams is that it reduces communication, co-operation, and assistance between team members.

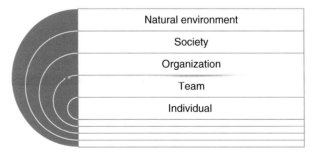

Figure 9.6

Levels in the team environment.

Figure 9.7

Temperature, air quality, and weather conditions can greatly affect teams.

The presence of *physical hazards* in the immediate environment of a team can have a strong influence on behaviour. There are many examples showing that people can get used to living and working in dangerous conditions, without ever becoming complacent. Operating in hazardous environments can lead to increased co-operation within teams. Some risk factors in the environment can be controlled, while others cannot. Teams working in these environments will need to take on board a range of preventative procedures and measures to mitigate the dangers and maximise the team's safety.

Atmosphere refers to the immediate non-physical environment that stirs an intellectual or emotional response within individuals. It can, for example, determine whether a team experiences a particular working environment as good or bad, comfortable or uncomfortable, encouraging or discouraging, relaxing or stressful. Short-term changes in team ambience may be influenced by recent project successes or failures, or external events, while longer-term atmosphere will be influenced by the composition of a team and the physical space in which they operate. The nature of the space that you work in will tend to induce similar responses from you and your co-workers. Using the analogy of restaurants, it's common to hear that such and such a place has a "great atmosphere" while another does not. The differences between the two may not be easy to describe but are nonetheless tangible. Different types of projects may thrive in different physical spaces that have their own atmosphere.

Personal space, the space around a person that they believe to be psychologically theirs, represents an important subset of the ambience experienced by individuals. Every person has their own private space but the boundaries of this space are not exact and depend on what we believe is a reasonable distance between us and other people. At the centre of this personal space is our individual self- and body awareness. Your personal space will grow or shrink depending on your relationship with and to those around you. In Western societies, the following five classes of personal space have been defined, depending on the distance between individuals (Hall, 1966; Forsyth, 2019) (Figure 9.8):

1 *Intimate zone*: Extreme closeness, less than 0.5 m.
2 *Personal zone*: Reasonable closeness, from 0.5 m to 1.2 m.
3 *Social zone*: Immediate proximity, from 1.2 m to 4 m.
4 *Public zone*: Reasonable distance, 4 m or more.
5 *Remote zone*: Great distance between individuals.

To put this into context, you will allow your partner or child closer to you than you would your co-workers, and you would let your co-workers in closer than you would a stranger.

Teams that have a relatively small space at their disposal generally experience better bonding between members than if the space is larger, as a small area calls for greater intimacy. This can mean better team cohesion, although it can also prove volatile if two very incompatible personalities are forced to be too close together. Extrovert individuals are more likely to tolerate less space between themselves and individuals in the team whom they do not consider to be close friends. If team members feel there is little closeness within a team, then they will tend to position themselves further from each other, have little eye contact, and be formal in their communication, and vice versa for a team that is more bonded.

Figure 9.8

We all have our personal space.

Gender differences can play a role in team closeness and communication. In mixed groups, for example, it is not uncommon for those of the same gender to unconsciously gravitate towards each other. Other factors to take into account are the positions or roles of individuals within a team and, as mentioned, different cultural views. In some cases, teams may be working in such a confined space that individuals struggle to maintain a desirable distance between themselves and others and suffer as a result.

Overcrowding can be associated with confusion and preventing teams from achieving their goals. In such situations where space is at a premium, it can require careful planning, clever use of space, and good personal discipline to avoid interfering with each other and losing track of where items of importance are. It is advisable to have at least one place where private discussions can take place, as people will otherwise feel uncomfortable having to share details in a public setting.

In meetings, the psychology associated with seating arrangements can matter and either support or constrain good communication. One form of seating arrangement can increase the level of mutual interaction, personal connection, and trust, while another form of seating arrangement can reduce interaction and make things more distant and formal. Teams require an area over which they have authority and within which they carry out their work. This area may be subdivided into smaller areas with different access levels (Forsyth, 2019). These can be categorised into a *primary area* that no one except those who belong to a team can access; a *central area* into which members of a team may invite third parties; and a *general area* in which a team shares with others. Team members can also designate certain parts of their primary area for particular activities or as places where people are guaranteed to have their personal space respected.

Reflection points

- What effect do the circumstances and environment of your team have on your team?
- What dangers may affect your team?
- How does the understanding of "space" in the context described here differ between individuals?
- Where are the boundaries between your personal spaces as team members?
- How is the primary area of your team defined?

Open communication in teams

During the course of the book we have discussed the development of particular communication skills and how they relate to teams. Let's take a moment to summarise our findings. In essence, the communication skill set that is required for effective teamworking revolves around the skills (and opportunities to practise them) of self-disclosure and effective interpersonal communication. The ability to communicate well within a team is the ability to encourage constructive interaction among team members and ensure their participation in the teamwork. Successful and sustained communication requires a mix of all these skills, both within individual members and the team as a whole.

Many find it difficult to open up and may have never had any communication skills training. At the extreme, there may be someone who has never discussed personal matters with anyone, not even with family or close friends. In teamwork, it is easy for those who are quiet and reserved to withdraw and allow those who are louder or more prominent to dominate the conversations. These more reserved members can choose the *quiet life* by abdicating responsibility to others who find it easy to take centre-stage and talk about themselves and their opinions. This allows them to avoid having to confront others and discuss issues that may particularly concern them. Keeping to yourself, however, will not help you to acquire the requisite skills, and may encourage others to have undue influence within the team. Far better to take the plunge, try to open up and work on improving communication, even with those in a team who you may not naturally trust or with whom you are in conflict. This can require courage and determination. Once you find your voice, however, it is very likely that others will take more notice of you and show you greater respect. This will lead to more opportunities for self-disclosure and the level of open communication will increase as fellow team members become more receptive and encouraging.

There are several techniques to practise self-disclosure and open communication. One of them is to initiate a conversation with another team member. Open up to him or her and as your confidence grows you may open up to the whole group. You'll also find it useful to prepare what you are planning to say in some detail before discussing your feelings, experiences, and behaviour within the team. The idea is not to limit or constrain your self-disclosure, but to help you rehearse opening up in team settings. Self-disclosure and open communication are useful for the development of both the individual and the team. Be ready to deal with negative feedback; real, unintended, or imagined (see Figure 9.9)

Open communication is important for driving the team communication process and to support sound decision-making. We have discussed the importance of empathy in teamwork to create trust and support. In interactive communication, responses are expected to be given with empathy and understanding. It is not necessarily easy to sustain empathy without practice. There are several ways in which you can develop your skills as a facilitator of open and inclusive team communication:

- Practise empathy and communication skills outside of work.
- Make a conscious effort to show empathy (or use other related skills) at an appropriate point during a team discussion and notice the impact. Practising these skills will, over time, help you to make them an essential part of your competence as a communicator.

Figure 9.9

Be ready to deal with both positive and negative feedback.

- Ask someone outside the team to monitor your communication to give you feedback.
- Look for opportunities to reward team members or the team as a whole for increased levels of communication and interaction.
- Maintain your skills and review them regularly once you have acquired them.

Reflection points

- What is appropriate to say in a team?
- What is not appropriate to say in a team?
- Write down a few guidelines for anyone working collaboratively in a team.
- Describe these guidelines to your group.
- Ask fellow group members to describe how well or poorly they feel you meet these guidelines.
- Discuss what can be done to ensure interactive communication in a team.

Taking the initiative in teams

Effective project teams require team members who proactively maintain a positive attitude towards an open and interactive communication. This creates an atmosphere of cohesion, unity, and purpose. They generally show initiative and flourish, while allowing others to flourish too. However, a healthy team spirit is not a given and requires effort and patience to build-up and to maintain. Some team members are naturally eager but others may be more reticent (Figure 9.10). In this context, Gerard Egan categorised the following roles, each of which has its own distinctive positive and negative characteristics: (a) *the detractor*; (b) *the observer*; (c) *the participant*; (d) *the contributor*; and (e) *the leader* (Carkhuff, 1974 in Egan, 1976: pp. 233–242).

Detractors do not contribute anything positive to a team and its work and have a negative effect on communication and performance. Their input is destructive and typically motivated by self-interest and lack of willingness to take responsibility for their actions or for the team advancement. They will oppose initiatives such as communication training and the team may consume considerable time and energy trying to deal with them. Favourite pastimes include making critical judgements of others who take initiative and generally undermining fellow team efforts.

Observers avoid active communication with others. They may answer when asked but when they do, they will generally show a lack of effusiveness. Their lack of initiative can be an obstruction to effective teamwork. Their neutrality may be a conscious choice or may stem from other factors such as the lack of confidence. In many cases other team members accept this behaviour, especially if it comes from someone they are familiar with, and maybe have tried to engage with before. If the "observer" is a new team member, however, someone should be assigned to help them find a way to better contribute to

Figure 9.10

Some team members are naturally eager but others may be more reticent.

the team. This can involve encouragement and positive feedback on incremental improvements in team communication. If other team members do not succeed in helping the observer to participate, then the team will struggle with the goal of open and inclusive team communication and performance may suffer, as a result. Observers can lack the confidence and motivation to step out of this role on their own, and so will typically need the support and encouragement of others to be able to do so.

Participants are active and constructive team members who strive to strengthen team cohesion and are focused on team performance. They understand that communication within a team is partly their responsibility and they will aim to have a positive impact. Participants co-operate and interact, are willing to open up about themselves when asked to do so, and can be self-reflective when challenged. The participant does not, however, show much initiative, so if a team mainly consists of participants, then the team may not be particularly innovative.

Contributors take the need for team initiative seriously and do not wait for others to ask or encourage them. They build relationships with each member of the team and understand that good inclusive communication is important for the teamwork. Hence they are the driving force in teamwork, skilful in communication, and are willing to take considerable risks. If there are many supporters in the same team, co-operation can become very lively. They are organised and join the team not to see what happens, but to make things happen.

Leaders take a communicational lead within the team. They possess all the attributes of the supporters, but with a heightened sense of responsibility and with the skills to improve the communication techniques of themselves and others. They model good communication in their engagement within the team. Leaders continuously examine the team's communication performance and encourage improvement through support. They serve as a role model for other team members and match their words and actions to demonstrate the use of skill sets to others.

Reflection points

- Which of the above categories describes your participation in teamwork?
- How do individuals avoid participating in challenging communication?
- How do teams avoid dealing with challenging situations?
- Review your learning experiences whilst being a part of your communication group and tell each other what you have learnt and what remains to be learned.

Continuous improvement

We all belong to groups and teams of different sorts and need to participate in various kinds of communication on a daily basis. Improving how we interact with others is a lifetime's work and if you are open to interpersonal challenges you can always find new skills to master. In this book, we have explored a variety of aspects that are vital to your understanding of the nature of groups and of team interactions. We hope that you have been inspired to explore, to a deeper level, the essential factors to working with, leading, and managing project teams. You should now be familiar with some key theories and we hope you are on your way to collating a set of methods that you can use to improve and develop your communication skills, in co-operation with others (Figure 9.11).

We hope that your colleagues, friends, and family will soon notice a difference in your improved communication skills and better understanding of team dynamics. And we hope that we have managed to shed light on the psychological and social factors that are critical aspects of professional project management and in management in general.

We encourage you to continue your professional development and to learn more about the extensive range of theories and practices available on teams, co-operation, social interactions, and performance. As part of that process, we hope that you will continue along the path of personal growth and to observe your use of communication skills and the team dynamics in the teams which you lead. You are now in a good position to move forward and assist others in developing their own communication skills.

Figure 9.11

You can use your team to improve and develop your communication skills.

Reflection points

- What are the main things you learnt from reading this book?
- What have you not learnt from reading this book?
- How will you use what you have learnt from reading this book in your work?
- How will you use what you have learnt from reading this book in your everyday life?

References

Baron, R. S. (1986). "Distraction-conflict theory: Progress and problems" in *Advances in Experimental Social Psychology*, 19, 1–40.

Belbin, R. M. (2007). *Team roles at work*. Oxford: Elsevier.

Burn, S. M. (2004). *Groups: Theory and practice*. Belmont, CA: Thomson Wadsworth.

Cottrell, N. B. (1972). "Social facilitation" in C. G. McClintock (Ed.), *Experimental social psychology* (pp. 185–236). New York: Holt, Rinehart & Winston Publishing Company.

Egan, G. (1976). *Interpersonal living*. Monterey, CA: Brooks/Cole Publishing Company.

Forsyth, D. R. (2019). *Group dynamics* (7th ed.). Boston, MA: Cengage.

Goffman, E. (1959). *The presentation of self in everyday life*. Garden City, NY: Doubleday.

Hall, E. T. (1966). *The hidden dimension*. New York: Doubleday.

Harris, T. E. & Sherblom, J. C. (2005). *Small group and team communication* (3rd ed.). Boston, MA: Pearson.

Jackson, S. E., May, K.E., & Whitney, K. (1995). "Understanding the dynamics of diversity in decision-making teams" in R. A. Guzzo, E. Salas, & Associates (Eds.), *Team effectiveness and decision making in organizations* (pp. 204–261). San Francisco: Jossey-Bass.

Ringelmann, M. (1913). "Research on animate sources of power: The work of man" in *Annales de l'Institut National Agronomique*, 2. XII, 1–40.

Sanders, G. S. (1981). "Driven by distraction: An integrative review of social facilitation theory and research" in *Journal of Experimental Social Psychology*, 14, 291–303.

Sanna, L. J. (1992). "Self-efficacy-theory: Implications for social facilitation and social loafing" in *Journal of Personality and Social Psychology*, 62, 774–786.

Schmitt, B. H., Gilovich, T., Goore, N., & Joseph, L. (1986). "Mere presence and social facilitation: One more time" in *Journal of Experimental Social Psychology*, 22, 242–248.

Steiner, I. D. (1972). *Group process and productivity*. New York: Academic Press.

Steiner, I. D. (1976). "Task-performing groups" in J. W. Thibaut, J. T. Spencer & R. C. Carson (Eds.), *Contemporary topics in social psychology* (pp. 393–422). Morristown, NJ: General Learning Press.

Triplett, N. (1898). "The dynamogenic factors in pace-making and competition" in *American Journal of Psychology*, 9, 507–533.

Weiss, R. F. & Miller, F. G. (1971). "The drive theory of social facilitation" in *Psychological Review*, 78, 44–57.

Whitehead, T. N. (1938). *The industrial worker: A statistical study of human relations in a group of manual workers*. Boston, MA: Harvard University Press.

Williams, K. Y., & O'Reilly, C. A. (1998). "Demography and diversity in organizations: A review of 40 years of research" in *Research in Organizational Behavior*, 20, 77–140.

Zajonc, R. B. (1965). "Social facilitation" in *Science*, 149, pp. 269–274.

Index

experiential confrontations 172
experiments 25–6
expert power 113, 116
expert teams 80, *81*
external experts 147–8
external stakeholders 97–8
extra-team communication 96, 97
extroverts 44

facilitators, and communication 14
fearful-avoidant personalities 61
feedback: constructive 34–5, 115, 186;
    mutual 149; positive 55
feelings 61–2, 86; *see also* emotions
Festinger, Leon 48, 68, 71
Fiedler, Fred E. 167–8
fifth level communication skills 36
fight or flight, and teams 53
first level communication skills 33
Fischer, Bill 59
followers, and leaders 57
formal authority 114
forming stage 10, *70*, 71–2, 78, 83
Forsyth, Donald R. 25
founded teams 5
fourth level communication skills 35
French, J. P. R. 113
Freud, Sigmund, *Group Psychology and
    the Analysis of the Ego* 27
*Fundamental Interpersonal Relations
    Orientation* (FIRO) scale 46

Galton, Francis, *Hereditary Genius* 163
gender 166, 197, 203; and stereotyping
    51, 197
generalised language 107
goals 67, 82, 195
good communication 99
Great Man Theory 163
grieving stage 75
group cohesion 9–10, 68
group norms *see* collective norms
*Group Psychology and the Analysis of the
    Ego* (Freud) 27
groups: defining *3*, 80; and subgroups
    169, 194
groupthink 25, 138, 142, **143**, 144, 146, **148**
Gruenfeld, Deborah 126; *Approach/
    Inhibition Theory of Power* 126

Haslam, Alex 121
Hawthorne Effect 22
Hayward, Tony 97
Hereditary Genius (Galton) 163

hierarchies 120, *121*
homogeneity 197
honesty 109
human beings 188–9
human capital 80
Human Resources departments 32

Iceland 141–2, 144
Icelandic National Assembly (2009) 141
idealised influence 167
identification **125**
improvement 207, *208*
inclusion, need for 45–6
individual consideration 167
influencing: and integrity 128–9; by
    leaders 160; transformational 161; via
    attention 99
informal authority 114
informal groups 4
information, questions about 138
information authority 116
informative support 52
informing stage 75
in-groups 169
inhibition-related tendencies 126
initiations/testing 71–2
initiative, taking 35
innate tendencies 162–3
inspirational motivation 167
integrity 128–30
intellectual stimulation 167
interactional theory 164
Interaction Process Analysis (IPA) 22–3
interchange compatibility 57
internalisation **125**
International Red Cross/Crescent 78–9
interpersonal communication 17–18, 34,
    86, 91
interpersonal relations 14; and
    conformity 57; importance of 12
interruptions 106–7
intimate teams 5
intra-team communication 94, 95
introverts 44, 87

Janis, Irving 25, 142
job enrichment 188
Joiner, Brian L., *The Team Handbook* 71
joint review meetings 199
Jung, Carl G. 44
junior members, involving 76–7

Keech, Marian 71
Kelly, Harold 28